INDUSTRY *and*
POLITICS *in*
RURAL FRANCE

INDUSTRY *and* POLITICS *in* RURAL FRANCE

Peasants of the Isère
1870–1914

Raymond A. Jonas

Cornell University Press

ITHACA AND LONDON

First published 1994 by Cornell University Press.

International Standard Book Number 0-8014-2814-9
Library of Congress Catalog Card Number 93-30896
Printed in the United States of America
Librarians: Library of Congress cataloging information appears on the last page of the book.

♾ The paper in this book meets the minimum requirements of the American National Standard for Information Sciences—Permanence of Paper for Printed Library Materials, ANSI Z39.48-1984.

For Carl *and* Lucy Jonas

Contents

Abbreviations

ADI   Archives Départementales de l'Isère, Grenoble
AN   Archives Nationales, Paris
CGT   Confédération Générale du Travail
CNRS   Centre National de Recherche Scientifique
GFS   Groupe Féministe Socialiste
IRSH   *International Review of Social History*
POF   Parti Ouvrier Français
PUF   Presses Universitaires de France
RGA   *Revue de Géographie Alpine*
SFIO   Section Française de l'Internationale Ouvrière

Preface

This book is about peasant society at a crucial moment—
the moment of its disaggregation. The onset of this disaggregation
throughout much of rural France coincided with the mid-nineteenth-
century crisis, a crisis of rural overpopulation, signaled by dearth,
under- or unemployment, and the abandonment of farming for
work in towns and cities. In the southeast, most notably in the
department of the Isère, rural industry arrested the demographic
effects of the crisis—it gave people an alternative to migration—at
the same time that it accelerated its social effects by initiating the
conversion of peasants into workers. The new rural industry
brought a thriving and dynamic local economy to towns, villages,
and hamlets, but at the price of ongoing contact with urban commercial networks, with money culture, and with labor and political
organizations—in effect, at the price of the dissolution of peasant
society. Rural industry also destabilized gender relations because
the wages earned by the women who worked in the new mills
became the means, at least potentially, to disengage them from the
agrarian and patriarchal patterns of rural life in which they had
been enmeshed.

Conventional political leaders sensed the political opportunities
created by rural industry almost before anyone else and sought to
make the most of them. Conservatives overlooked the fact that
most workers in the rural textile industry were women and extolled

rural industry as an answer to prayers because it reinvigorated peasant society, halted the "rural exodus," and thus arrested French "decadence" by creating the conditions that enabled peasants to maintain themselves on the land. Leftist leaders appreciated the potential significance of women's new public role, yet their response was ambiguous. In his 1906 New Year's editorial on the theme "this human flock" the Socialist Max Cance announced that the organization of working women would be his party's top priority for the year. But this objectivizing, passive, and oddly pastoral image was deeply misleading and reveals a certain bad faith. These working women had acquired a new profile in rural society by their sheer numbers and by the importance of the wages they earned. Their work had given them, as Cance and others belatedly recognized, a certain authority to reshape household relations, public opinion, and village society. At first their efforts were halting and bore the halo of archaic forms of protest—the weapons of the weak. But by the first decade of the twentieth century, the moment of Cance's epiphany, the women of the mills had learned how to influence public debate and to command public attention through the occupation of public spaces and the skillful manipulation of political symbols. That their efforts could ultimately be undermined had to do almost exclusively with events beyond their control. The outbreak of war in 1914, a case of collective arrested development if ever there was one, put men, as soldiers, back at the center of public attention.

Chapter 1 provides a brief overview of the theories to be examined. Chapter 2 explores two landscapes, the physical and the political. After a survey of the geographic setting and the status of agriculture, I analyze certain national and local political issues from the Second Republic through to the last general election before World War I in an effort to answer the question: What was the trajectory of public opinion during this period, at least as voters expressed it at the polls? Chapter 3 is a brief history of the transfer of silk production from its traditional center in the city of Lyon to the rural hinterland and an examination of the reasons for it. Chapter 4 concerns the industrialization of the countryside as silk merchants substituted factory-based weaving for domestic weaving and, later, mechanical looms for hand looms. Chapters 5 and 6 survey the demographic and economic effects of the industrialization of the countryside. Here I examine mutations in the organization of peasant households brought about by the declining fortunes of the smallholding farmer and the emergence of a rural industrial wage economy. Here and in the following chapters I also examine aspects of the feminization of the public realm in village society—an inevitable consequence of women's predominant place in the work force of the rural mills. Chapter 7, which describes some of the important events in the development of militancy among rural textile workers, reveals the quite deliberate connections made between worker solidarity and village society. It shows how militancy shaped the political attitudes of those who, even though they were not themselves employees of the textile industry, were very much dependent on a local economy driven by the textile mills. Chapter 8 reconsiders the larger issues raised in Chapter 1.

Young scholars accrue many debts. I am grateful to the individuals and institutions who generously advised, supported, and encouraged me while I worked to complete this project. In the early stages of research I benefited from the advice of several scholars in the United States, notably Ted Margadant and Lynn Hunt, and in France: André Burguière, Maurice Agulhon, Michèle Perrot, and Yves Lequin. Much later I had the pleasure of meeting and discussing with Pierre Barral our mutual interest in the department of the Isère. Colleagues at the University of Washington, notably Fritz Levy and John Toews, provided helpful commentary on the manuscript. Christopher Johnson, Lee Shai Weissbach, and Julian Archer all commented on portions of this work presented at conferences. Michel Peronnet, Geneviève Gavignaud-Fontaine, and Pierre Barral provided me with a forum at the Université Paul Valéry (Montpellier III) to present portions of this work.

I also express my thanks to the Archives Nationales, the Bibliothèque Nationale, and the Archives Départementales of the Isère and the Ain. Mlle Chambelland of the Musée Social in Paris gave me permission to work in the museum's collection. M. Petitmengin of the Ecole Normale Supérieure permitted me to use the school's library; research in France was greatly expedited by his kind consideration. In the United States I relied heavily on the staff and holdings of the Doe Library at the Berkeley campus of the University of California, the Green Library at Stanford University, and the Suzzallo Library of the University of Washington. I owe the means to complete much of the basic research to a Bourse Chateaubriand awarded by the French Embassy to the United States. An award from the Mabelle McLeod Lewis Memorial Fund allowed me to devote myself fully to writing at a crucial stage. The Graduate School Research Fund of the University of Washington also provided support for travel, software, and equipment, without which most of the collection and analysis of demographic data would have been impossible. Designation as the University of Washington Social Sciences Research Professor gave me a quarter's break from teaching to complete some of the final revisions.

Others to whom I am particularly grateful are Patricia, Anthony, Elizabeth, and Katherine Jonas, who helped in countless ways. William O'Donnell generously drew on his vast experience in design and graphic art in advising me on the maps used here. Warm thanks, again and especially, to Lynn Hunt, who read the original chapters with speed, charity, and a keen editorial eye. David Pinkney graciously agreed to read subsequent drafts and offered advice that substantially improved them. An anonymous reader's remarks forced me to rethink and reconceptualize my work in a way that led to a crucial final revision. Peter Agree, editor at Cornell University Press, skillfully saw the project through.

Portions of this work have appeared in "Peasants, Population, and Industry in France," *Journal of Interdisciplinary History* 22 (Autumn 1991): 177–200; "Visualizing Population in History: The Example of Population and Rural Industry in Southeastern France," *Historical Methods* 24 (Summer 1991): 101–109; and "Equality in Difference? Patterns of Feminine Labor Militancy in Nineteenth-Century France," *Proceedings of the Western Society for French History* 15 (1987): 291–98. These sections are used here by permission.

Raymond A. Jonas

Seattle, Washington

INDUSTRY *and*
POLITICS *in*
RURAL FRANCE

I

Carnival
in Vizille

February is the time of carnival, but in February 1877 the working women of Vizille, a town in the Isère, did not think of banishing mythical demons. Concealed by the cloak of carnival as well as by the cover of darkness, they charivaried the owner of the largest mill in Vizille. The official record does not say in what manner they articulated their moral disapproval, but we may assume that the din was sufficient to awaken most of the town. When they were satisfied that they had made their point, they went home and went to bed. The next morning they went on strike.[1]

Yet another example of the persistence of the archaic in nineteenth-century France? Perhaps. One might be sorely tempted by such an idea. After all, Eugen Weber cautions us about the dangers of assuming that enlightenment and "modernity" had penetrated *la France profonde,* where superstition, habits of deference, fear of the outsider, atavisms of all kinds, and a pronounced localism prevailed. Weber's discussion of charivari, the primitive practice of howling, noisemaking, and intimidation visited upon members of village society who contravene consensually established standards of conduct, makes it clear that young men carried out this work of rough justice. Under the July Monarchy, in the early nineteenth

1. Archives Départementales de l'Isère (henceforth ADI), 166 M, 1, 1 February 1877.

I

century, their demonstrations easily shaded into the political, with participants occasionally abandoning the random noises of charivari to break into political song—the "Marseillaise," for example—or marching on the homes of political notables. The last political charivari in France took place in 1849; after that it reappeared only as a "carcass," no longer a living thing.[2]

Strange, then, to find charivari thriving in the early Third Republic. Was it a profound and persistent backwardness in Vizille that was to blame? Doubtful. Vizille, first in revolution in the eighteenth century, needed no instruction in these matters. In 1788 the notables of the Dauphiné had gathered at Vizille to revive their provincial assembly shortly after their dramatic defiance of royal edict on the Day of the Tiles—events that had allowed the Dauphiné to proclaim itself the "cradle of the Revolution."

Then was it by an ironic twist of fate that the cradle of modern revolution became, within the space of a century, the home of a living museum of traditional mentalities? Or was political charivari reinvented? But if so, why did women revive this form of popular justice, this "weapon of the weak" that traditionally had been wielded by men? When and how did women seize control of the tribunal of public opinion?

The immediate passage from charivari to strike in Vizille in 1877 suggests that if carnival meant catharsis, for these women catharsis was incomplete. Ritualized revolt of the subordinate failed to supplant or blunt an incipient rebellion. In the passage from the cover of darkness to the full light of day, their resistance passed from the ritual to the real.

Making sense of the abrupt intrusion of "archaic" charivari in late nineteenth-century France is in part a matter of placing the act in the context that renders it intelligible. This context is far from static. For even though the Isère remained deceptively stable in appearance—it was an agrarian department throughout the nine-

---

2. Eugen Weber, *Peasants into Frenchmen* (Stanford, 1976), pp. 399–406. Charivari, including its politicized forms, was not alien to the Dauphiné. See Emmanuel Le Roy Ladurie, *Carnival in Romans* (New York, 1979). On ritual and displacement see Victor Turner, *Dramas, Fields, and Metaphors: Symbolic Action in Human Society* (Ithaca, 1974) and *Image and Pilgrimage in Christian Culture* (New York, 1978). For a critique see James C. Scott, *Domination and the Arts of Resistance* (New Haven, 1990), esp. pp. 184–187.

teenth century—it was the setting of a significant social and political transformation potentiated by pervasive but small-scale industrialization. The Lyon silk industry was the initiator of change. The manufacturing portion of the Lyon Fabrique, as the city's silk industry has traditionally been known, abandoned the city of Lyon over the course of the nineteenth century. The departure was motivated by several considerations, not the least of which was the obstacle posed by the Lyon silk artisans to the merchants' desire to gain undisputed control of the industry. In marked contrast to the militant Lyon silkworkers, the peasant-workers of the rural departments of the region appeared willing to accept the direction of the Lyon silk merchants. Industrial progress and social peace seemed within reach to any merchant willing to relocate to a rural department, safely beyond the influence—or so it seemed—of the militant Lyon workers.

Peasants, for their part, were receptive to Lyon's initiative. If the first half of the nineteenth century constituted a kind of golden age for French peasants, the second half was conspicuously lacking in luster. Before the mid-century crisis, peasants had come under increasing pressure as population continued to grow and agricultural resources remained static. With the extension of the national railroad network under the early Third Republic, challenges to small-scale agriculture only became more acute. Rural industry thus offered significant new income at a time when the challenge to survive from the fruits of agriculture alone began to seem overwhelming. By the closing decades of the nineteenth century, tens of thousands of rural workers drew wages from dozens of silk mills scattered throughout the foothills of the Isère.

Most of them were women. Men also worked in the silk mills, but they were few and most of them held categorically distinct positions, those involving maintenance or supervision. Or they worked as boys beside their mothers and sisters. The rank-and-file silkworker was nearly always a woman, and here we encounter two significant mutations in rural society. The first is the dual economy established through the spread of rural industry. Agriculture and industry persisted side by side in a relationship that could be characterized as at once symbiotic and parasitical. The term that deserves emphasis depends on the ruthlessness with which mill managers were willing to pursue competitive advantages in price on the backs of their workers and on peasants' capacity to endure such exploitation as preferable to a definitive departure from the land. For the moment let us agree that relations were in some sense organic and that neither rural industry nor peasant agriculture is likely to have survived, much less thrived, without the other.

The second mutation concerned gender roles and public spaces. For as women left farm, hamlet, or village for a day or a week at the mill, they inevitably transformed the social and sexual definitions of the rural landscape. Men became stewards of the fields and guardians of the hearths. Women took to the roads that led to the mill. In doing so, they claimed for themselves a much wider social territory. The feminine public would extend—intermittently, but often with great force—well beyond the marketplace, the wash-place, and the church. It came to embrace village streets and rural roads, cafés and mill yards, meeting halls and town halls.

This extension of the feminine public was perhaps not deliberate at first, but it followed directly upon working women's new work-related routines. It offered new opportunities to shape public opinion; women seized these opportunities as they presented themselves and as circumstances allowed. All the same, institutional forums of power, especially formal political outlets, remained closed to women. In some cases, as a practical matter, the lack of such formal outlets left women with little choice but to make use of an ancient repertoire that men had long since abandoned. The charivari episode and many others, as we shall see, may be understood not as atavisms but as creative reappropriations of the archaic for want of an alternative.

The Socialists of the Isère, however, refused to abandon a working class whose profile deviated from the canonical. The fact that the Isère's only significant proletariat was dispersed across a vast territory was challenge enough. That the Socialists' most likely clientele could not vote offered a significant disincentive to a party that was giving in to the temptation to measure its success in electoral terms. Rolande Trempé's miners of Carmaux individually embodied the transition from peasant to proletarian, for the same person filled both roles.[3] Thanks to the sexual division of labor in the silk industry of the Isère, the transition from peasant to prole-

3. Rolande Trempé, *Les Mineurs de Carmaux*, 2 vols. (Paris, 1971).

tarian took place at the level of the household, not that of the individual, as part of an overall household strategy; the opposition of peasant and proletarian overlapped that of male and female. Socialists would have to elaborate and implement a sophisticated strategy in order to appeal to the woman as worker (or worker as woman) without alienating the husband, son, or father as elector, peasant, and property owner.

2

Geographical and Temperamental Landscapes

They were seasonal laborers but mistrustful flatlanders used a less charitable name: *boquaux*. Twice a year these "outlanders" descended from the Alpine foothills of the Isère to the broad plains east of Lyon to labor in the fields of large landowners.[1] Today no one would see a visitor from a village perhaps twenty miles away as quite so alien; technology (Paris is just over two hours away by high-speed train) and the politics of immigration have completely redefined the identity of the alien in France. But until the middle of the nineteenth century, seasonal agricultural laborers defined the boundaries of otherness in the department of the Isère.[2] The nineteenth-century pejorative slang is instructive: it encapsulates the sense of distance, of geographical variety, and of the already precarious status of peasants who depended on income from seasonal labor.

If one were situated at the exact geographical center of France, the Isère would be located almost due east (see Map 1). But since in geography, as in so many other things French, the center of the compass is fixed on Paris, the Isère is known as a department of the southeast. When one takes a regional perspective—that is, from

1. See Jean Ginet, "La Main d'oeuvre agricole saisonnière dans le Bas-Dauphiné," *RGA* 21 (1933): 338–339.
2. On peasants' receptivity to anti-Semitism see Michael Burns, *Rural Society and French Politics* (Princeton, 1984), which devotes special attention to Isère.

Map 1 France and its departments

the city of Lyon, at the confluence of the Rhône and the Saône—the Isère extends southward and eastward. Its northern and western boundaries are marked by the Rhône River; its eastern edge abuts the peaks of the Alps. The Isère's southern boundaries are less easily described; they were drawn in accordance with political sensibilities rather than natural limits.

The name Vercors, the designation of the Isère's natural fortress and the shelter of choice to the Resistance during World War II, helps to convey a sense of the ruggedness of the eastern half.[3] A few elevation figures complete the picture. The city of Lyon is only 160 meters above sea level. Grenoble, the departmental capital, some 100 kilometers to the southeast of Lyon, sits only 60 meters higher. Travel beyond Grenoble to the east perhaps only another 50 kilometers and one is in the midst of peaks reaching to nearly 4,000 meters.

The Isère's western half, beginning at Grenoble, is known as the Lower Dauphiné (Bas-Dauphiné); it lacks the steep contours of the Alpine east. In the Bas-Dauphiné, plains and rolling hills predominate. Fundamental differences between east and west have potentiated others.

Quite obviously such conditions impose constraints on customs and habitat. In the Alpine east, harsh climate and terrain limit the sizes of settlements and do nothing to encourage communication: there are simply no large settlements in the region. The most important commune in the region, Bourg-d'Oisans, struggled to maintain a population that had fallen below 2,500 at mid-century.[4] Indeed, the higher elevations in the Isère are the locations of choice for those who prefer the ascetic way of life. The monks of the Grande Chartreuse settled in the Alpine east of the Isère precisely because its inhospitality ensures solitude.

In the Bas-Dauphiné, gentler contours and more temperate

3. The boundaries of the department have been changed once. Under the Second Empire, in 1852, four communes in the northwestern corner of the department, Villeurbanne, Bron, Vénissieux, and Vaulx-en-Velin, were attached to the department of the Rhône. The act merely made official what had been publicly recognized for some time—that these communes had become satellites of Lyon. See Edmond Esmonin and Henri Blet, eds., *La Révolution de 1848 dans le départment de l'Isère* (Grenoble, 1949), p. viii.

4. ADI, 123 M, 3, 6, 8, 10. The population was 2,766 in 1866. It then declined steeply but recovered to 2,609 just before World War I.

weather, especially in the river valleys, have permitted larger settlements and greater mobility. Indeed, parts of the Bas-Dauphiné have a distinctly meridional flavor, a description especially merited by those communes that trace their date of settlement to Roman times. Grenoble is customarily regarded as the boundary between the two halves of the department, a perspective entirely appropriate because that city possesses both Alpine and southern features characteristic of the two regions.

Agriculture: Crops

Agriculture in the nineteenth century was as varied in the Isère as anywhere else in France, thanks to the subsistence farmer's compulsion to grow *un peu de tout,* a little of everything. Potatoes, wheat, rye, and grapes (for wine) were among the more popular crops. Farmers also produced some less common ones: chestnuts, mulberry leaves (for silkworms), dairy products, and—a local specialty—walnuts, *noix de Grenoble,* of strictly regional renown. Given the variations in climate, soil, and resources in the Isère, not all of these things could be grown everywhere. Even in the nineteenth century there was some specialization, at least where one's holdings permitted a degree of commercial farming, and the specific advantages afforded by the various regions of the department contributed to the creation of three large agricultural zones. The first of these zones is the Isère's easternmost region, corresponding roughly to the part of the department that lies east of Grenoble. The second zone occupies the middle ground, most of the arrondissements of La Tour-du-Pin and St-Marcellin. The third zone includes the remaining territory—essentially the plains east of Vienne and the Rhône but west of the foothills.[5] The first zone contained both the least and the most valuable lands. People at the higher elevations generally engaged in forestry and livestock herding. The cantons that make up the Vercors and beyond, such as Villard-de-Lans, Monestier-de-Clermont, and

5. This schema differs only slightly from that offered by Edouard Bovier-Lapierre in *De l'influence du milieu physique sur le développement économique* (Paris, 1906), p. 171.

Clelles, were very poor. Cattle in the region were sturdy enough to withstand the harsh climate and difficult terrain but were not good milk producers. Prices for farmland in the area, mostly suited only to pasture, reflected the severity of conditions in the area and were among the lowest in the department, dipping below 1,000 francs per hectare in 1908.[6] The same could be said for the canton of Le Touvet, on the steep right bank of the Isère near Chambéry. This agricultural zone east of Grenoble, however, also encompassed several fertile river valleys that offered some of the department's very best agricultural land. The fertile, terraced hillsides of the Grésivaudan, as the valley of the Isère above Grenoble is known, produced·not only the customary grains but grapes of good quality.[7] First-quality land could also be found beside the Drac and, to a lesser degree, the Romanche. The eastern zone of the department thus presents extremes of agricultural wealth and poverty.

In the middle elevations, land of better-than-average productivity yielded a greater variety of crops. In this second zone warmer temperatures and more gradual contours present the observer with an entirely different picture. Beside the river Isère farmers raised grapevines and chestnut trees as well as fruit and walnut trees in a setting that feels semiarid by mid-July. This is where meridional France begins. The land is not always the best, but a combination of factors, including adequate water and sunlight along with less abrupt changes in terrain, make the area more livable if sometimes only marginally more productive than the higher zone. Elsewhere in the hilly second zone there was less room for variation. Here one could find grains, rye, and hemp—hemp especially before the middle of the nineteenth century. Extension of cleared land at the expense of woods and scrub produced extra pastureland for sheep in the Bièvre during the eighteenth century.[8] But the combination of very

6. Figures for land values may be found in Pierre Barral, *Le Départment de l'Isère sous la Troisième République 1870–1940* (Paris, 1962), p. 128.

7. The Grésivaudan also produced large quantities of hemp in the mid–nineteenth century. Along with the cantons of Tullins and St-Marcellin, the region averaged as high as 1,500 kilograms of thread per hectare. See Edmond Esmonin's comments in Esmonin and Blet, *Révolution de 1848*, p. x.

8. Bernard Chorier, "Réaction aristocratique et poussée sociale dans une cellule rurale du Bas-Dauphiné: St-Hilaire-de-la-Côte, 1659–1835," in Chorier, *Structures économiques et problèmes sociaux du monde rural dans la France du Sud-Est* (Paris, 1966), p. 264. Chorier (p. 307) describes how the meridional char-

small farms and very high population densities, as high as 200 persons per square kilometer in the canton of Morestel, required peasant households to make the most of resources that had been severely taxed for generations. Polyculture was the prudent choice under such circumstances, at least for the short term, with potatoes and grains, including buckwheat, among the preferred crops. The draining of swamps, particularly around La Tour-du-Pin, helped to increase the area of land available for cultivation or pasture.[9]

The Isère's third agricultural zone, beyond the plain of Lyon in the department's northwestern corner and west of the foothills, was the department's ideal grain-producing area. Included for administrative purposes in the arrondissement of Vienne, this area bore some resemblance to the heavily commercialized grain-producing plains of Bresse to the north. This was the only part of the department where medium- to large-scale farming was carried out. In the years before the rural exodus, mechanization, and the development of a national market in grain, there was a considerable seasonal circulation of goods and persons in the western half of the department, as when the *boquaux* descended from the foothills to help bring in the harvest.

Of course, crop patterns rarely follow such neat divisions, partly because markets can influence planting decisions as much as geography or microclimates. Wheat, grapes, and walnuts were the three great crops, and more precise knowledge of their distribution tells us about the status of the peasantry.

Wheat is an unusual case precisely because it was so common. Large-scale commercial farmers grew 40 percent of the Isère's wheat on 20 percent of its land area; in the plains east of Vienne every fourth hectare was planted in wheat. The figure serves as an index of the quality of the region's soil and terrain, and the methods of cultivation practiced by the region's farmers. To these factors must be added a major commercial advantage: proximity to the major market of Lyon. All of these factors combined to make these

---

acter of the Bièvre, as much a matter of crops as of terrain and climate, disappeared over the course of the nineteenth century, when over three-quarters of the cultivable land was planted in grains.

9. Bovier-Lapierre, *De l'influence,* pp. 158, 171. In the department of the Ain, these swamps were actively managed in a system of pisciculture that produced an affordable fish for *Lyonnais* of modest income.

plains profitable and enormously productive, the "granary of the Dauphiné."[10]

The remainder of the wheat crop was farmed in much less capital-intensive settings. Wheat was planted and harvested nearly everywhere, even where one would think that the quantity and quality of the yield would discourage the practice. Grenoble, with half of the department's land area, produced only one-fifth of its wheat crop; higher altitudes, colder air, and uneven contours led to dismal yields on the one hectare in twenty committed to wheat. Farmers around La Tour-du-Pin and St-Marcellin produced more substantial quantities of wheat, though mostly for local consumption. Even peasant families with the tiniest parcels of land to cultivate planted grain for their own use.

The farmers of the Isère also produced fair quantities of that other French staple, wine. In 1905 they cultivated, harvested, and processed over 580,000 hectoliters of it. Grenoble led the way in hectares under cultivation and in hectoliters produced, though not in quality. Grésivaudan's peasants and farmers accounted for one-third of the department's production in 1905. The Grésivaudan, the river valley north of Grenoble, was the Isère's most important winegrowing region. But in France wine, like wheat, is ubiquitous. The farmers of Vienne produced 25 percent of the department's volume from vines grown beside the Rhône, on far fewer hectares than the *grenoblois* planted. La Tour-du-Pin and St-Marcellin each accounted for one-fifth of the Isère's wine production.[11]

The Isère's other high-volume crop was walnuts. Despite all appearances to the contrary, *les noix de Grenoble* are not grown in the area of Grenoble, or even in its arrondissement. Like a good deal of Lyon silk and most Milwaukee beer, Grenoble nuts are associated with the city simply as a matter of convenience. Fully 80 percent of the crop, some 36,404 metric quintals, came from the farms around St-Marcellin, below Grenoble along the banks of the river Isère.[12]

---

10. The expression is Philippe Vigier's in *La Seconde République dans la région alpine* (Paris, 1963). Precise production figures may be found in François Roualt, *Géographie agricole du département de l'Isère* (Grenoble, 1907), p. 53.

11. Figures on wine and vineyard hectarage are from Roualt, *Géographie agricole*, p. 152. For figures from the earlier period see Vigier, *Seconde République*, 1:58.

12. See Vigier, *Séconde République*, 1:129.

We must take care not to leap to the conclusion that agriculture in the department was a highly specialized and commercialized affair; it was not, nor could it have been. For the vast majority of farmers the first priority was to produce the food that the household would need. In most cases, this priority compelled the prudent family to plant a variety of crops, foremost among them wheat. This preoccupation did not rule out farming for the market, but, as one source put it, agriculture in the Bas-Dauphiné was essentially an "enriched" polyculture "in which wheat dominated."[13] The unglamorous potato also had its place in this scheme. Peasants in the Isère produced some 136,461 tons of potatoes in 1838. Nine in ten of these potatoes were to be consumed on the farm that grew them.[14] Nearly all small farmers were compelled to produce some goods for market, if only to satisfy debts payable in cash, but most small farmers did not produce principally for the market. Market agriculture involved some risks; subsistence farming was farming for the risk-averse and for those who could not afford to fail.

When these peasants needed to increase their income, then, they thought not of risky market-oriented agriculture but of ways to multiply their sources of income. The raising of silkworms in the Bas-Dauphiné under the Second Republic conformed neatly to this logic.[15] So did hiring oneself out to harvest wheat, at least through the first decades of the Third Republic.[16] The rural textile industry fitted into this pattern of rural life through the second half of the nineteenth century and beyond.

The point is neatly supported by an 1899 letter to the prefect of the Isère from farmers in the town of St-Didier-de-la-Tour. The peasants, in search of a sure thing, requested permission to grow tobacco, a strictly controlled substance under government monopoly, and therefore highly profitable. They supported their argument with the simple observation that St-Didier-de-la-Tour, unlike most other areas, lacked rural industry. They complained of their disadvantageous position and pleaded with the prefect "to include St-

13. Louis Champier, "L'Equilibre économique du Bas-Dauphiné septentrional de la fin du XVIIe siècle au milieu du XIXe," *Evocations*, October 1949, p. 497. See also Pierre Barral, "Le Dauphiné des notables," in Bernard Bligny et al., *Histoire du Dauphiné* (Toulouse, 1973), p. 352.

14. Esmonin and Blet, *Révolution de 1848*, p. ix.

15. See Vigier, *Seconde République*, p. 59.

16. See Ginet, "Main d'oeuvre agricole saisonnière," pp. 338–339.

Didier-de-la-Tour, which has no industry, and thus whose sole resource consists of agriculture, among those communes permitted to
grow tobacco in 1899."[17] Out of the dense agricultural thicket that
was subsistence farming, local specialties and preferences did
emerge: in the lower river valleys it was walnuts, on the upper Isère
it was wine, everywhere else—and particularly on the western
plains—it was wheat. But sometimes the best cash crop was silk.

Agriculture: Property

According to Louis Champier, the formula for the crisis
of peasant society in the Isère of the nineteenth century was simple:
increasing population and the ongoing partition of land under cultivation.[18] Champier's assertion raises questions about the size of
farm that could support the typical rural household.

"The average extent [of the farm] fluctuate[d] around the figure
of eight hectares," wrote Paule Bernard about the Bièvre (Bas-
Dauphiné) at the end of the nineteenth century. This small size "led
to increasing difficulties for the large rural family trying to live
solely on the products of the land."[19] By the end of the nineteenth
century, she writes, the repeated division of the family inheritance
created a dangerous situation for rural families. But if eight hectares marked the threshold of subsistence in that central part of the
Bas-Dauphiné, how did families with less land ever manage to
survive? And what about elsewhere?

Elsewhere matters were sometimes much worse. By all accounts,
efficient exploitation of the soil in the department of the Isère was
severely hampered by the persistence of a large number of *micro-
propriétaires:* those whose available land was unusually small. According to a source writing at the turn of this century, "property in
the Isère was excessively divided, a condition quite unfavorable to
the development and progress of agriculture," and this situation
did not improve substantially until well after the rural exodus had

---

17. ADI, 52 M, 60, 5 September 1898.
18. Champier, "Equilibre économique."
19. Paule Bernard, "Un Exemple d'industrie dispersée en milieu rural," *RGA* 40
(1952): 137.

gotten under way.[20] Farms throughout the department in 1892 averaged only four hectares, a figure far below the subsistence threshold of eight hectares cited by Bernard for the Bièvre. Four-fifths of all holdings in that year were smaller than five hectares, and 43 percent of households got by on a parcel of one hectare or less, an astonishingly low figure.[21] Either these households were on land of such exceptional quality that their two, three, or four hectares were as productive as eight hectares elsewhere, or they were deriving income from other sources, making considerable sacrifices, or both.

There are always variations to consider, however—variations over geography and over time. At the end of the nineteenth century, farms of five or fewer hectares dominated the agricultural landscape in the Grésivaudan, around Grenoble and to the south, throughout most of the arrondissement of La Tour-du-Pin, and along the banks of the Isère from Grenoble to Voiron and south to the department of the Drôme. Small property was the rule everywhere except for the arrondissement of Vienne, where markets, soil, terrain, and history favored larger, more efficient producers, and the higher elevations of the Vercors and the Massif de la Chartreuse, regions of pasture where terrain and soil pushed much higher the number of hectares of land area needed to remain above the threshold of subsistence. In two generations this situation would change as trends favored larger holdings, but for the first half of the Third Republic, farms larger than ten or fifteen hectares were limited to specific geographic areas.[22]

The pattern of landholding offers yet another perspective when it is placed across a temporal dimension. There can be little doubt about the trend for most of the nineteenth century. During the eighteenth century and the first half of the nineteenth, the size of the average farm in the Isère decreased with the general increase in population. Louis Champier assures us that this was the case in the northern half of the Bas-Dauphiné, and other sources confirm the

20. Comte de Galbert et Charles Génin, *L'Agriculture dans l'Isère au XIXe siècle* (Grenoble, 1900), p. 33. Bernard argues that agricultural conditions remained difficult despite the effects of the *exode rural* ("Exemple d'industrie dispersée," p. 137).

21. Barral, *Département de l'Isère*, pp. 95–96.

22. Ibid.

trend in the southern half and elsewhere.[23] In fact, there is little risk in stating that, in rural French communities at least, population was inversely proportional to farm size, because after the onset of the *exode rural* the trend was reversed (at least over the long run) as the average farm size tended to increase.

The corollary to this rule is that the number of persons in a given locality will be directly proportional to the number of farms. Jean Garavel studied records spanning 120 years in his village of Morette.[24] Morette is located in the canton of Tullins, in the arrondissement of St-Marcellin. At an elevation of about 400 meters, Morette is five kilometers from the river Isère. In this part of the Bas-Dauphiné, where the average size of the communes hovered at just fewer than 500 persons during most of the Third Republic, Morette's population of 422 in 1891 was not far from the mean.

The sizes of the farms in Morette varied in direct proportion to changes in the population. As the population of Morette increased in the first half of the nineteenth century, farms proliferated. In fact, the number of farms nearly doubled in the thirty-five years between 1827 and 1862, from 61 to 116. Perhaps just as important, and typical of pre-*exode* rural France, more than half of those new farms were maintained on fewer than five hectares.[25] The small peasantry was at its apogee in respect to numbers but was approaching its nadir in respect to the quality of life. Fertility and partible inheritance drove the peasant household beyond the strict boundaries that framed its existence.

After the 1860s the so-called rural exodus had gotten under way in earnest and the number of farms began to fall; in fact, the number fell quite steeply. Most directly touched were peasants on marginal farms. In Garavel's Morette, for example, the decline in the number of farms was registered exclusively in the category representing farms of fewer than five hectares. More prosperous middle peasants profited, in a jackal-like manner, from the crisis of the

23. According to Champier, "Au dix-huitième siècle il est certain que la population deviendra plus nombreuse encore—a chaque génération, par suite des partages successoraux, la part de terre allouée à chacun va se réduire alors que la technique n'évolue pas" ("Equilibre économique," n.p.).

24. Jean Garavel, *Les Paysans de Morette* (Paris, 1948). A table showing the results of Garavel's study may be found on p. 43. Population figures given for Morette are from ADI, 123 M, 3, 6, 8, 10.

25. Chorier has made a similar point about population increases and farm size elsewhere in the Isère in "Réaction aristocratique," p. 308.

small peasantry; virtually all other categories of farmers continued to grow after the 1860s and on through the 1890s. The number of farms of all sizes in the commune of Morette declined by 12 percent in the thirty years between 1862 and 1892, despite the fact that in the same period the number of farms of from five to ten hectares rose by nearly 18 percent, and comparable increases are found in all other categories of farms save the very largest. The number of farms smaller than five hectares, however, declined by one-third—a measure of the peasantry's steep slide into misery. Throughout the department similar conditions obtained through the turn of the century; in the thirty years between 1878 and 1908, land values in the department of the Isère declined on average by 33 percent.[26] These figures suggest two conclusions: that the crisis in French agriculture at the end of the nineteenth century was above all the crisis of the small peasantry; and that it was the middle peasants— those who worked farms of perhaps ten to twenty hectares—who were benefiting from the small peasants' distress by snatching up land at fire-sale prices.

Oddly, large landowners did not profit from the crisis of the small peasantry. Indeed, they were experiencing troubles of their own; it is more than a matter of chance that the onset of the rural exodus overlapped with a crisis in large agriculture. Liberal trade policies under the Second Empire drove down the price of grain; foreign grain arrived for sale at Marseille at prices below the production costs of local producers in the Isère. The economic crisis of 1860 thus opened a prolonged period of trouble for large-scale farming—one from which many large farms would never recover.[27] Many large landowners took this downturn as a signal to evaluate investments. Many sold their land, even though prices were declining, and shifted their capital to industrial enterprises.[28]

The twin crises of peasantry and large agriculture became com-

26. Specialists in rural France in the nineteenth century have noted the decline in land prices toward the end of the century—a consequence and not a cause of the rural exodus. For precise figures on declining land values in the Isère, see Barral, *Département de l'Isère*, p. 127.

27. According to one source, after 1860 large-scale agriculture "n'était plus une entreprise rentable": Champier, "Equilibre économique," p. 497. It should be pointed out that many farmers were tenants. The arrondissement of Vienne was the only area of the Isère where *faire-valoir indirect* constituted a significant element in the system of ownership and cultivation of agricultural land. See Vigier, *Seconde République*, p. 67.

28. Champier, "Equilibre économique," p. 497.

plementary and mutually reinforcing. Many landowning peasants also worked as seasonal laborers for the larger landowners of the Bas-Dauphiné. Large property owners looked to smallholders for seasonal labor and smallholders looked to large landowners for the additional income they needed. Typically it was the young men who descended to the plains of Vienne to work the harvest. Twice annually they visited the fields of Vienne: in June for the harvest of oats, wheat, and barley, in July for oats again and for threshing. In compensation for their labor, each team received one-tenth of the harvest (*la dixième gerbe*) or some other amount or ratio negotiated in advance.[29] Since these payments were generally made in kind, the peasants' annual employment gave them a large marketable quantity of grain that could easily be converted to cash. In fact, the seasonal laborer usually sold his share at threshing time and returned home with his earnings. In such a manner small polycultural farming and large market-oriented agriculture in the Bas-Dauphiné reinforced and sustained each other through the first half of the nineteenth century.

Now their misery was complementary too. The rural exodus, beginning in the 1850s, and the crisis of large agriculture, which commenced in the Bas-Dauphiné in the 1860s, marked the onset of decay. Because of their mutual dependence, small agriculture suffered with large; the position of small farm households became more precarious with diminishing opportunities to supplement their resources with income from seasonal farm labor. As the most marginal of small farmers departed, they took with them the hands that made seasonally labor-intensive large-scale farming possible.

The presence of rural industry offered an alternative for some peasants, but it also aggravated the problems of the large farm. The condition of relative labor scarcity created by the rural exodus, the inability of agriculture to match the higher wages offered by rural industry, and the invention and adoption of agricultural machinery, such as the reaper and binder, combined to put an end to the low-wage, labor-intensive conditions in which large and small prop-

29. The "teams" consisted of two persons: the *faucher* and the *ramasseur*. For a complete description of this complementary relationship between large and marginal proprietors, see Ginet, "Main d'oeuvre agricole saisonnière," pp. 338–341; see also Chorier, "Réaction aristocratique," p. 137; Barral, "Dauphiné des notables," p. 351.

ertyholders together had thrived.[30] New conditions after mid-century favored the middle peasantry, or at least did not undermine it. The rural Isère was becoming more socially homogeneous, but it was doing so at the expense of both the top and bottom of the rural social order. Successive thinnings of the ranks at the extremes was helping to create in the Isère—with a few important exceptions—a more uniform rural society.

The Lyon silk industry made its appearance in time to witness the twin crises of large agriculture—undercutting of the Bas-Dauphiné grain producers—and the onset of the *exode rural*. Wage labor in rural textile mills helped to maintain some otherwise marginal peasant households; but it could not maintain all households everywhere. For those within the orbit of rural industry, the shift from a household strategy that depended on men's seasonal labor in agriculture to one that depended on women's seasonal labor in industry was far from trivial. For those outside the reach of rural industry, and they were legion, all hopes rested on finding a better life elsewhere. Survivors in the Isère were middle peasants and those marginal households whose location and resources in land and labor meshed most neatly with local opportunities.

The Political Landscape, 1848:
An Exception to the Rule?

It was the spirit of René Hébert, not the specter of communism, that haunted the working-class city of Vienne in February 1848. The news of the February Revolution in Paris inspired a group of workers—would-be sansculottes and *bons bougres* of Père Duchense—to round up more than a dozen priests and run them out of town. Vienne could thus lay undisputed claim to a peculiar title: headquarters of anticlericalism in the Isère under the Second Republic.[31] Perhaps it was the admonishment of the spirit of

---

30. On technological innovations in Bas-Dauphiné agriculture see Ginet, "Main d'oeuvre agricole saisonnière," pp. 340–341.

31. Vigier, *Seconde République*, p. 203. On dechristianization in the Isère under the First Republic, see Michel Vovelle, *La Révolution contre l'église* (Paris, 1988), pp. 97, 114. For discussions of the estrangement of workers from the church see François Lebrun, ed., *Histoire des catholiques en France due XVe siècle à nos jours*

Jacques Barnave, but elsewhere in the Isère silence was the first reaction to the news of the overthrow of Louis-Philippe in 1830 and the proclamation of the Second Republic at the Hôtel de Ville in Paris in 1848. The exception, as in so much else, was the city of Vienne, where a genuine workers' movement was alive and thriving on traditions of militancy dating back to the beginning of the century, back even to the Year II. Outside of Vienne there was no immediate public celebration.[32]

Public opinion, at least as measured by political expression of it, underwent a profound reorientation in the Isère between 1848 and 1914. In time a consensus may emerge about the place of the Second Republic in the creation of the republican tradition in France; indeed, Maurice Agulhon's view that it was the crucial period of apprenticeship for the Republic may already prevail.[33] I take his position as a starting point for tracing the subsequent development of republican politics under the Third Republic. In this sense, the history of the Republic in nineteenth-century France was in part the history of the reaction of the provinces against the Revolution, at least in its Parisocentric or Montagnard phase; the Republic was the means provincial France finally discovered to impose its will on Paris, the periphery on the center.[34] This is not to

---

(Toulouse, 1980), esp. pp. 286–287, 297–299, 318; and Gérard Cholvy and Yves-Marie Hilaire, *Histoire religieuse de la France contemporaine*, vol. 1, *1800–1880* (Toulouse, 1985). On the lasting appeal of anticlericalism in Limoges, see John M. Merriman, *The Red City* (New York, 1985), pp. 160–161.

32. The envy of all those who have ever tried a hand at electoral geography is André Siegfried, whose *Tableau politique de la France de l'Ouest sous la Troisième République* (Paris, 1913) is still a source of inspiration more than seventy years after its publication. Readers interested in a more detailed discussion of electoral geography as a subdiscipline of French historiography should begin with François Goguel's *Géographie des élections françaises* (Paris, 1951). Georges Dupeux's *Aspects de l'histoire sociale et politique du Loir-et-Cher* (Paris, 1962) is innovative in many respects. Tony Judt's *Socialism in Provence* (Cambridge, 1979) brilliantly suggests new ways of understanding peasant society and the meaning of Radical and Socialist votes within it. William Brustein, "A Regional Mode of Production Analysis of Political Behavior," *Politics and Society* 10 (1981): 355–398, makes some meaningful regional comparisons while constructing a utilitarian model of the French voter. Brustein pursues these points in *The Social Origins of Political Regionalism* (Berkeley, 1988). For a criticism of Brustein's approach see Laird Boswell, "How Do French Peasants Vote?" *Peasant Studies* 16 (1989): 107–122.

33. Maurice Agulhon, *1848; ou L'Apprentissage de la République* (Paris, 1973), inexplicably translated as *The Republican Experiment* (Cambridge and New York: Cambridge University Press, 1983).

34. Syndicalism was another possible response to the Jacobin tradition. On the

say that provincial France was hostile to all manifestations of the republican left. As the conservative republican Adolphe Thiers might have put it, the Republic would be Girondin or it would not be.

Here the aim is to identify the boundaries of the Socialist constituency, to locate the moment when the Socialist and nonsocialist wings of the republican left in rural France parted ways. If we are to understand this moment, we must first understand the established political tendencies in the Isère in 1848 and then follow through to the periods of the Radical Republic and on to the emergence of a distinct Socialist left toward 1914. If we are to make sense of the sudden popularity of Socialist politics after 1900, we must know more than how this popularity extended or departed from established local political traditions. In certain crucial respects, opinions expressed at election time only imperfectly represented popular attitudes, in part because the apprenticeship of 1848 was incomplete. How could it not be, when it did not include women? The Socialists recognized this difficulty, implicitly and explicitly, and prepared their success by molding their identity around a constituency consisting of the working women and men of the Bas-Dauphiné. To appreciate the novelty of socialism in the Isère we thus must recognize important continuities, without overlooking crucial discontinuities, departures, and adaptations. And 1848 is the place to begin.

When the watchful silence of February 1848 was broken, memories of the Great Revolution did play a role. The spirit of July–August 1789 inspired some peasants to exploit opportunistically the change of regimes in February 1848. They settled certain local grievances at what seemed to be a propitious moment. In some parts of the Bas-Dauphiné, for example, peasants demanded the distribution of communal land; in other places the suspension of governmental authority was taken as a signal to gather wood from private forests. But these incidents were quite limited in scope; generally the news of the revolution in Paris engendered little activity and few public expressions of support. Nor, for that matter, did the February Revolution give rise to the sense of foreboding in the Isère that it did in departments commonly associated with "conser-

anti-Jacobinism of the syndicalists see Jeremy Jennings, *Syndicalism in France* (New York, 1990), esp. p. 60.

vative France," where the memory of the Great Revolution was both unpleasant and easily revived.[35] If the Dauphiné had been the "cradle of the Revolution" in 1788, sixty years later it nurtured less ambitious aims.

Odd as it may seem, the Catholic church was among the first to rally to the Republic. Less than two weeks after the February Revolution the bishop of the diocese of Grenoble made a dramatic show of support for the new Republic. On 4 March he circulated a directive to parish priests ordering them to recognize the provisional government of the new Republic, to drape tricolor bunting from church towers, to sing the Te Deum, and to offer funeral services in honor of the victims of the revolutionary street fighting in Paris in February.[36] The Isère seems always to have favored a Gallican and progressive Catholicism. Despite vigorous official opposition, under the Restoration voters had elected the abbé Grégoire, symbol of the Revolution's constitutional church, to represent them in the Chamber of Deputies in 1819.[37] Another Catholic church would reveal itself after 1875 under the leadership of the reactionary bishop Fava at Grenoble, but during the Second Republic Gallican and politically moderate forces prevailed within Catholicism in the Isère.[38] A gulf seemed to separate radical Montagnard Vienne from

35. On the initial response of the peasants see Vigier, *Seconde République*, pp. 199–201. On conservative France see, e.g., Jean-Clément Martin, *La Vendée et la France* (Paris, 1987).

36. Philippe Vigier and G. Argenton, "Les Elections dans l'Isère sous la Seconde République," in Esmonin and Blet, *Révolution de 1848*, p. 12. For the reaction of Catholic leadership in Paris and elsewhere see Antonin Debidour, *Histoire des rapports de l'église et de l'état de 1789 à 1870* (Paris, 1898), pp. 481–484.

37. In fact, the margin of victory for Grégoire was provided by ultraroyalists, whose votes for him are an example of *la politique du pire*. He was rejected by the Chamber for reasons of "political morality." See Robert Badinter, "Eloge de l'abbé Grégoire," *L'Express*, 15 December 1989, p. 21; René Rémond, *The Right Wing in France from 1815 to de Gaulle* (Philadelphia, 1966), pp. 66–68; and Georges Hourdin, *L'Abbé Grégoire: Evêque et démocrate* (Paris, 1989), pp. 139–141. On the origins of the abrupt rightward shift that established the pattern for church attitudes under the Third Republic see Jacques Gadille, *La Pensée et l'action politiques des évêques français au début de la IIIe République, 1870–1883* (Paris, 1967).

38. The crucial difference between the epochs was the experience of Catholics under the Second Empire, which gave new life to reactionary and ultramontaine forces within the Catholic church. See Norman Ravitch, *The Catholic Church and the French Nation, 1685–1985* (London, 1990), and Ralph Gibson, *A Social History of French Catholicism, 1789–1914* (London, 1989).

Grenoble and the rest of the Isère. The workers' revival of the tactics of the dechristianizers of the Year II revealed a zeal to remember what the church sought desperately to efface. Yet a republic that could count among its supporters such disparate elements as the descendants of the sansculottes and an apparently enlightened or at least prudent Catholic church had high chances of success. As news of the change of regime reached the towns and villages, republicans quietly replaced local officials from the July Monarchy, largely without incident.[39]

Support for the moderate and liberal republic of the February Revolution carried through to the elections of April. The candidates chosen represented the republican ideal as incarnated in the Parisian daily *Le National*—another way of saying that few candidates of "the people" appeared on the republican list, which was dominated by representatives of the middle bourgeoisie.[40] Dissent came from the workers of Vienne and its suburbs, who turned out in large numbers to vote for the candidates proposed by the Comité des Travailleurs. Like the anticlericalism of February, this event went without echo elsewhere.[41]

In December 1848 the voters of the Isère voted again, this time for candidates for the office of president of the Republic. Among the five candidates only two really mattered: General Louis-Eugène Cavaignac and the emperor's nephew Louis-Napoléon. The Isère contributed to the landslide that gave Louis-Napoléon nearly 82 percent of the vote. Cavaignac, saddled with all manner of baggage, including the "45-centimes tax," won barely 15 percent of the vote.[42]

Yet though the Isère voted with the rest of France, it soon found

39. Vigier and Argenton, "Elections," p. 11.

40. AN, C 1331, and Vigier, *Seconde République*, p. 187; for more on the makeup of the republican list see Vigier and Argenton, "Elections," p. 25.

41. On the Comité des Travailleurs see Vigier and Argenton, "Elections," p. 251. The workers of Vienne represent a militant tradition different from the one that was to grow up among the silkworkers. They are famous for their involvement in one of France's few incidents of Luddism. The incident is reported by Raoul Blanchard in "Une Emeute ouvrière dans l'Isère," *Revue d'Histoire de Lyon* 13 (1914).

42. Alexandre-August Ledru-Rollin, François-Vincent Raspail, and Alphonse Lamartine collectively mustered approximately 2 percent. See Vigier and Argenton, "Elections," p. 44.

itself marching alone. Its exceptionalism took the form not of an abrupt shift of alignments but of the persistence of alignments during a period of radicalization elsewhere in France. By 1849, opposition to the direction the Republic was taking—or was not taking—seemed to favor the polarization of political alignments. Throughout France the "morning-after republicans," those rendered suspect by their tardy conversion to the republican creed, were more and more boldly reverting to their prerepublican ways. Meanwhile republicans of conviction shifted leftward toward the "Démoc-socs," radical republicans labeled "red" because of their progressive stance on social issues and their commitment to fulfillment of the "social" promise of the Republic. The republicans of the Isère, however, remained faithful to the original moderate vision of the February Revolution. As Philippe Vigier has put it:

> The originality of political attitudes in the Isère in May 1849 is demonstrated not only by their fidelity to the republican cause but also by the *variety* of republicanism that triumphed there. Most departments voting against the Party of Order voted by a kind of natural force of reaction to elect Red Republicans, the Montagnards. The Isère, for its part, remained faithful to those it elected in February, to the last man moderate republicans [*hommes du National*].[43]

The Second Republic has been referred to as a period of political apprenticeship for republican France.[44] If so, the people of the Isère did not undergo a radical apprenticeship, and the Isère of the Third Republic did not inherit a radical legacy. Why were the citizens of the Isère satisfied with the Republic in its moderate incarnation? The easy answer is that the Isère already had a political tradition in 1848—one it had inherited from the First Republic. That political tradition was republican but legalist, just as the resistance of the *dauphinois* to the crown in 1788 had not strayed from the narrow bounds of legality even if their actions ultimately had revolutionary effects.[45]

43. Ibid., p. 56.
44. The idea of the Second Republic as a period of republican apprenticeship can be found in Vigier's *Seconde République;* the terminology is from Agulhon, *1848,* where this idea is developed persuasively.
45. For more on this legalist tradition, see Barral, "Dauphiné des notables," p. 346; see also pp. 369–370. Lynn Hunt offers several insights into the links between the Second and Third republics and the Revolution of 1789 in *Politics, Culture, and Class in the French Revolution* (Berkeley, 1984).

At least as important as an explanation for the moderation of the inhabitants of the Isère in a region otherwise identified as "red" is the fact that it was spared the worst effects of the economic crisis of mid-century France. While other parts of France were facing hardships in 1848 and after, the Isère was enjoying at least relative prosperity. Thus the economic basis of discontent elsewhere in France was attenuated in the Isère. The only exception to this rule was Vienne, which was more industrialized and thus more vulnerable to economic bad times; moreover, Vienne's population was more heavily nonnative and therefore did not share local traditions. The virtue of this explanation is that it not only can account for the political moderation of the Isère but also can explain why Vienne was the only place in the department where the Démoc-socs received any support in 1849.[46] Thus the unique behavior of Vienne can perhaps best be understood as the reanimation of the political traditions of the Year II in the midst of an industrial crisis and a short-lived collapse of political authority. Elsewhere it was as if, through some prodigious application of will, the people of the Isère had effaced the memory of the politics of the First Republic in favor of the memory of the ideals of 1788 in order to make way for the invention of a tolerant, moderate regime.

The Meaning of the Radical Republic

The dishonorable circumstances in which the French army found itself fell like a dense fog over any enthusiasm felt at the declaration of the Third Republic after the Franco-Prussian War and the collapse of the Empire in the fall of 1870. The fact that industry and commerce were struggling to survive in the economic quagmire created by the Prussian siege of Paris did little to lift the public mood. Even after the armistice, industrialists in the Isère could not be sanguine about the future; they blamed the Commune and the occupation for their troubles.[47]

Recovery and reconstruction would come only after peace, and there was little apparent enthusiasm in the Isère for the neo-Jacobinism of Léon Gambetta. The year 1870 was not 1792; Bis-

46. See Esmonin and Blet, *Révolution de 1848*, p. xxvii.
47. For information on the state of business and industry at the change of regimes see AN, C 3021; F 12, 4509A.

marck was not the Duke of Brunswick; Sedan seemed far from Valmy. For these and a host of other reasons, voters rejected war-mongering republicans in favor of the "Peace List," even if those candidates were avowed monarchists, openly hostile to the new Republic. The result was a second *Chambre introuvable;* like that of the Restoration, it included many representatives of political and religious reaction. Artifact of the overwhelming desire for peace it certainly was, but royalists saw it as the confirmation of a belief they had long cherished and nurtured—*la France profonde* was royalist.

In fact, the allure of monarchist candidates vanished with the Prussians. Republican voters delivered their warning shots in the by-elections of 1871 and 1872, each of which resulted in the substitution of a republican deputy for a monarchist in the Assembly at Versailles. The general elections of February 1876 ought to have shamed the royalists back to their châteaux. That, at least, was the opinion of "an old peasant" from a part of the Isère not noted for advanced political opinions, who wrote to Marshal (and President) MacMahon to explain that he was a republican not from convic-tion but because Bonapartists and monarchists had discredited themselves: "My sons and I swear never again to listen to monar-chists, much less to vote for official candidates. . . . The Empire crumbled under the weight of so many lies and so much shame, . . . the Republic was proclaimed and welcomed here by everyone."[48] The sentiment must have been widely shared, for when Marshal MacMahon prorogued the assembly elected in 1876, the voters responded with an unequivocal message. Of the Isère's eight elec-toral districts, eight elected republican deputies.

The Isère thus began the Third Republic with something of a consensus—if only a negative one—that the days of monarchy and Bonapartism were over. Whatever their differences on other issues, enfranchised citizens in the Isère intended that political battles henceforth would be fought out within the institutional framework provided by the Republic. The voters of the Isère assisted the birth of the Third Republic as they had witnessed the death of the Second—united in their support of a democratic republican ide-al.[49]

48. See "Un vieux paysan du Dauphiné" to Marshal MacMahon, AN, F1C III 5. The letter is signed "Jean-François, cultivateur, près Virieu-sous-la-Bourbre."
49. The point is confirmed by an incident recorded in the early 1880s. In 1882

In March 1882 the National Assembly voted to give municipal councils the power to choose the person to serve as mayor. Until then, political life in France had been stifled at its most basic level by a top-down administrative structure. The office of mayor was filled by a state appointee and not by a person selected by popular mandate. Thus the village's chief executive was a representative of the state rather than an advocate of the people. The law of 4 March 1882 changed that situation by giving municipal councils, themselves popularly elected, the right to elect their mayors. The new law had the unintended consequence of fostering the growth of coalitions and, ultimately, political parties at the municipal level. Besides increasing the authority of local government, the law encouraged and enlivened local political life by favoring electoral coalitions for the purpose of controlling the office of mayor.[50] Like the law that gave the Fifth Republic a popularly elected president after the referendum of 1962, the law of 1882 fostered the development of disciplined parties and of party coalitions with a view toward controlling executive power. Only three years after the 1882 law, the first splits in the republican family of the Isère appeared as first the Radicals and then the Socialists formed distinct parties and electoral committees.[51] A political complement to the Ferry school law, the law of 4 March 1882 made village politics a kind of schoolhouse, a training ground for political action. It created conditions that fostered the growth of political organization, a necessary counterweight to the personal authority of village notables, the wealthy and powerful. It also served as the interface between the world of formal politics, dominated by the enfranchised, and the informal world of public opinion, open to the participation of all.

---

the subprefect at St-Marcellin warned the prefect of the Isère that the populace of his arrondissement was troubled by rumors of the imminent collapse of the Gambetta ministry. The popular fear, as reported by the subprefect, was that Gambetta's government would be replaced not, as one might have guessed, by a conservative one but "par un cabinet d'une nuance plus avancée." Utterance of a sycophant? Certainly, but it contains a kernel of truth. Political preferences in St-Marcellin remained on the tame side until 1906. See ADI, 53 M, 16, 24 January 1882.

50. Jean-Marie Mayeur, *Les Débuts de la Troisième République* (Paris, 1973), pp. 119, 217.

51. Of course, the example of party politics and interparty politics was set at Grenoble, where the challenges but also the rewards of organization were greater. The Groupe Ouvrier Socialiste of Grenoble was formed then, and by 1889 the police recognized it as a significant force in shaping public opinion; see ADI, 55 M, 1, 19 May 1889.

Radicals thrived in a climate that finally allowed the little people to step out from under the shadow of the notables. It was probably not an accident that Léon Gambetta chose the Isère to make his famous *"nouvelles couches sociales"* speech, which heralded the political arrival of the "little people," that broad middle class of shopkeepers, peasants, artisans, and workers which was to assume its share of power in the new Republic under the elastic political rubric of "Radical."[52] The Isère, like many other departments in the southeast of France, was full of "little people," of small property owners and aspiring property owners.

But radicalism was far more than a social phenomenon. A vast political territory on the left of the existing republican alignment had become fair political game with the amnesty of the Communards; the Radicals were the first to stake it out. The Radicals already enjoyed wide support among workers, in part because of the absence of any genuine alternative. The rhetorical restraint of the periods of Moral Order and the Opportunist Republic, coming as it did atop decades of Bonapartist officiousness, created an atmosphere in which Jacobin rhetoric could sound daring and new.[53]

But it would be a grievous mistake to reduce radicalism to a rhetorical phenomenon. Radical politics were not mere plays on historical themes; its issues were far from empty of practical meaning. Radicals seized upon the question of the role of the church in French life because it mattered. In the Isère, the church maintained a high public profile in areas remote from those of traditional religious concern. Several religious orders maintained permanent facilities in the Isère; among them (to mention only a few) were Trappists at Roybon, Capuchins at Meylan, and Jesuits (until 1880) and Sisters of the Sacred Heart at Grenoble. But the most famous order, then and now, was the Carthusian. These monks supported themselves through the sale of the liqueur that bears the name of their

52. The best single source on Gambetta is J. P. T. Bury's *Gambetta and the Making of the Third Republic* (London, 1973). On the features and consequences of the Radical social program see Judith Stone, *The Search for Social Peace* (Albany, 1985).

53. Some Jacobin themes retain their appeal. Note the recent debate surrounding the wearing of the chador in public schools in France. See "Vous avez dit école laïque?" *L'Express,* 3 November 1989, pp. 6–12. Anticlericalism has acquired a new power to mobilize now that it has been combined with fear of immigrants.

mother house, La Grande Chartreuse, near Grenoble.[54] A reclusive (and therefore seemingly mysterious) Catholic order supported by large and profitable sales of liquor presented an enticing and unusually large target with little visible constituency; it was unlikely to go unnoticed for very long. For a left easily seduced by the ideal of temperance and other late Victorian themes, it invited attack. Emile Combes's Radical ministry, in its radical application of the 1901 law on associations, succeeded in catching the Carthusians in this very wide net. Their expulsion in 1903 was an event of national importance.[55]

The proper relation between church and state was a consuming national political issue in these years. The fear that the church stood behind various movements hostile to the Republic reached its zenith during the Dreyfus affair.[56] Under the Combes ministry it became a national obsession. These incidents had their local echoes.

For the church, the Commune of 1871 had been an epiphany. The church suddenly realized how alienated from it the working people of France had become; the church came face to face with the fact that working-class France was a missionary country populated by heathens. The working class became the object of missionary zeal.[57] New parish churches staked out the pagan territory of the working classes in Paris's eastern neighborhoods. For a bourgeoisie stunned by working-class militancy, Catholicism became a colonizing ideology. In the Isère the church collaborated closely with business in a partnership perceived as mutually advantageous. Catholicism became party to the disciplining of workers.

54. The Carthusians had been expelled once before, under the Revolution. Each time they returned under friendly regimes, the first time in 1816, the second time in 1940. On the legislation concerning the Carthusians see François Goguel, *La Politique des partis sous la Troisième République* (Paris, 1946), p. 120. On the expulsion itself see Barral, *Département de l'Isère*, p. 414; and Paul Dreyfus, *La Vie quotidienne en Dauphiné sous la Troisième République* (Paris, 1974), pp. 214–224. For unauthorized religious orders in the Isère, see AN, F 7, 12316, prefect to Minister of the Interior, 6 July 1887.

55. See Jean-Marie Mayeur, ed., *La Séparation de l'église et de l'état* (Paris, 1966), p. 99; François Lebrun, *Histoire des catholiques en France* (Toulouse, 1980).

56. See Georges Bonnefous, *Histoire politique de la Troisième République*, vol. 1, *L'Avant-guerre* (Paris, 1956), esp. p. xi; and Goguel, *Politique des partis*, esp. p. 129.

57. See Jean-Baptiste Duroselle, *Histoire du catholicisme* (Paris, 1985), p. 109.

Well before the 1870s, involuntary religious practice was common in the textile factories.[58] Mill owners made prayer obligatory and sometime attendance at mass as well. Some of the earliest of the textile factories in the Lyon region had chapels built into the factory/dormitory compound. The best and most widely imitated example was the factory of C. J. Bonnet at Jujurieux, in the department of the Ain. At his factory, built after the Lyon insurrections of the 1830s, Bonnet employed only unmarried women, recruited throughout the region, who agreed to live at his compound. He was an employer to these women, but he also functioned *in loco parentis*. As a kind of benevolent patriarch he looked after his workers' spiritual well-being. Religious ritual was incorporated into the daily routine. Religious supervision was constant, both on the job and off. Bonnet operated his mill in this fashion without official interference under the Orléanist monarchy, the Empire, and the early Republic. Most employers in the silk industry chose not to offer housing to their workers (though many did); but in his blending of religion and work, the sacred and the profane, Bonnet had many emulators.

Early in 1886, soldiers armed with hammers, nails, and lumber boarded up and sealed the doors to a chapel in the village of Châteauvilain (Isère). The chapel was not a parish church; it was part of a private residence within a mill complex, where the 300-plus workers were expected to pray and attend mass as part of the factory routine. Resentment of such compulsory practices, allied with the desire to capitalize politically on anticlericalism, almost certainly led the Radical mayor of Châteauvilain to notify authorities of the chapel's existence, a clear violation of the law.[59] The factory owner, one Giraud of Lyon, refused to seek authorization for the chapel, even after he had been advised of his legal obligation to do so. Giraud and his mill manager pointed out that the chapel had been in use for over forty years—since the days of

58. On similar efforts in the Nord see Patricia Hilden, *Working Women and Socialist Politics in France, 1880–1914* (Oxford, 1986), esp. pp. 114–115.

59. The law in question, an obscure and heretofore unenforced one enacted on 18 Germinal of the year X, required that private chapels have the express approval of the government, which had to be requested by a bishop. Obviously the law was intended to make such chapels rare. The text of the relevant portion of the law is reproduced in *La Croix*, 15 April 1886, p. 1.

the July Monarchy—without complaint; any challenge after so many years of us could only be politically motivated. This refusal eventually led to the chapel's forcible closure by order of the prefect of the Isère.

By late March, Châteauvilain, a village of barely 600, was alive with rumors of the chapel's surreptitious reopening. The mill owner was challenging the right of the state to prohibit the construction and use of a place of worship. He would insist on his right to build and use the chapel as he wished. He invited the local parish priest to return to lead prayer and to celebrate mass in the chapel.

On 8 April, on the evidence of these persistent rumors, the subprefect at La Tour-du-Pin dispatched two brigades of soldiers to the mill. When the prefect and the soldiers arrived, they had to break into the mill manager's private residence, to which the chapel was attached. Their entry was blocked from within, so they had to break down a wooden door. At this point the narrative becomes clouded. It is unclear if the manager made his last stand in the chapel sanctuary itself (as an illustration in *Le Temps* would have it) or simply within the walled grounds of his residence. Some facts, however, are indisputable. Fischer, the manager, fired first. When the soldiers sought to break down an outer door, Fischer fired his handgun three times: twice into the air, once into the door. Within, Fischer enjoyed the protection of many of the women who worked for him in his mill. They placed themselves between the soldiers and their employer; they resolved to prevent his arrest. As the soldiers burst through the door, the women closed ranks to shield Fischer. The soldiers pressed forward, and in the ensuing confusion they fired at least three shots. One shot gravely wounded Fischer. One of the workers, Henriette Bonnevie, died from a gunshot wound to the chest. A second women was shot in the thigh.[60]

The incident at Châteauvilain drew the attention of the national as well as local press, and it soon became a political issue. How could the events be shaped to convey an instructive political message? The anticlerical press sought to emphasize the religious control of the workplace. The clerical press argued that the republican

---

60. Details on the incident at Châteauvilain can be found in AN, F 7, 12387, telegram, 12 April 1886; *Le Temps*, 9 April 1886; "Les Troubles de Châteauvilain," *La Croix*, 10–16 April 1886.

impartiality with respect to religion had turned to harassment—*La Croix* called it simply "the religious war."[61] Other stories emphasized the courage of the women: one had it that a saber-wielding soldier was stopped in his tracks when Josephine Martinet cried out, "Strike me if you dare, [but] I'll defend my master!"[62]

Of course as much depended upon the reception of the tale as upon the manner in which it was told. In a region such as the Isère, which *La Croix* was forced to admit was not notably devout, readers were more likely to be receptive to the anticlerical dimension of the narrative. Whether the mill owner at Châteauvilain obliged his workers to attend religious services is not clear, but the mere existence of the chapel suggests its semiofficial status. The Châteauvilain incident of 1886 revealed the importance of the issue of religion in the workplace and helped to make it a political issue by demonstrating its potentially dramatic appeal to voters. By extension, Châteauvilain pointed the way for the political champions of anticlericalism, the Radical Republicans. From the expulsion of the Jesuits through the inventories of church property (which led to the expulsion of the Carthusians from the Isère in 1903), Radicals would establish their political identity through their anticlericalism. Indeed, by 1902 Radical candidates would control the majority of the Isère's seats in the national Assembly.

Whether employers inserted religious practices into the daily factory routine for reasons of personal piety or out of a misguided sense of mission, it amounted to a controlling discourse, an attempt to use religion to define the boundaries of workers' conduct. Some mill owners collaborated with the church in establishing chapters of Albert de Mun's Catholic Circles, though with limited success. There were ten workers' Catholic Circles in the Isère in the 1880s with a total membership of 402. In 1906 the Syndicats Libres de l'Isère, a federation of Catholic trade unions, could claim 231 members, well behind the Rhône, with 2,731 members, and the Nord, with 12,943.[63] Workers were far from infinitely malleable,

---

61. "La Guerre de religion," *La Croix*, 15 April 1886, p. 1.

62. "Le Drame de Châteauvilain," *La Croix*, 14 April 1886, p. 2.

63. On the Catholic Circles and membership figures see AN, F 7, 12477; Patricia Hilden, "Class and Gender: Conflicting Components of Women's Behavior in the Textile Mills of Lille, Roubaix, and Tourcoing, 1880–1914," *Historical Journal* 27 (1984): 361–386. Information on the *syndicats libres* is in AN, F 22, 68. No

however. Ironworkers at Allevard, for example, were reportedly obliged to send their children to Catholic schools or face dismissal from their jobs on the slightest pretext. The official who reported this practice noted that the only form of retaliation available to the workers was the vote. If the choice of schools is an act open to scrutiny, the vote is not. Candidates recommended by the employer were regularly and roundly defeated at Allevard, and thanks to the secret ballot, it was impossible to assign blame.[64]

Thus national political issues had local relevance. The Radicals are often accused, unfairly I believe, of falling short of the more rigorous ideological standards successfully imposed by the Socialists in the same period. There could be considerable variations among candidates, but certain features of the Radicals' program could not be temporized, most notably their attitude toward the church.[65] The persistence in the Isère of violations of freedom of conscience in the name of religion lent substance to the sine qua non of the Radical program: anticlericalism. In these years, as the Dreyfus affair had shown, it was impossible to talk about church and state without taking about the nature of the regime itself.[66] But it was the church's high profile locally, far more than Dreyfus, that made radicalism real, not mere posturing.

Given the uses of religion in the workplace, workers are unlikely to have remained indifferent to religious issues. Indeed, it would be unfair to charge, as many people did, that the Radicals' insistence on raising the religious issue was a diversion, a smoke screen behind which they concealed their identification with the interests of

---

delegates from extreme right-wing groups in the Isère attended the 1909 Congrès de la Fédération Syndicaliste des Jaunes de France. See AN, F 7, 12793, 5 November 1909. Circulation of *La Croix de l'Isère* ran to 22,000, according to Michael Burns, "Politics Face to Face" (Ph.D. diss., Yale University, 1981), p. 180. As a whole, the evidence suggests that the Isère was something of a disappointment to Catholic leaders in this and other respects.

64. On Allevard see AN, BB 18, 1902, Procureur de Grenoble, 7 July 1892. For information on the *guesdistes*'s attitude toward compulsory religious services in factories, see Claude Willard, "Les Attaques contre Notre-Dame de l'Usine," *Mouvement Social* 57 (1966): 203–209.

65. Jean-Marie Mayeur describes anticlericalism as the single issue most likely to unite republicans of all shades. "N'est-ce pas cet anti-cléricalisme qui fonde chez beaucoup . . . l'adhésion à la stratégie de défense républicaine?" (*Débuts*, p. 186).

66. On the importance of the Dreyfus affair in rural France, see Burns, *Rural Society and French Politics*.

the bourgeoisie. On the contrary, the Radicals' attacks on the church, however motivated, were surely greeted sympathetically by many workers who were confronted by the concerted efforts of the church and the employers to rechristianize them.

Thus anticlericalism was both a social and a political issue. Although in retrospect the perception of the church locked in mortal combat with the Republic may appear exaggerated, at the time it was an important way of defining the boundary between public and private. In this sense, the map of votes for Radical candidates is larger than the extent of support for radicalism—it defines the community of individuals committed to a secular public realm.

1910: Drawing the Boundaries
of a Socialist Constituency

Nineteen-ten was a banner year for socialism in the Isère. For the first time in their history, the Socialists of the Isère elected three deputies to the National Assembly, but that is not why the year stands out; in 1914 five Socialists would go to Paris. The real story was about the Socialist candidate who ran a hard campaign without any hope of taking a seat in the Chamber of Deputies. Her name was Elisabeth Renaud.

Cofounder, with Louise Saumoneau, of the Groupe Féministe Socialiste (GFS) in 1899, Renaud was a schoolteacher of working-class background. Saumoneau's acceptance of the common Socialist assertion of the priority of socialism over feminism made her hostile to bourgeois women, even bourgeois feminists, on the grounds that they were class enemies; Renaud's position was more nuanced. Saumoneau, like Paule Mink, saw the collaboration of working-class women with bourgeois feminists as a bourgeois trap. However well intentioned, such an alliance was objectively counterproductive insofar as it diverted working-class energies from the primary tasks of class struggle and social revolution. For Saumoneau, feminism could never be a goal in itself but must be seen as part of a larger effort toward the liberation of working-class women and men from the oppression of capitalism.[67] This strategy

---

67. See Steven C. Hause and Anne R. Kenney, *Women's Suffrage and Social Politics in the French Third Republic* (Princeton, 1984), esp. pp. 69–70; Marie-

of feminist containment dominated French Marxist (*guesdiste*) attitudes under the early Third Republic; working women were to see their place as subsumed within the politics of the working class. In the Nord, as Patricia Hilden has shown, such attitudes led to the estrangement of working women from the *guesdiste* Parti Ouvrier Français (POF).[68]

Elisabeth Renaud had distanced herself from this position without breaking with Saumoneau, and in the Isère she would become the standard-bearer of a different kind of Socialist feminism. Charles Sowerwine has described her socialism as eclectic, a fitting label for a person who felt comfortable in the company of *guesdistes* and *allemanistes*, who supported the participation of the renegade Socialist Alexander Millerand in the "bourgeois cabinet" of René Waldeck-Rousseau, and who finally found her way to a variant of the socialism of social justice associated with Jean Jaurès.[69]

It would be misleading to characterize Renaud's politics as a rejection of the ideals of class struggle. But her politics were unmistakably heterodox, a fact as rich in significance for an understanding of socialism in the Isère as it is for an understanding of the direction her thinking took after the collapse of the GFS in 1905. The Socialist Federation of the Isère offered her the candidacy in the second arrondissement of Vienne. Renaud threw herself into the campaign, running on a platform constructed of both feminist and socialist planks. She had no chance of winning, not only because of her legal disqualification from office but because the second arrondissement of Vienne was not one that any Socialist was likely to win. Indeed, that is why Vienne was chosen for just such a gesture. But what a gesture! By running a feminist, the Socialists had taken a huge risk of alienating conventionally minded voters. But they also had made a bold statement. In one stroke they showed that their commitment to feminism was by no means purely rhetorical, and so did the 2,871 men who cast ballots for Renaud.[70] The

---

Hélène Zylberberg-Hocquard, *Féminisme et syndicalisme en France* (Paris, 1978), p. 111; Charles Sowerwine, *Sisters or Citizens?* (Cambridge, 1982).

68. Hilden, *Working Women*, pp. 213–216.

69. See Sowerwine, *Sisters or Citizens?* pp. 83–84; see also Marilyn J. Boxer, "Socialism Faces Feminism: The Failure of Synthesis in France, 1879–1914," in *Socialist Women*, ed. Boxer and Jean H. Quataert, pp. 95–97 (New York, 1978).

70. See ADI, 8 M, 41; Barral, *Département de l'Isère*, p. 556; Sowerwine, *Sisters or Citizens?* pp. 124–125.

Renaud candidacy showed that the Socialists of the Isère were far from dogmatic but willing to adapt to circumstances, to enlarge the meaning of their cause, to gather rather than to exclude, to make overtures to a constituency defined in more than purely electoral terms. It was a gesture that turned heads, forced people to ask themselves "Why not?" and earned the Socialists the respect of the disenfranchised throughout the department.

It would be tempting to view Renaud's candidacy as a case of tokenism (to employ an anachronism), a cheap and easy gesture in the direction of feminism, with little ultimate consequence. After all, there was no sequel to the Renaud candidacy in the elections of 1914. But this judgment would be unfair. Feminism had to compete for space on an agenda that for obvious reasons was very crowded in 1914. Moreover, to dismiss the Renaud incident would be to miss the meaningful reorientation, paralleled in other Socialist policies, that the Renaud candidacy embodied for Socialists in the Isère. To understand the full significance of the Renaud candidacy, one needs to know about earlier positions taken by the Socialists. As recently as 1906, positions hostile to the open and heterodox socialism represented by Renaud prevailed in the Socialist Federation of the Isère.

Socialism in the Isère goes back to 1880, when the Workers' Federation of Grenoble was organized. After fits and starts, the real growth of the party began in the 1890s, after visits by party luminaries such as Paul Lafargue, which had the additional effect of ensuring the continued development of what had become the Federation of the Isère in 1896, affiliated with Jules Guesde's Parti Ouvrier. Electoral victory came astonishingly soon. Alexandre Zévaès, a student from Paris and favorite of Guesde himself, ran an energetic campaign for election as deputy in 1898. He won in the runoff round, thanks in no small measure to the support of Radical voters, who preferred Zévaès to the incumbent moderate Republican and his Catholic rival.[71] Two years after its founding, the Federation of the Isère had its first deputy.

The federation built its reputation in part upon its intransigent opposition to collaboration with bourgeois parties, despite the evi-

71. ADI, 55 M, 1; Barral, *Département de l'Isère*, pp. 424–427; on *guesdisme* see Claude Willard, *Le Mouvement socialiste en France, 1893–1906* (Paris, 1965).

dent fact that Zévaès owed his success to many bourgeois votes. A political firestorm broke out in 1899 after the Socialist Millerand accepted a seat in the Waldeck-Rousseau cabinet, and the Federation of the Isère loudly condemned such collaboration. Zévaès himself spoke unequivocally on the issue: "We must choose between the path of ministerialism and the path of revolution."[72] That was one way of framing the choice, but the political consequences of such a formulation cost Zévaès dearly. In 1902 he lost his seat in the Chamber of Deputies.

His defeat forced the Federation of the Isère to confront questions being debated by Socialists at the national level. The Dreyfus affair and the related issue of the proper relation between church and state heightened the sense of an embattled Republic. Such an atmosphere favored candidates who took a "sensible" position on the question of republican defense, allying themselves at election time with all good republicans. "Good republicans," including Socialists such as Jean Jaurès, favored a republican bloc in the face of the "clerical reaction." *Guesdistes* insisted on holding the line on class collaboration, even with republicans of "advanced opinions." Was the rhetoric of class struggle a dangerous indulgence in 1902? For many voters it was, and it proved fatal to the Zévaès candidacy.

Zévaès drew the right electoral conclusions from his experience, but the majority in the Federation of the Isère did not. The faction gathered around the charismatic Zévaès showed a strong interest in electoral politics and favored electoral alliances with the Radicals in order to improve the chances of candidates friendly to them and, of course, to improve the party's showing at the polls. They promoted doctrinal changes that would have broadened their appeal and would have moved the Federation of the Isère closer to the Radicals by stressing nonclass issues, such as anticlericalism. The other (older) faction of the party, with close ties to the national POF leadership, strongly disapproved of such a deviation from the federation's program and from the tactics of class struggle.

The dispute came to an open quarrel after the disappointing results of the 1902 elections. For a brief time Zévaès seized control of the federation's newspaper, *Le Droit du Peuple*. The paper dra-

---

72. *Premier congrès général des organisations socialistes françaises* (Paris, 1900), pp. 131–135, cited in Barral, *Départment de l'Isère*, p. 428.

matically reflected the change in editorial policy as it began to run pieces with an anticlerical bent alongside those on the condition of workers, and featured human-interest stories of the *petits divers* genre (drownings and scandals) more typical of the provincial press. "Power lies at the center" was the embedded message; Zévaès's editorial shift pointed the way. Paul Lafargue descended on the Isère to put an end to the disarray. He called an extraordinary federation congress to sort out the mess.[73] It ended when Zévaès walked out.

He formed a rival faction and ran against federation candidates, unsuccessfully, in the next general elections. Perhaps worse than the split itself was the confusion it sowed among local Socialist sections. Although the Federation of the Isère had recovered and fully reconstituted itself by 1906, it was not so strong as it would otherwise have been—for one thing, its candidates had to run against the "renegade" Zévaès and his allies. Thus though the Socialists' performance at the polls improved in 1906, surely it was not what it would have been had the Federation of the Isère not split and had not candidates of rival brands of Socialism—*zévaèsiste* and orthodox—opposed one another for office.[74]

In the elections of 1906, having reinforced its ideological rigor in its struggle with Zévaès, the Federation of the Isère tested a new electoral strategy, one aimed at maximizing not its chances to win seats in the Chamber of Deputies but the propaganda value of election campaigns. At the 1905 national party congress at Chalon-sur-Saône it had supported a resolution to run a candidate in every electoral district in the 1906 general elections, or at least wherever it was within the means of the party to do so. The danger in this policy, as the more parliamentarian Socialists did not fail to point out, was that in spreading its resources so widely the party would hurt the chances of candidates in districts (*circonscriptions*) where the Socialists were strong and had a chance to win.

73. See the daily *Droit du Peuple* for 1902; Barral, *Départment de l'Isère*, p. 430. Zévaès went on to pursue a varied career as politician, historian, and attorney. His legal career manifested a persistent opportunistic streak and appetite for controversy (one of his clients was the assassin of Jean Jaurès). Barral interviewed Zévaès before his death, and I am grateful to him for the opportunity to discuss the personality and career of Zévaès.

74. In the second district of Grenoble, Brizon (SFIO) took nearly 4,000 votes and forced the *zévaèsiste* Cornand into a runoff round against a Catholic candidate. See AN, C 6355.

The Federation of the Isère, now part of the French Section of the Socialist International (SFIO), anticipated by some months the policy worked out by the SFIO at its Chalon-sur-Saône congress. At their annual congress the Socialists of the Isère decided that "a [Socialist] candidate will be presented for the first electoral round in all of the electoral districts of the Isère." In this and other matters they faithfully reflected the attitude of the old POF. They reasserted the federation's authority over candidates' dealmaking, for example, when they proclaimed that "no arrangements may be made with other political parties. The federal committee will announce the Federation's stance for the second round of the election." This carefully orchestrated bottom-up procedure, relying upon the *guesdiste* militants in the federations to anticipate motions at the national congress, was intended not only to limit the independence of federation candidates; it was also used to limit the power of Socialist deputies at party congresses.[75] The Socialists in the Isère thus showed at once several traits readily traceable to their *guesdiste* origins: their suspicion of other parties, the maintenance of the electoral variant of the policy of class struggle, their suspicion of deputies, and the persistence of the policy of ranking party functionaries above deputies. The resolution approved at the SFIO congress was thus a victory for the *guesdiste* faction of the party, which held that elections were above all opportunities to propagandize; deputies were to understand that the winning of seats in the legislature, given the long-term goals of the party, was to be regarded as incidental.

The SFIO congress's decision was also something of a victory for the historian, since the historical interest of this election resides less in the number of successful SFIO candidacies than in the number and location of Socialist votes. Because the Federation of the Isère was obliged to run candidates in all *circonscriptions,* the elections of 1906 allow us to chart the popularity of socialism in its infancy. Thus while it is clear that some candidacies could be little more than tokens, the fact that the Socialist point of view was so widely represented gives us an opportunity to assess the strength of the Socialists thirty-five years after the Commune, ten years after the founding of the Federation of the Isère.[76]

75. See AN, F 7, 12499, 19 January 1905.
76. For details on the debates at Chalon-sur-Saône see Georges Lefranc, *Le*

Even if their meager monetary resources had to be shared among the several *circonscriptions,* the Socialists seem to have compensated for the shortage by making the most of their human resources. The Socialist candidate in the arrondissement of St-Marcellin in 1906 was accompanied by several other party members at more than seventy public meetings. In his campaign in St-Marcellin, Paul Mistral had the help of the militants Louis Michallon, Pierre Brizon, François Dognin, Cartier, and Faure, among others—a tactic that elevated program over personality but that also showcased the dynamism and breadth of talent of the movement.[77] The Socialists employed similar strategies in their efforts in the three arrondissements around Grenoble. Altogether in 1906 SFIO candidates were responsible for bringing some 12,000 voters to the polls in the Isère, roughly 8 percent of those eligible to vote in that year.[78] In 1910 Socialists would win four seats in eight; in 1914, five in eight. For the next three generations the Isère would be a Socialist department.

An Open and Pliable Left

With the Zévaès schism fading, Socialists began to adapt more comfortably to electoral politics and their new role as premier party of the left in the Isère. They began to shake off the rigid orthodoxy of the early years when they were staking out a territory on the extreme left and hostility to Radicals was part of a strategy of political differentiation. In 1906 and later they supported Radical candidates in runoff rounds, just as Radicals supported them.

Outside of election periods as well as during them they showed

Mouvement socialiste sous la Troisième République, 2 vols. (Paris, 1977), 1: 144–146.

77. See "Campagne électorale," *Droit du Peuple,* 15 October 1906. This observation seems to contradict André Siegfried's claim that most voters had difficulty distinguishing programs from the personalities who represented them. According to Siegfried, "most voters have neither the judgment nor the habit of abstract thought needed to make decisions exclusively on the merits of doctrine: they have considerable difficulty separating ideas from the men who espouse them" (*Tableau politique,* pp. xxiii–xxiv).

78. Results for 1906 are taken from AN, C 6355–6357.

themselves open to initiatives in favor of feminism, as the Renaud candidacy showed, and as their choice of Angèle Roussel as a delegate to national congresses affirmed.[79] And for peasants, as we shall see, they dropped their earlier insistence that the small farmer was doomed to disappear, gobbled up by a rapacious agrarian capitalism. Now they represented themselves as defenders of the small farmer against the expropriation of the capitalist farmer, a position publicly elaborated first by Paul Mistral as *conseiller général* and who, as mayor of Grenoble and as deputy after 1910, would personify socialism in the Isère in the interwar period.[80] *Le Droit du Peuple,* daily newspaper and "official organ of the Socialist Federation of the Isère," shed its rigidly ideological tone. Although it never came close to the shamelessly populist style Zévaès had given it under his brief stewardship in 1902, its readership now was clearly intended to extend beyond the committed militants. With this new voice the Socialists of the Isère discovered and courted new constituencies: among committed republicans ready to look beyond radicalism, among women, among peasants, as well as among the communities of peasants and textile workers in the vast hinterland between Grenoble and Lyon.

79. Sowerwine, *Sisters or Citizens?* p. 125. I support Sowerwine's characterization of the Federation of the Isère as "responsive to women."

80. Mistral was himself of peasant background. For an early statement of this position on peasant property, see *Droit du Peuple,* 11 April 1902.

3

*From the Workshop
to the Factory:
The Silk Industry in
the Nineteenth Century*

For the insurgent Lyon silk workers (*canuts*) of the
1830s the future could be described in stark terms: "Live working
or die fighting!" The alternatives conveyed by the slogan omitted a
third possibility, admittedly of little appeal to the *canuts:* that the
future of the industry lay beyond Lyon.[1] And while the Isère's share
in overall silk production was negligible in 1830, within two generations the silk industry would become its major industrial employer. Silk, along with coal and metallurgy, drove the economy of the
Lyon region. In a much more lopsided way it drove the industrial
economy of the Isère. In fact, by 1886 it would employ more workers than the next three industries combined. More persons supported themselves as textile workers than in any other line of work
except agriculture.[2]

1. The standard texts on the insurrections of the Lyon *canuts* in 1831 and 1834
are Ferdinand Rude, *L'Insurrection lyonnaise de novembre 1831* (Paris, 1944), and
Robert Bezucha, *The Lyon Uprising of 1834* (Cambridge, Mass., 1974).
2. The Isère in the nineteenth century had four major industries: mining, paper
milling, glovemaking, and silk fabrication. In 1886 the glove industry employed
some 5,000 persons. Paper milling employed nearly 4,000. Mines and quarries
occupied another 2,700. In the same year the textile industry employed 590 supervisors, 8,700 male workers, 18,500 female workers, and some 2,600 children, male
and female. See AN, F 12, 4509A. (I have rounded off the figures.) Yves Lequin
asserts that the silk industry, along with the coal and metallurgical industries of the
Loire Valley, "appear [to have been] the motors of industrial growth for the entire
region": *Les Ouvriers de la région lyonnaise, 1848–1914,* 2 vols. (Lyon, 1977),
1:26–27.

These observations suggest the impact of the textile industry on life in the rural Isère. If one wishes to understand the shift in public opinion and the adjustments in everyday life, one must first understand how attitudes were shaped by the way people lived and worked. For tens of thousands of persons, and by extension for thousands of rural households and farmsteads, the textile industry was an economic fact of everyday life. Interest in the expansion or contraction of the industry extended well beyond those who had invested time or capital in it. The stagnation or vigor of the industry mattered to the many individuals and families whose welfare depended directly or indirectly on the prosperity of the land and the loom. And as people became more open to the new and broadening influence of industrial labor, their ways of living and thinking began to change. Many of the Isère's hamlets and villages first opened to the world as producers of textile goods. But the commercial link served as a conduit for other things as well. Contact with towns and cities, contact with others and their ideas, all of these became possible and frequent once the rural world opened itself to industry. The textile industry exposed the rural community to the ideas and movements of the cities. The economic and cultural autarky of the peasant communities was battered down by the gentle but persistent action of the shuttle and the loom.

At least two perspectives on the silk industry of the Isère are of interest. First of all, technological and organizational developments substantially altered the character of the industry in the nineteenth century. The industry, its location, its tools and techniques, its products, and its personnel all changed during the years from the Restoration to the Republic. The Fabrique of the old regime would barely have recognized the Fabrique of the Belle Epoque. Second, the commercial rhythm of the market for silk goods under the Third Republic, the rise and fall of demand reflected in the pace of expansion, merits attention because of its local impact. Thus there are two perspectives: one on the silk industry as an industry, the other on silk fabric as a commodity.

The Silk Industry:
Old Problems, New Methods

The history of the silk industry in the nineteenth century can be divided into two overlapping periods. The first involved the organization of production, the second concerned industrial technology. In each case the consequences of the change were far-reaching, even though it took several decades for these consequences to be fully absorbed.

The organizational change involved the transfer of the production of silk from the city of Lyon, where it had flourished for years, to the surrounding countryside. This change did not take place all at once, nor were its ultimate consequences immediately foreseen. But from the beginning, at the start of the nineteenth century, the advantages to be gotten from the use of a labor force based in the countryside were sufficiently attractive to propel the movement forward. By the 1890s the city of Lyon as a center for the production of silk fabric had been completely eclipsed by rural producers. An organizational restructuring had taken place, leaving control of the industry in Lyon but shifting production to the countryside.

The second noteworthy change in the silk industry during this period was based on a technological innovation. The hand loom powered by the weaver was replaced by the mechanical loom powered by some inanimate source of energy. This innovation dramatically increased the productive capacity of the individual worker. At the same time it forced perhaps the most profound change in the structure of rural weaving. Since the operation of the mechanical loom required power, typically the torque of a water wheel, the activity of weaving would henceforth need to be centralized. For the first time in the history of the silk industry, factory-based production became the norm. Inevitably the individual weaver was rendered uncompetitive outside of certain specialty areas.

By the 1890s the transformation of the Lyon silk industry was complete. The Fabrique had made the transition from urban weaving organized in traditional artisanal form to rural weaving organized in modern industrial form. Contrary to trends in other branches of industry, industrialization of the silk industry did not require relocating in large urban agglomerations. The novelty was that the Lyon silk industry broke with its traditional forms of production not by urbanizing but by ruralizing. The full consequences of this transformation of the silk industry can be grasped only by examination of each of its two main features in some detail.

A Country Retreat

There is no agreement on when the silk industry first began to recognize the advantages of a rural labor force. Some sources date the movement from the first decade of the nineteenth century; others prefer earlier dates and cite evidence from the late eighteenth century. The entire question could be dismissed as irrelevant if it did not shed light on the *motives* of the captains of the silk industry. Economic realism, foreign competition, and fear of the collective power of the silk weavers of Lyon have all been offered as explanations.

The first explanation, economic realism, is popular with some nineteenth-century sources and is given some credence by eighteenth-century sources. It also supports the claims of those who, in the tradition of the historian Alfred Cobban, see the Bourbon monarchy as a dynamic and progressive force.[3] The Lyon Fabrique was a state-regulated industry under the old regime. A royal *arrêt* of 13 February 1765 aimed to eliminate "all obstacles that might interfere with the progress of industry." Accordingly, the decree authorized silk weaving by inhabitants of the countryside outside the city of Lyon. A desire to remove the fetters on industry inspired the lifting of economic restrictions under the old regime and permitted rural weaving.[4]

According to other sources, foreign competition for markets also helped to spur rural production. Lyon had long dominated the world market for silk fabric and the goods fashioned from it. However, Lyon's access to markets was impeded by war during the early years of the Revolution and by the continental system and the British blockade under the Empire. Lack of consumer confidence and insecure alliances also served to impede commercial expansion. Worst of all, when the blockade was finally lifted, it was clear that foreign competitors, particularly the English, had benefited from

3. See Alfred Cobban, *History of Modern France*, vol. 1, *Old Regime and Revolution, 1715–1799* (Harmondsworth: Penguin, 1982).

4. Paul Pic and Justin Godart, *Le Mouvement économique et social dans la région lyonnaise*, 2 vols. (Lyon, 1902), 1:186–187. On the inevitability of those events, their economic rationality, and the vain hopes of the Lyon artisans, see Marius Morand, "L'Outillage de la Fabrique lyonnaise du tissage de la soie," *RGA* 3 (1916): 318.

the cover provided by wartime blockades to build their own silk industries. With the cessation of hostilities, they proceeded to invade French markets. Competition came from more distant producers as well: the Russian and American silk textile industries can trace their origins to the beginning of the nineteenth century. Manufacturers in the United States proved to be especially tenacious competitors with the French for dominance of the North American market. Blessed by certain natural and unnatural advantages, they progressively undermined the French position in North America in the second half of the nineteenth century.[5] Faced with shrinking profit margins, the silk merchants of Lyon sought to reduce costs. Rural-based production offered immediate cost advantages that would allow them to produce more cheaply than their foreign rivals.

But certainly the most dramatic explanation of the silk merchants' motives is political: the silk chieftains simply fled the organized power of the silkworkers of Lyon. According to this explanation, the organized weavers of Lyon were a constant source of irritation and an unbearable restraint on the authority and prerogatives of the silk merchants: they repeatedly resisted attempts to cut wages and to alter the traditional relationships and operations of the silk industry. The artisans demonstrated their collective power most dramatically in the insurrections of 1831 and 1834, events of such scale and violence that they are overshadowed only by the June Days and the Paris Commune in the history of civil violence in nineteenth-century France. It was feared that by the very force of their collective efforts the weavers would come to control not only the production of silk fabric but ultimately the conditions of its sale as well. Even worse than the economic threat the to the silk industry was the social and political threat to the ruling class of a major provincial capital.[6] After the insurrections of the 1830s it was no longer possible to think of the problems of the silk industry as

5. For the details on foreign competition see G.-A. Nicolas, *L'Organisation sociale de l'industrie du tissage de la soie* (Paris, 1923), p. 29, and Joseph Jouanny, *le Tissage de la soie en Bas-Dauphiné* (Grenoble, 1931), p. 31.

6. For a discussion of the issue of artisanal control see Jouanny, *Tissage de la soie*, p. 34. On the social threat posed by the artisans see Paul Clerget, "Les Industries de la soie dans la vallée du Rhône," *Etudes Rhodaniennes* 5 (1929): 29. On protest and insurrection see Rude, *L'Insurrection lyonnaise*, and Bezucha, *Lyon Uprising*.

merely internal problems. The working class of Lyon could be every bit as dangerous as the working class of Paris. Thus by shifting the center of production away from Lyon, the masters of the Fabrique hoped to undercut the workers of Lyon. According to this view, the practice of rural weaving was instituted because the political militancy of the Lyon artisans would be broken only when their craft monopoly on weaving was broken. The displacement of the Lyon silk industry was a strategic political move in the class warfare of the nineteenth century.

Each of these explanations conveys an element of the truth. The earliest evidence of silk weaving outside of Lyon dates from 1750, just a few years after riots among silkworkers in 1744.[7] Thus it is not necessary to wait for the nineteenth century for evidence of experiments with rural weaving; nor do we have to look to the 1830s for evidence of the exasperation such experiments engendered among the weavers of Lyon. It is also apparent that the *arrêt* of 1765, the official royal approval of rural silk weaving, lags some fifteen years behind the first appearance of rural weaving. Obviously the royal *arrêt* was simply an endorsement of an existing practice, not a license to institute a new one.

With the cessation of hostilities in 1815 and the resumption of commerce, competition on world markets intensified. England could no longer count on disruptions to trade on the continent to shield it from the full competitive strength of Lyon. Lyon, in its turn, faced considerable competition from England, Switzerland, and Germany and could no longer claim the American and Russian markets uncontested. Under these conditions, the temptation to preserve profits by cutting production costs must have been irresistible; they were probably inevitable if the silk industry was to survive. And though labor costs were not the only factor of production capable of adjustment, they were the handiest and the largest. The results ought to have been predictable. The motto of the insurgent *canuts*, "Live working or die fighting!" suggests a mood of mingled defiance and exasperation.

Thus, ironically, the future of Lyon's major industry lay outside of Lyon. Even so, it is a good deal easier to imagine the disadvantages of such a shift than to discern its advantages. Transportation

7. Pic and Godart, *Mouvement économique*, p. 186.

costs surely counted for something: it must have been cheaper to bring raw materials to a single facility than to deliver them to hundreds. Lyon's transport infrastructure had already been developed, that of the countryside had not. And something ought to be said for centralized supervision of the pace and quality of work. Even if urban workers could be troublesome, the problems of supervision must have weighed heavily against decentralized production. And what about skills? Farmers would surely be lacking in basic skills. In Lyon these skills were passed down from parent to child; thus the labor force was highly trained in the art of weaving and entrepreneurs did not have to assume training costs. No such claim could be made for the peasants. Still the trend was clearly against the weavers of Lyon. Why?

One factor was what might be called the accrued labor costs of political militancy. The labor power of the Lyon *canuts* could be had only at considerable expense. The Lyon silk weavers were articulate and well organized, and their tradition of militancy and collective action made them a force with which the merchants had to reckon. Rural weavers had none of these things, at least at the beginning of the nineteenth century. Few were literate, they were scattered across the countryside, and, at least before 1848, they lacked well-developed, independent political traditions. The putting-out system, for such it was, capitalized on the very isolation of the rural weaver, who remained ignorant of wages and conditions elsewhere and in any case lacked the means to do very much about them. And political traditions aside, as a rule proximity to the city worked against low wages. City life was expensive; urban workers had to be paid more. Rural workers could live on less; they could be expected to work for less.[8]

Rural weaving was cheaper also because it was not the weaver's sole source of income. These workers, after all, were peasants. Before the advent of weaving they had managed to get by on their small plots of land and whatever seasonal employment they might find as agricultural day laborers. Weaving, for them, was often simply another *travail d'appoint*, a part-time job. It was a way to earn cash when one grew only for subsistence or produced such a small quantity of marketable produce that one relied on other

8. Ibid., p. 192.

sources for cash income. For these peasants weaving was not the primary occupation. They produced their own food, housing, and clothing, so that in a sense agriculture was subsidizing industry. It seems only fair to point out that industry was also subsidizing small farming.

Rural weaving had another advantage: peasant-workers always had their farms to support them during lean times. Whenever the market for silk cloth slackened, as it did periodically, the peasants could return to their fields. When demand resumed, they could return to their looms. For this reason, according to one source, rural weavers could withstand long periods of unemployment.[9] The possibilities for control of fixed costs in such a system should be obvious. Production levels could be tailored precisely to meet demand without the risk of losing workers and without the dislocation such layoffs would cause in the city.

As for the techniques of weaving, though it is true that rural weavers could not hope to match their urban counterparts in skill, they were not novices either. At first only simple assignments and cheap materials were entrusted to rural weavers, and even then the quality of the finished fabric often left much to be desired. But the resulting savings in labor costs made French silk competitive and so justified the investment in "trainees."[10] The skills of rural weavers improved with time, and paradoxically the *canuts* of Lyon contributed to the improvement of rural weaving techniques. Out of work after 1831 and 1834 because of slackened demand or because of blacklisting, many Lyon artisans returned to their native villages. There, through example and direct instruction, they contributed to the improvement of rural weaving skills.[11]

In fact, the peasant who was completely ignorant of the techniques of weaving was a rarity, at least in the region east of Lyon. Hemp was commonly among the array of crops cultivated by *bas-*

9. Ernst Pariset, *Histoire de la Fabrique lyonnaise* (Lyon, 1901), p. 306. Observers disagree about the proportion of time allotted to weaving and to farming. Some insist that farming was the part-time occupation, on the grounds that the hands of a true peasant would be much too rough to handle silk fabric. Undoubtedly the situation varied from case to case.

10. Jouanny, *Tissage de la soie*, p. 31. See also Pariset, *Fabrique lyonnaise*, p. 307.

11. See Gilbert Garrier, *Paysans du Beaujolais et du Lyonnais* (Grenoble, 1973), p. 206.

dauphinois small farmers for household needs. They used it to produce a rough but durable fabric. Hemp was, in a sense, a subsistence crop in that much of it was never intended to reach market but was "consumed" by the household. But it was also one of the bases of rural industry in the first half of the century; the popularity of hemp is attested to by the fact that it was the most popular raw material for fabric in the area before the extension of silkworm raising. Many families had at least one member weaving hemp as wintertime employment.[12] In certain parts of the Isère hemp weaving was carried out on nearly an industrial scale. In 1810 the Manufacturers' Advisory Council wrote that nearly all of the peasants around Voiron wove hemp for market. But by the 1840s, hemp as a cash crop and hemp weaving for market were under attack from hemp imported from Russia and Italy. Hemp weaving for domestic use continued for a while, but finally fell out of favor with the increasing availability of cheap cotton fabric from the northeast.[13]

Of course, weaving skills were not lost. Moreover, an important need remained, for the sheer scale and extent of the cottage industry in hemp suggests that supplemental income of some kind was essential to the petty farmer of the Bas-Dauphiné. The industry had once employed as many as 12,000 persons in the area around Voiron alone. At least as many were engaged in the same activity in the arrondissements of La Tour-du-Pin and St-Marcellin. Is it any surprise, then, that the silk industry of Lyon established itself in those parts of the Isère where hemp weaving was already an established tradition?[14]

The protests and revolts of the Lyon *canuts* in the 1830s had terrified Lyon's silk merchants. The merchants despaired of being able to control the silkworkers and believed that they would remain

12. The split between farming and winter hemp weaving in the department of the Ain (directly north of the Isère) is the subject of Abel Chatelain, "L'Emigration temporaire des peigneurs de chanvre du Jura méridional avant les transformations des XIXᵉ et XXᵉ siècles," *Etudes Rhodaniennes* 21 (1946): 166–178. Many contracts for agricultural *domestiques* contained a release clause allowing them to be released from their responsibilities during winter for hemp combing. See p. 172.

13. A full description of *l'industrie toilière* can be found in Pierre Léon, *La Naissance de la grande industrie en Dauphiné*, 2 vols. (Paris, 1954). See esp. 1:424, 555.

14. For detailed figures for 1848 see ADI, 162 M, 2. On Voiron see Léon, *Naissance de la grande industrie*, p. 581. For La Tour-du-Pin and St-Marcellin see Lequin, *Ouvriers de la région lyonnaise*, 1:17.

a source of trouble and a challenge to their authority as long as they possessed a measure of control over the production of silk fabric. Merchants saw peasant weavers as less demanding and more malleable. Scattered across the countryside, rural weavers were deprived of contact with one another and hence lacked the opportunity to organize and negotiate collectively. Moreover, the peasant weaver was believed to respect authority by habit and to perform tasks unquestioningly. For these reasons silk merchants thought that the rural weaver would make an attractive alternative to the troublesome, potentially revolutionary urban worker.[15]

The advantages of rural weaving far outweighed the disadvantages. If the techniques of rural weavers left something to be desired, at least they were not complete novices, having served a kind of apprenticeship at the loom weaving hemp. The low wages that peasants would accept more than compensated for the unevenness of their skills. Finally, and perhaps most important, the isolated rural weaver was believed to be more docile and less troublesome and therefore the ideal rejoinder to the Lyon weavers' bothersome encroachments on the prerogatives of the silk merchants. Peasant labor gave the silk merchants the flexibility and leverage they needed to break the militancy of the Lyon *canuts,* cut production costs, and meet foreign competition head on.

The Limitations of Cottage Industry

Clothing fashion follows politics; or is it the other way around? It is sometimes suggested that changes in political temperament are reflected in fashion. Whatever the general validity of this statement, it was palpably true in the case of the July Monarchy.

15. On the perceived attributes of rural workers see Clerget, "Industries de la soie," p. 22. Clerget argues that the putting-out system was developed as a kind of revenge on the *canuts* for the revolts of 1831 and 1834. Others point out that the process was already under way and that the revolts of the 1830s only hastened the movement. This account seems fair to me as long as one acknowledges that even before the revolts of the 1830s the silk merchants intended to break the militant *canuts* and that the cottage industry was developed with this goal in mind. Thus rural weaving should be seen as both cause and consequence of the revolts of the 1830s. For an account hostile to the Lyon weavers see Pariset, *Fabrique lyonnaise,* p. 317. Other views can be found in Nicolas, *Organisation sociale,* p. 30, and Pic and Godart, *Mouvement économique,* p. 190.

Louis-Philippe's preference for sober dress over the flamboyant styles of the restored Bourbon monarchy not only demonstrated a degree of good political sense but also earned him the nickname of "bourgeois king." Louis-Philippe's choice of style reflected an awareness of the increasing numerical and political importance of the broad middle class. The example set by the royal family rapidly became the standard for French fashion. The silk industry immediately sensed this shift in public mood and official dress. Elaborate brocades, long the mainstay of the Lyon Fabrique, lost in popularity to more modest designs. The conventional tastes of the bourgeois king coincided with the emergence of a middle-class market for silk fabric.

Foreign rivals never seriously challenged Lyon's dominance of the market for the high-quality fabrics that had made the reputation of Lyon and had been the pride of its artisans. The Swiss, the Germans, even the Italians had earned their share of the market by concentrating on enlarging its lower end and catering to it. They produced a fabric of medium quality for consumers to whom price was a consideration. And while the market for high-quality fabrics merely held its own in the nineteenth century, the middle-class market boomed. French dominance of the market for silk fabrics declined as an expanding market in the nineteenth century grew away from traditional French strengths. By the first decades of the Third Republic, the heyday of the "new social classes," it was clear to all concerned that the future of the industry lay in the production of inexpensive fabric. The future of the Lyon silk industry depended upon growing with this expanding, soon to be dominant segment of the market.

Success in production of cheap (*bon marché*) fabric depended upon holding down the costs of materials and labor, doing so would entail a more thorough rationalization of the production process. Since most silk used was imported from Asia, Lyon was not in a position to influence its price. A reduction in the cost of raw materials could be realized only with the introduction of new production techniques that could make the most of available materials. Under the existing system, the production of silk thread began with the unraveling of the cocoon of the silkworm. If the cocoon were perfect, it would be formed of a single length of silk "thread." Perfect cocoons thus yielded perfect thread. Flawed cocoons had to be discarded as unusable because they yielded only thread fragments. One of the reasons that silk fabric was so expensive was that its price reflected not only the labor-intensive way it was produced but also the wastage represented by these discarded cocoons.[16]

It was only a matter of time before manufacturers realized that they could recover these costs by taking the thread fragments produced by these defective cocoons and spinning them, like cotton fibers, into a single thread, called schappe. In fact, the process had existed for some time, but it was not until the nineteenth century that the technique was used on a large scale. By then middle-class tastes increasingly drove the market, and these cheaper materials now found buyers "trading up" from the ordinary cottons and linens.

Economies in production created new markets. Silk could be woven with less expensive materials—schappe, wool, cotton—in various combinations of warp and woof.[17] Such combinations produced a fabric that could claim some of the qualities of fine silk, notably weight and strength, without the trouble and expense associated with the production of traditional all-silk fabrics. Moreover, since these fabrics would take a dye *after* they were woven, merchants gained flexibility in planning for the market. Undyed fabric could be held in the warehouse ready to be dyed once it was clear which colors would be most favorably received by consumers in Paris and elsewhere. Silk merchants now could respond better not only to consumer demand but to fluctuations in worker productivity. Thus these new materials and new techniques gave merchants greater control over the rhythm of production as well as over the vagaries of the marketplace.

The speed with which entrepreneurs adopted these new methods

16. After they passed inspection, the cocoons were placed in basins of warm water. The warm water loosened the gum that gives the cocoon its integrity in its natural state. When the gum dissolved, the freed thread of the cocoon was fed into a mechanism that combined threads and twisted them. When the combined threads were left to dry, residual gum served to bind them together. This process produced a single thread of unusual weight and strength—the trademark of silk. On the processes involved in the production of silk thread see M. Beauquis, "La Filature de soie française," in Ministère du Travail et de la Prévoyance Sociale, *Bulletin de l'Inspection du Travail* (Paris, 1908), esp. p. 151.

17. Crêpe and mousseline are produced from a warp and woof of raw silk; satin and serge from a raw silk warp and cotton woof; pongee and batavia from a warp of raw silk and woof of schappe. See Pariset, *Fabrique lyonnaise*, p. 389.

Table 1. Average annual imports of silk floss and scraps, 1827–1887 (thousands of kilograms)

Period	Weight
1827–1836	74
1837–1846	149
1847–1856	448
1857–1866	617
1867–1876	1,400
1879	3,627
1883	4,917
1887	5,300

Source: Ernst Pariset, *Histoire de la Fabrique lyonnaise* (Lyon, 1901), p. 36.

and materials is readily apparent in the yearly importation weights of the *bourres de soie*—silk floss and scraps. From 1827 to 1887, the average annual importation weights, in kilograms, rose from virtually nil to over 5 million kilograms per year (see Table 1). The average annual import weight doubled every ten years. This trend continued through the early years of the Third Republic. By that time silk was being imported on a massive scale.

Making more efficient use of raw materials and the introduction of fabrics with a combination of silk and nonsilk threads were not the only ways to reduce costs and produce a cheap product for mass consumption. Marginal labor costs could be reduced by an increase in the productivity of the individual worker. The rural weaver's productivity, however, was difficult to control. By all accounts, the amount of time a rural weaver was likely to devote to weaving depended on the entrepreneur's control.[18] For most peasants, farmwork took precedence over weaving, so they were a good deal less reliable than full-fledged workers whose loyalties were not divided between land and loom.

Thus the alternation between farmwork and weaving, the very reason for the cheapness of peasant-workers' labor, was also the reason for their limited productivity. One observer estimated that

18. The classic statement of adaptation to factory discipline is provided by E. P. Thompson in "Time, Work-Discipline, and Industrial Capitalism," *Past & Present* 38 (1967): 56–97.

the productivity of the rural loom was at best one-half that of an urban loom.[19] Control over the factors of production was clearly only partial and tenuous as long as entrepreneurs relied on cottage industry for their fabric. Because rural weavers' allocation of time to weaving was inelastic, so was the volume of their production. And since the volume of production of the individual weaver was relatively inelastic, the entrepreneur could increase the volume of cloth produced only by increasing the total number of weavers. And, of course, such a solution offered no compensating reduction of costs. There are few economies of scale in the putting-out system.

Factory-based production could solve these problems because the factory was a controlled and disciplined setting, a setting designed for full-time work. Thus the introduction of the factory was not in the first instance a function of motorization and mechanization but a means to control and regularize labor productivity. Factory routine compelled farming to conform to the routine of industry rather than the other way around; it made silk production orderly and dependable. Factory development thus deprived peasants of the freedom to choose how to employ their time by putting them in a setting where their movements were subject to the schedule of the mill and the rhythm of the loom; mechanization and inanimate power provided their own impetus later. The development of the powered mechanical loom, which could not realistically be adapted for cottage use, accelerated the switch to factory-based production.[20] These processes, however, ought to be perceived as historically distinct.

Once entrepreneurs bought and installed their own looms in mills, new forces began to weigh against cottage industry. The switch to factory-based production obligated entrepreneurs to support expenses previously shouldered by domestic weavers themselves. Little wonder that during periodic contractions, silk merchants deliberately shut down putting-out networks first because of the higher fixed costs their own factory-installed looms represented. As one silk merchant put it in testimony before the Chamber of Deputies, the choice was obvious: "When an industrialist has both factory weavers and domestic weavers, if the [amount of]

19. Pariset, *Fabrique lyonnaise*, p. 308.
20. Léon, *Naissance de la grande industrie*, p. 506.

work diminishes he stops the domestic weavers first."[21] No amount of self-exploitation could save rural weavers idled by entrepreneurs who now had large investments to amortize. Thus in good times domestic weaving thrived alongside factory weaving because there was sufficient work to occupy everyone, but given the self-interest of entrepreneurs, shrinking markets were disproportionately hard on domestic hand-loom weavers. Each market cycle reduced the contingent of domestic weavers. A rising tide raises all ships but neap tides left domestic weavers stranded.

Hand looms remained popular, though increasingly they were factory-based. At the end of the Second Empire, areas of distributed cottage weaving far outnumbered factory-based weaving sites, yet the concentrations of looms in factories made factory-based weaving far more important than cottage weaving. Indeed, the ratio of workers in mills to weavers in cottages was roughly 3 to 1. The imbalance would be even greater if productivity were compared.[22]

The development and introduction of the mechanical loom accelerated this process. The mechanical loom, powered either hydraulically or by steam engines, was first used in other branches of the textile industry, particularly cottons. The abandonment of dyeing before weaving and the lapse in popularity of the complex woven-in designs, which demanded skill and careful attention on the part of the weaver, served to eliminate the principal design advantage of the hand loom. It also served to discount the creative superiority and craft skills of trained silk artisans. Meanwhile, a weaver could produce three times as much cloth on a mechanical loom as on a hand loom in the same amount of time. Yet the mechanical loom was *une machine douce*—gentle and precise enough in its movements to operate without stressing the fragile threads. Thus the mechanical loom was perfectly adapted to the developments in the uses of raw materials of the same period.[23]

---

21. Assemblée Nationale, *Commission d'enquête sur l'industrie textile*, 5 vols. (Paris, 1906), 2:18. An 1866 report out of Cessieu made a similar point. Cessieu had one mill employing 105 workers and another 165 looms scattered about the surrounding area, of which only 100 were currently in use. This is an important demonstration of the forces favoring factory weaving. The people who worked in the mill got work first. This arrangement protected the mill owner's capital investment and, over time, sent domestic weavers a message. See ADI, 138 M, 11, 1866, La Tour-du-Pin.

22. ADI, 138 M, 10.

23. Nicolas, *Organisation sociale*, pp. 37–38.

The first mechanical looms put to use in production in the Isère were installed in factories at Rives and Tullins in 1826. A total of eight mechanical looms were erected along with twenty-two hand looms— ratio that hardly conveys much confidence in the new technology but reflects its expense. Later in the same year a factory at Renage was outfitted exclusively with the new mechanical looms. Soon Isère led all other departments of the Lyon region in the number of mechanical looms installed. Of the more than 18,000 mechanical looms in operation in the seven departments of the Lyon region in 1879, 11,000 were in the Isère. By the 1890s they had easily outdistanced the hand loom in the production of silk fabric.[24]

Aggregate figures for the nineteenth century tell the story. The number of hand looms operating in the major silk-producing departments of the Lyon region—Ain, Isère, Loire, Rhône—increased through most of the nineteenth century. In 1840 these four departments had 21,000 hand looms. Over the next thirty-two years the number of hand looms increased fourfold, to 80,000. Thus hand-loom production continued to increase well after the introduction of the mechanical loom, as if producers aimed to increase production in any way possible. The long expansion of the rural silk industry came to an abrupt end in the slump that followed the Franco-Prussian War, a slump followed in short order by the onset of the Long Depression. Hand looms then went into a fairly steep decline. Their numbers fell to 40,000 by 1898, when the mechanical loom and the factory system can finally be said to have taken over the bulk of production.[25]

The Decline of Cottage Industry, the Rise of the Factory System

The introduction of mechanical looms and of new materials were among the most important developments in the silk industry in the nineteenth century. Both innovations reduced the cost of weaving silk fabric; the first by increasing the productivity of the individual worker, the second by blending fine silk with raw silk,

24. Léon, *Naissance de la grande industrie*, p. 506; ADI, 138 M, 10, 16.
25. Nicolas, *Organisation sociale*, p. 41.

cotton, or wool, and thus reducing the necessary quantities of expensive fine silk thread.

Each of these innovations assumed changes in the system of production. Mechanical looms required substantial capital investment.
The use of new raw materials and the operation of mechanical
looms demanded closer managerial or technical supervision. Neither was practical under the old artisanal mode of production in
either its urban or rural incarnation. Both higher rates of capital
investment and increased managerial direction pointed toward centralized production, toward factory production. Moreover, unlike
hand looms, mechanical looms depended on some inanimate
source of power, typically from a steam engine or water wheel—
another call for capital investment and concentration of looms. The
rationalization of the silk industry in the nineteenth century encouraged the abandonment of cottage industry. It also signaled the
abandonment of the old artisanal base for all but the most specialized tasks. The adoption of the factory system marked the advent of modern industrial techniques to silk production.

The establishment of the textile factories was much more complicated than the putting-out system. The beauty of the putting-out
system was its simplicity: the laborer provided skill and power, the
entrepreneur handled the transportation of the raw materials and
finished fabric. With the introduction of the factory system, all of
these factors—power, transport, skill, labor—had to be reconsidered.

The department of the Isère could supply all these things; in fact,
it was the relative abundance of each of them that made the Isère so
attractive as a location for new investment. The department's central and eastern portions are crisscrossed with waterways. Hydraulic power, such as the power created by water running under a
paddle wheel, was plentiful and readily accessible in the Isère.
Boosters coined the term *houille blanche,* literally "white coal," to
describe the tremendous energy potential of the rivers of the Alpine
region; the words convey the enthusiasm with which businessmen
viewed the investment opportunities of the area. Silk entrepreneurs
preferred the rivers of the foothills leading down to the area known
as the Bas-Dauphiné. There the rivers were not so plentiful or
powerful as they were in the mountains, but they were powerful and
plentiful enough to drive literally thousands of looms. In these

foothills and plateaus dwelled a small property-owning peasantry accustomed to combining agricultural work with other kinds of employment, including weaving. Finally, the foothills of the Bas-Dauphiné were well served by a good system of roads. Under the Second Empire, railroad lines linked Grenoble to Lyon and Valence (Drôme) and to the small towns in between.

Thus the Bas-Dauphiné offered perhaps the Lyon region's best combination of infrastructure and human and natural resources. Upheavals in Lyon in 1848 and 1849 only added to its allure. Entrepreneurs demonstrated their enthusiasm by erecting dozens of factories in the areas between the plain east of Lyon and Voiron, two dozen kilometers northwest of Grenoble. They took care, in a territorial fashion worthy of competitors in the natural world, to maintain a respectable distance between themselves and their nearest rivals. In 1850 a businessman opened the first factory to house hydraulically powered mechanical looms for the working of silk, at Moirans, just south of Voiron.[26] His example was quickly followed, and soon factories were in operation on riverbanks across the Isère, or at least across the Bas-Dauphiné: on the Bourbre, near Bourgoin-Jallieu, Ruy and La Tour-du-Pin; on the Morge at Coublevie, Voiron, and Moirans; on the Fure at Rives, Renage, and Tullins; on the Ainan at St-Bueil, St-George-en-Valdaine, and St-Albin; and on a handful of streams such as the Tréry at Vinay. In all of these places mechanical looms driven by the power generated by flowing water wove silk fabric.[27]

Not far from these factories, a few individual weavers continued to weave and thus entered into vain competition with factory workers at the mechanical looms. Some of them gave in and became factory hands. Far more male weavers abandoned weaving and devoted themselves fully to farming. Weaving became the occupation of women and children. Hydraulic power had allowed personnel recruiters to drop "strength" from the list of worker requirements—although one is justified in wondering if it had ever been more than a convenient means to bar women from the trade. Whether this barrier was real or constructed no longer mat-

26. Philippe Vigier, *La Seconde République dans la région alpine*, 2 vols. (Paris, 1963), 2:45. Other factories were erected at La Sône, Rives, St-Antoine, and Chavanoz: Léon, *Naissance de la grande industrie*, p. 516.
27. AN, F 12, 4509a.

tered; technology shattered it. Power looms, hydraulic or steam-powered, had rendered thousands of women eligible for industrial employment—at wages below those offered to men. Ironically, the (usually) male rural weavers whose cheap labor had helped to force the *canuts* of Lyon to submit to the will of the merchants were in turn being replaced by female workers who were paid still less.

Industrial development in the Isère followed a "ruralized" pattern—industry was distributed, not concentrated. Distributed energy resources facilitated this pattern. Had it not been for a similarly broad distribution of waterways, labor distribution could not have had such an influence on industrial location decisions. A greater concentration of industry would have been inevitable. Because of "white coal," the energy trapped in the rivers and streams of the Alpine foothills of the Isère, there were few locations where both cheap energy and cheap labor were not close at hand. Thus industrialization did not entail rapid urbanization.

The silk industry in the Isère fits perfectly the model in which returns to scale are low. Thus, if French business culture seems to conflate the concepts of *ferme* and *firme,* as Robert Smith has pointed out, there were also practical linkages and limits to scale. Entrepreneurs in the Isère would probably have gained little simply by expanding their facilities. Indeed, they stood to lose much, because as scale increased, they increased the chances that they would have to use wages to soften the relative inelasticity in the local labor supply—in effect, to bid with cash to persuade peasants to weave rather than farm. Small firm size represented a rational, even shrewd adaptation to the distributed nature of two important factors of production—energy and labor.[28]

Who were these entrepreneurs who established the new silk fac-

28. On some issues related to the persistence of cottage weaving see Paule Bernard, "Un Exemple d'industrie dispersée en milieu rural," *RGA* 40 (1952): 133–157. For a fresh look at the debate on firm size see John Vincent Nye, "Firm Size and Economic Backwardness: A New Look at the French Industrialization Debate," *Journal of Economic History* 47 (1987): 649–669. Robert J. Smith has suggested that a third term links and determines the dimensions of *ferme* and *firme;* namely, *famille:* "Family History and the Rise and Fall of an Industrial Enterprise: Bouchayer-Viallet of Grenoble, 1870–1972," paper presented at the 1989 meeting of the Western Society for French History. On questions of labor supply and French industry see William Reddy, *The Rise of Market Culture* (Cambridge, 1984).

tories and installed the looms? Not the silk merchants of Lyon, at least not at first. Then as before these individuals preferred to restrict their interest to the commercial (and controlling) end of the business. The task of industrial development was entrusted to others, the same middlemen who had organized and developed the putting-out system. Under that system, Lyon entrusted the raw materials to a *tâcheron*, a middleman, who in turn entrusted them to the individual weaver. Now, with the factory system, the Lyon merchant still provided the raw materials to a middleman, now more often called a *façonnier* (in at least one case *façonnière*), who was the owner of the factory and looms and who undertook to hire factory workers in a subcontracting arrangement. In many instances, the production of putting-out networks was simply consolidated into mills. A comparison of the distribution of sites in 1866 with sites in 1886 suggests that this was frequently the case during the intervening period of consolidation.[29] Thus the silk industry retained a strict separation of commercial and productive functions even during this period of industrialization. With few exceptions, Lyon's capital investment was limited to raw materials. Equipment costs were absorbed by the *façonniers*, as were the responsibilities of managing a labor force.[30] Control of the direction of industry remained in Lyon and the *façonniers* had to compete with one another for Lyon's orders.

The Fate of the Rural Textile Industry:
Silk as a Commodity in the World Market

The market for silk fabric, like the market for most luxury commodities, is volatile. It is subject not only to wide swings in taste and fashion but also to disturbances created by apparently unrelated events and forces. The market for silk is easily upset by events in distant parts of the globe. The American Civil War, for example, had a devastating effect on one of the Lyon Fabrique's major markets: the South's patrician class had always been an important customer for Lyon's goods. As a consequence, demand

29. ADI, 138 M, 10, 16.
30. Jouanny, *Tissage de la soie.*

and profits plummeted as the cost of the war and the Union blockade effectively closed off both supply and demand in the American
South.

The end of the Crimean War, paradoxically, had a similar effect.
During the conflict, American grain producers supplanted the Rus-
sians as major suppliers on the European grain market. The resumption of normal relations and commerce between Russia,
France, and Britain abruptly closed the European market to American grain. The subsequent disruption of the American economy put
demand for European luxury goods, including French silk, into a
steep decline. Silk production had to be cut back, orders barely
trickled out of Lyon, and for a time nearly half of the looms were
inactive.[31] Events in faraway places could have unexpected and
significant consequences for the prosperity of the silk industry, its
merchants, and its workers.

The silk industry weathered the disruptions of the American
Civil War; the looms were almost fully active in the closing years of
the Second Empire. Prefectoral reports on the economic situation
in the months before the onset of the struggle between the French
and the Prussians emphasized, quite predictably, the salutary effects
of political order and domestic tranquility. Early in 1870 the prefect of the Isère could report that the rate of unemployment was
normal for that time of year. Wages, he reported, were "abundant."
Barely a year later the subprefect of the arrondissement of La Tour-
du-Pin catalogued the commercial "devastation" wrought by the
Franco-Prussian War. During the war, he reported, "business trans-
actions . . . suffered greatly." Industrial production had fallen pre-
cipitously and hovered at around one-half to two-thirds of prewar
levels. Even the largest textile establishments, presumably better off
because of competitive advantages derived from larger scale and
because as large employers of women they had not been hurt by
military recruitment, were facing production cuts of from one-third
to one-half. The situation was little improved some three months
later, despite the armistice. At that moment, the prefect noted,
industry and commerce had received a great boost. Events in
Paris—the prefect characterized the revolt of the Paris Commune as
"theater," but this was before *la Semaine Sanglante*—dragged busi-

31. Léon, *Naissance de la grande industrie*, pp. 808, 817.

ness activity back to its wartime levels. The prefect looked forward to the settlement of the problems of Paris and the return of the tranquility that would permit the resumption of the industry's former level of activity.[32]

The early years of the Third Republic, its first decade or so, turned out to be unremarkable in most respects. Unremarkable times are good for business. Commerce resumed with the cessation of hostilities and the end of the civil war in Paris. The 1870s marked the beginning of the silk industry's shift from hand looms to mechanical looms. The principal reason for the failure of handloom production was economic: it simply did not produce enough fabric to remain profitable for the merchant. For the same reason, it could not provide a living for the worker, who was paid at piece rates. One merchant recalled that "twenty years ago we paid 1.50 and 2 francs per meter to hand-loom weavers. Today we don't even sell the same fabric for 1.35 francs. It's impossible [today] for a hand-loom weaver to make a living."[33] The mechanical loom drove down piece rates as it raised individual productivity. The market for silk simply bypassed the productive capacity of the hand-loom and of the weaver who operated it.

The story is perhaps best told by the numbers of hand looms in operation in the region as a whole. In 1872, which may be regarded as the high point for hand-loom production, some 80,000 hand looms were in operation. By 1900, barely half of those looms would still be producing fabric, and most of them were not in the countryside but in the city of Lyon, where hand looms were often used for the most specialized tasks, the most elaborate designs. For the mass production at which rural workers and looms excelled, the hand loom was being rendered technologically obsolete.[34]

The end of the 1870s came and went with the industry still enjoying good health. A contemporary observer close to the silk industry marveled that in 1878 alone some 10,000 mechanical

32. See AN, F 12, 4509a, 2 February 1870; prefect's letter, June 1871. This dossier contains similar reports for the other arrondissements.

33. Testimony of M. Cherbin, a representative of the Lyon silk industry, in Assemblée Nationale, "Commission d'enquête," 2:18.

34. See Robert Thiervoz, "L'Industrie en Valdaine et ses répercussions démographiques, sociales, et électorales," *RGA* 42 (1954): 90–92; Pariset, *Fabrique lyonnaise,* p. 424. Figures for hand looms are from Nicholas, *Organisation sociale,* p. 36.

looms had been installed in the departments surrounding Lyon. By the 1880s, however, the limits of growth had been reached. Indeed, there is some evidence that the depression of the 1880s had hit the silk industry somewhat earlier than other industries. In 1884 one commentator noted that the rate and volume of orders had been in decline since the dawn of the new decade. "Textile producers have been watching the volume of orders drop for three years now," he noted. He blamed the industry's problems not on a general economic crisis but on the caprices of fashion: "The silk industry is a fashion industry. It is only natural that it follow the whims of fashion."[35]

Sources inside the silk industry also tended to cite the growth of foreign competition as among the principal causes of the silk industry's malaise. Whatever the reason, the depressed condition of the economy and the vagaries of the luxury market were perhaps most painfully reflected in wage stagnation followed by gradual wage decline in the 1880s. Factory owners tried to maintain margins in the more competitive circumstance by cutting wages. In the summer of 1885, as prices languished, the prefect of the Isère chose the euphemism "restrained" to describe the trend in wages. By April of the following year prices had not budged and the prefect, now moved to speak with candor, described wages as "barely remunerative." Five months later he reported on a situation that had only worsened. Euphemisms would no longer serve. Wages were frankly in decline.[36]

Even in these circumstances the textile industry continued to expand, mostly because merchants remained optimistic about the long-term prospects for French silk in the world marketplace but also because there apparently was still money to be made filling contracts for the Lyon Fabrique. Reduced wages, however, made the labor recruiters' task difficult. The larger factories, especially those that employed a thousand workers or more, relied most heavily on wages to attract laborers because they often needed to recruit their workers over a greater area. They were also the first to

35. *Républicain de l'Isère*, 14 February 1884. This was the year of an unsuccessful multifactory strike among silkworkers. For mechanical looms in 1878 see Pariset, *Fabrique lyonnaise*, p. 388.
36. ADI, 163 M, 1.

notice an effective wage floor. It was no longer realistic to expect to attract workers away from their farms to live in crowded dormitories for up to a week at a time, at least not as long as wages were falling. It was during the lull of the mid-1880s that employers first encountered resistance to wage reductions, though most of the resistance was unorganized and manifested in recruitment difficulties rather than labor unrest.[37]

The 1880s forced an adaptation to new conditions: new facilities were being added, but they were of a particular kind. On the face of it, the megafactories, employing a thousand workers and more, should have enjoyed economies of scale, since the costs of doing business were spread across many more looms. These calculations, of course, assumed that there were enough workers to keep all of the looms busy. The large mills, more than others, depended upon wages to draw the workers in, and the lean years of the 1880s had demonstrated the limits of recruitment. Because Lyon farmed its orders out on a competitive basis to the factory owners and their managers, it was the merchants of Lyon and not the individual factory owners and managers who were ultimately responsible for wages. The desire to win orders required factory owners to work within narrow margins. Smaller margins, of course, usually meant lower wages. Efficiency suffered when labor was in short supply, and labor was in short supply when wages languished.

If wages were too low to attract workers, and if competitive pressures prohibited an increase in wages, then employers would have to go to the workers. Toward the end of the nineteenth century factories could continue to expand and be profitable only by shifting away from a boarded labor force, a fact demonstrated by the closing of one of the Isère's largest textile factories during this period. Once it was evident that the larger factories could not attract workers without raising wages above profitable levels, entrepreneurs opportunistically stepped into the breach and set up new mills that were smaller and thus required fewer workers to operate

37. The major exception was the general strike of the winter of 1884, which, as we shall see, began as a protest against falling wages. Daily wages at a facility at Moirans, one of those involved in the strike, averaged between 0.67 and 1.17 francs per day, according to an envoy of the prefect. See AN, F 12, 4658, "Rapport sur les grèves de Paviot," 25 February 1884. Reports on wages and prices can be found in ibid., 4509a, reports of 19 May 1885, April 1886, and September 1886.

profitably. They were also located near the workers' homes, so that lengthy commutes and boarding were unnecessary. The strategy worked. It was soon confirmed that it was much easier to find perhaps 300 employable persons in a rural commune than to recruit and transport 1,000 such workers to a larger facility at Voiron or Vizille. The 1890s, on the whole a more prosperous period for the rural silk industry, particularly in its latter half, saw several smaller factories constructed in towns from which workers had commuted to dormitory factories in years past. Among these new factory towns were Virieu, Vinay, St-Etienne-de-St-Geoire, and La Côte-St-André.[38]

Thus competition for orders and languishing prices during the Long Depression put downward pressure on wages and intensified the trend toward ruralization of the silk industry. In a period of falling wages and in a more competitive international market, the French silk industry survived by becoming less conspicuous, by integrating more fully with the countryside. It was less dependent upon workers drawn from great distances when it operated on a more modest scale. The survivors of the Long Depression were not the massive dormitory factories preferred at mid-century but the more "organic" small facilities that insinuated themselves into the patterns of rural life. In sum, there was quite definitely a labor market in nineteenth-century France, but it operated within strict limits, limits determined in the first instance by a labor force whose radius of mobility, as if on a tether, was short and rendered somewhat inelastic by a primary commitment to the land; it was determined in the second instance by the factory owner's ability and willingness to pay.[39]

A Favorable Cycle: La Belle Epoque

The stagnation of the 1880s persisted into the first years of the next decade. In the early 1890s factory owners grumbled about protective legislation that governed conditions for women workers. Such legislation was believed to hamper French producers'

---

38. On the trend toward smaller factories see Jouanny, *Tissage de la soie*, p. 56.
39. Reddy, *Rise of Market Culture*.

competitive efforts. Soon, however, the silk industry joined in the general prosperity of the Belle Epoque. The late 1890s were highly profitable for the silk industry in France. From the towns of Bourgoin and Jallieu the word went out that the industry was in a "very prosperous" cycle. Factory owners gleefully reported that business in all respects was excellent and "left nothing to be desired." Wages rose to levels 25 to 30 percent higher than those of the preceding decade. By all measures, the industry appeared to be entering a kind of Golden Age.[40]

Undoubtedly the best measure of this expansion is the increase in the number of looms in operation during these years. Investment in mechanical looms, perhaps spurred by lower interest rates, increased tremendously after 1893. Immediately after the Franco-Prussian War, the French silk industry had some 5,000 mechanical looms in operation. This number had grown by 19,000 in twenty-two years, reaching 26,000 by 1893. Much of this growth may be attributed to modernization, not simple expansion; these figures represent, in part, the replacement of hand looms, which had been rendered obsolete for most commercial purposes by the 1890s. In the years surrounding the turn of the century, however, the Lyon Fabrique put into use an additional 16,000 looms. On the eve of World War I the French silk industry could boast some 42,000 mechanical looms, perhaps as much as one-third of the world's productive capacity in these machines.[41]

Meanwhile, the Lyon silk merchants were moving to increase profits by replacing independent *façonniers* with managers hired to operate factories that they owned themselves. Thus, whereas it was estimated that Lyon merchants directly controlled only one of every two and a half mechanical looms in 1894, by the turn of the century they were thought to own close to two of every three.[42] Now

40. The effects of the Spanish-American War were reportedly felt at Voiron: ADI, 53 M, 18, May 1898. Quotations from ibid., report of 1–15 February 1899.

41. Figures on *métiers mécaniques* for 1871 and 1893 can be found in Natalis Rondot, *L'Industrie de la soie en France, 1894* (Lyon, 1894), pp. 111–112. For 1914 see Jouanny, *Tissage de la soie*, p. 133. Lequin estimates that the importance of the Isère as the Fabrique's principal place of production was accentuated during these years. One-third of the Fabrique's mechanical looms operated in the Isère by 1914. See *Ouvriers de la région lyonnaise*, 1:85.

42. Pariset, *Fabrique lyonnaise*, pp. 398–399.

façonniers would not only be competing with one another for orders, they would also be competing with Lyon itself.

New Competitive Conditions

The overall picture of the Fabrique at the turn of the century was one of renewed vigor. But within six years it would again be in the midst of a profound crisis. Observers close to the industry first began to complain publicly of trouble in 1904: the source was foreign competition. Among France's most formidable competitors were Germany, Italy, and Switzerland. The Swiss in particular had made major inroads into markets long established as exclusive French preserves, even the French domestic market itself. The response, in some respects predictable, was protest against protective labor legislation and tariff barriers inadequate to safeguard the home market. The protection of the home market had always been an issue dear to the silk industry. One representative of the Lyon industry tied the two issues together in his testimony before a commission sponsored by the Chamber of Deputies: "Today Swiss, German, and American producers compete here under conditions more favorable than we. Thus, to the extent that we are hemmed in by labor laws, to that same extent we ought to reserve our markets for products that we ourselves produce."[43] The thrust of his statement might be rendered as "If we must have protective legislation, then at least also give us the profits to pay for them."

Protective tariffs imposed by other countries undoubtedly limited the ability of the French to expand their market share and in some cases closed off formerly open and lucrative markets. According to industry representatives, producers paid 7.50 francs per kilo on entry into Germany, 5 to 10 francs in Belgium, at least 25 francs on entry into Spain. In order to gain access to the vast American market producers would have to pay upwards of 17.5 francs to a limit of 25.60 per kilogram—a figure that one source claimed would double the retail price. Retaliatory tariffs may have been the preferred emotional response, but for an industry as dependent

---

43. Assemblée Nationale, 2:10. See also AN, F 7, 12767, 2 March 1904. For other complaints about labor legislation see Pariet, *Fabrique lyonnaise*, pp. 35–36.

upon foreign markets as the French silk industry such a move could have devastating repercussions. French producers exported an amount of silk fabric equal to more than one and a half times the value of the French domestic market, so they were quite vulnerable to a tariff war. In fact, some silk merchants publicly admitted to fear of the consequences of a complete closing of the American market.[44]

Fears of tariff wars simply did not exist for some foreign competitors. Propelled by the burst of commercial and industrial growth that accompanied the defeat of the South and westward expansion, industrialists in the United States had a vast domestic market to conquer. Legislators in the United States had little to fear by making the home market less accessible to manufactured goods, a point of view expressed in the McKinley Tariff of 1890. Worse yet, the provisions of this tariff were broadened by the Dingley Tariff of 1897. The American tariffs were a milestone in the erosion of the position of the Fabrique in the world market.

The U.S. Congress enacted the Dingley Tariff for the express purpose of encouraging American industry. In this effort they were fabulously successful. An American silk industry took off behind the protective trade barrier. In the past, American industry had suffered from the disadvantage of a relative scarcity of skilled labor. Tariffs helped to eliminate the importance of the gap in production costs which resulted from high labor costs. Moreover, as American silk manufacturers were close to China and Japan, they were advantageously placed for the purchase of raw silk. And as the latest entrants in the competition for a share of the market for silk fabric, they were not burdened with outdated equipment. In the eight years after the turn of the century the Americans built some 400 mills containing approximately 40,000 new mechanical looms, bringing their productive capacity close to that of the French. These figures alone ought to be enough to persuade us that the French producers and merchants were not exaggerating their claims in the hope of swaying their legislatures—but there is more. By 1914 American workers were weaving $250 million worth of raw silk per

44. Pariset, *Fabrique lyonnaise*, p. 11. For information about the relative importance of markets see Pariset's Table 1. A discussion of some of the interests and issues involved can be found in Jean-Marie Mayeur, *Les Débuts de la Troisième République* (Paris, 1973), pp. 123–124, 129, 205.

year, a stunning achievement when one considers that the total value of *world* production was estimated at 874 million francs in 1904.[45] Not only did the American tariffs render a major French market less accessible, they were making possible the growth of what would become France's most formidable competitor in the production of silk.

The combined weight of these forces—the emergence of competitors in Germany, Switzerland, Italy, and the United States and the perhaps overly ambitious expansion of French productive capacity in the 1890s—would deliver a stunning blow to the French silk industry before 1914. The first signs appeared in 1905, when the word "crisis" was already being employed to describe the condition of the industry. "The causes of the crisis are well known: excessive international competition, the plethora of production that results from it, the high price of raw materials, the caprices of fashion."[46] The French response was not entirely adequate. Many French textile firms had undergone retooling in the 1880s and 1890s. And although for this reason a substantial part of the industry's equipment was on a par with that of its competitors, a substantial part of it was not. Some cautious French textile manufacturers were still installing hand looms as late as 1890, oblivious of the competitive challenges of the new era. In 1900 one observer estimated that as many as 7,000 hand looms were still in operation in factories or on farms in the Bas-Dauphiné.[47]

The outlook appears to have brightened in 1906, but by the end of the summer of 1907 crisis conditions had returned. The problem seems to have originated, in part, in the United States. There a financial crisis hampered American industry through most of 1908

45. The 1904 world production estimates are from Pariset, *Fabrique lyonnaise*. On Lyon's European competitors, esp. Switzerland, see René Gonnard, "L'Industrie lyonnaise de la soie et la concurrence mondiale," *Revue Economique Internationale*, 15–20 August 1905, p. 261. Some of this ground is also covered in Lequin, *Ouvriers de la région lyonnaise*, p. 89. Aspects of the growth of the U.S. textile industry are discussed in Elie Reynier, *La Soie en Vivarais* (Paris, 1921), p. 235 and passim. In the face of such barriers as the Dingley Tariff, sometimes the best response was to relocate *behind* them. This was the action taken by Duplan & Cie, established in the United States in the 1890s. See Jouanny, *Tissage de la soie*, pp. 56–57.

46. Gonnard, "Industrie lyonnaise," p. 299.

47. Jouanny, *Tissage de la soie*, p. 48. See also Gonnard, "Industrie lyonnaise," p. 285.

and the reverberations of the Americans' difficulties were soon felt on European markets. Stocks of silk fabrics built rapidly while prices, naturally, tended to fall. The market share of the French producers seems to have been shrinking, too. According to local sources in the Isère, "there has been a nearly total stoppage of production since the end of the month of October 1907, brought about by the cancellation of orders in the midst of production and by all manner of difficulties in deliveries. The silk industry has undergone a general crisis."[48] With no end to the "general crisis" in sight, employers undertook drastic solutions. Factory owners cut the employees' workweek by one day, thus unintentionally realizing half of a demand dear to the French labor movement (*"la semaine anglaise"* without pay!).

A recovery of sorts ultimately did take place, but not before the crisis had forced the reorganization of the industry and numerous factories had closed. The shakedown touched hand-loom weaving most directly. Many hand looms were taken out of service after 1908, and by 1913 only 263 still operated commercially in the Bas-Dauphiné, a loss of thousands of looms in barely more than a decade.[49] The attendant suffering caused to rural weavers we can only imagine, but we know that those workers who still had looms were forced to accept wage cuts. Four hundred workers at Renage went out on strike after their wages were cut in April 1908. After only five days they returned to work under the conditions originally stipulated by the employer. Other workers unwise enough to launch such defensive strikes were not always so fortunate—some never had the opportunity to reconsider and return to their jobs. In March 1908 a factory owner at Voiron simply closed his factory after only two days when 103 workers went out on strike. Fifty workers on strike at La Sône received the same ultimate sanction in November of the same year. Of course, if weavers in the countryside were poorly off, then workers in the city of Lyon were undoubtedly worse off still. Forced to compete not only against rural workers but against foreign producers as well, those *canuts* who had some-how survived the nineteenth century were now given the bitter

48. "La Crise du tissage," *République de l'Isère*, 18 January 1908, in ADI, 52 M, 62.
49. Jouanny, *Tissage de la soie*, p. 48.

opportunity to receive wages that would merely allow them to *mourir en travaillant*, to die working. From 35,000 looms in 1856, a decade at least after their apogee, the number of looms at Lyon had fallen to fewer than 10,000 by 1900. Meanwhile, by renting gardens to silkworkers, charitable groups tried to recreate in Lyon what they believed to be the salutary conditions of rural workers— bitter fruit.[50]

In response to such widespread misery, the Chamber of Deputies was said to be prepared to vote unemployment credits for textile workers of half a million francs, a figure that labor leaders rightly dismissed as "ridiculous," given the depth of the crisis. From a high of approximately 129,000 employees in 1900, the total work force of the Fabrique had declined to 90,000 by 1914, for a loss of 30 percent in the space of fourteen years—a catastrophe by the standards of any industry, anywhere, at any time.[51]

Thus by the twentieth century the French silk producers were no longer alone in the world marketplace. Not only other European countries but the United States, too, had new, recently outfitted silk industries. France's share of the world market may have been as great as one-third, measured as a function of productive capacity, but one-third of the market was far less than the French share of only a few decades earlier. Moreover, French producers had to settle for much smaller profit margins if they were to prevent further erosion. Tariff barriers held a visceral appeal for many people in the industry, especially in view of the damage done to them by tariffs imposed by others. Given the dependence of French producers on the world market, however, they could not risk retaliation. In a situation in some ways analogous to that of the U.S. steel industry in the 1980s, excess world productive capacity in silk after

50. These *jardins-ouvriers* are described in A. Pessieux, *Etude monographique des créations sociales* (Valence, 1907), p. 388. On Renage and La Sône see AN, F 7, 12788, 3 April and 17 September 1908. The account of the strike at Voiron is in prefect to Ministry of the Interior, 9 March 1908, in the same dossier.

51. The discussion of unemployment credits is in AN, F 7, 12767, 2 October 1908, and *Petite République*, 24 March 1908, cited in F 7, 13819. Union organizers observed that "if workers had been organized in unions they would have been able to get by a bit more easily because of their union unemployment insurance." See "Les Avenières," *Droit du Peuple*, 31 January 1910. The estimate of the size of the work force in 1900 and 1914 is from Lequin, *Ouvriers de la région lyonnaise*, pp. 147–148.

1900 manifested itself in shrinking margins for owners and lower pay, shorter workweeks, and, in extreme cases, plant closings.

The silk industry had become such a part of rural life that the effects of the downturn rippled through the rural economy. Many communities suffered directly from the crisis of the industry but the workers themselves were the first to devise a response. They began to look more critically at an industry that demanded more and seemed to offer less. They were far from persuaded by a *patronat* that sought to divert attention and blame by pointing an accusing finger first at Lyon, then at faceless competitors safely beyond the frontier.

4

Peasants into Workers: Labor and the Silk Industry

The way of life in the rural Isère utterly captivated Victor Ardouin-Dumazet. At the turn of the century he toured France and, in the manner of the more famous Arthur Young, noted his impressions. What he found so enchanting about the Isère was the nearly transparent integration of industry with the ways of peasant society and rural life. Here at last was the sought-after solution to the perceived deleterious effects of urban industry: industry that neither polluted the urban environment nor uprooted the peasant from a healthful contact with the soil and the simple ways of rural life. Here is how Ardouin-Dumazet described the scene as he approached the textile town of Renage:

> At the base of the valley stand the buildings of the great industrialists Montessuy et Chomer, one of the most important textile manufacturers of the Lyon region. [Many workers] live in Renage itself . . . in houses separated by gardens or on farms scattered across the beautiful mountains of Parmenie. Clean and prosperous, this is a model workers' village.[1]

Here was the answer to the problems plaguing France. Renage's working model of the mixing of industry and agriculture in a rural

1. Victor Ardouin-Dumazet, *Voyages en France*, vol. 9, *Le Bas-Dauphiné* (Paris, 1903), p. 17.

setting offered a hygienic alternative to the social "contagions" of Paris and other big cities. For an observer obsessed by threatening concentrations of the laboring and dangerous classes in France's cities, Renage was a dream come true.

This was a dimension of life in the Isère that the strict categories of statistical sources could not adequately capture. In its analysis of the 1896 census returns, the French census bureau described the Isère as "largely rural." True enough. After all, population growth in the Isère's largest city, Grenoble, had pushed beyond the 50,000-person mark only in 1890, and one would have to go as far as Vienne, in the orbit of Lyon, before one would encounter another city that even approached that size. The Isère had only a handful of communes beyond the arbitrary statistical barrier that defined a commune as urban if it had more than 2,000 residents.

The census bureau's "rural" notation, however, derived not from the observation of the landscape or even the relative size of cities but from consultation of another index—occupational categories. Over half of the Isère's "active" (employed or employable) male population was engaged in agriculture. Therefore, the Isère must be rural.[2] Behind this judgment lay the assumption that agriculture means "rural" while industry means "urban," never mind the parallel assumption that industry means "male." Here we see a classic case of statistical categories masking meaningful information—in this case, industrial presence based on women's labor.

No one would quarrel with the description of the Isère as rural, only with the assumption that "rural" implies absence of industry. For what would the census officer have said of figures showing that in 1896, of the 287,000 persons in the *total* (male and female) active population, some 53 percent were engaged in nonagricultural occupations.[3] Would he be obliged to conclude that the Isère was an urban department? Many of the "farmers" of the rural Isère or their spouses or their sons and daughters were not full-time

2. Census data on the active male population in 1896 are from Direction du Travail, *Résultats statistiques du recensement des industries et professions (dénombrement général de la population de 29 mars 1896)* (Paris, 1899–1901), p. 23. The figures for Grenoble are from Christian Marie, *L'Evolution du comportement politique dans une ville en expansion* (Paris, 1966), p. 53. Grenoble had 46,407 persons in 1886, 54,249 by 1896.

3. Figures on total active population may be found in Direction du Travail, *Résultats statistiques* (1896).

herders or horticulturists. In fact, the most casual examination of the census data reveals that the peasant household that included a weaver, a glovemaker, a miner, or a factory hand was not at all rare. The Isère had a substantial, albeit rural, industrial sector.

But pity the poor statistician who must account for the extraordinary diversity of the economy of the Isère. The rigid census categories can hardly be expected to account for individuals who have multiple occupations. How, for example, might one classify the miner who worked his fields when he returned home from the mines? Or the peasant who stitched shoes at home? Or the small farmer who wove hemp into burlap? Or the *paysanne* who made gloves *à domicile?* Obviously the criteria of clarity, uniformity, and quantifiability imposed upon the census takers prohibited the full rendering of the occupational complexity of the peasant household.

Among the variety of industrial occupations open to the peasant of the Isère, weaving was the most important, numerically speaking. These peasants had long been accustomed to weaving; whether they wove wool for Vienne or hemp for Voiron, they were no strangers to the loom. Rare was the family in the Bas-Dauphiné that did not grow, harvest, and weave hemp for domestic use, a fact that rendered the transition to silk and to production for market all the easier.

So the apprenticeship of the silk weaver was the hemp weaving practiced at home. Was the weaver's art restricted to men? The *métier à bras,* the hand loom, was a cumbersome instrument that required considerable strength to operate—more strength than some women possessed, or so the *façonniers* said. But a peasant woman who in a pinch could drag a plow would not, one suspects, be intimidated by a hand loom. The argument that a sexual division of labor favored male weavers because a man's strength was needed may well be specious. In any event, the development of the mechanical or power loom undermined this particular masculinist discourse.

The mechanical loom enabled women to compete with men for employment because it dispelled such mystifications. When steam or a river-driven paddle wheel powered the loom, constructions of gender distinctions based on strength collapsed. For purposes of profit calculation, however, the advantage of the mechanical loom was that it tapped the reservoir of female labor and at a stroke vastly increased the available labor supply.[4]

So women's "qualifications" for textile labor significantly increased the size of the labor force. This was no small consideration in a country where natality remained stubbornly at or near the rate of replacement and each generation succeeded merely in replacing itself. By the 1870s women's role in the industrial labor force was already preponderant and by 1896 the pattern was well established. Of a total legal population (essentially everyone except temporary residents, such as soldiers garrisoned there) of 568,933 persons, roughly one of every two worked. Industry, as distinct from services and agriculture, employed some 37 percent of the active population; the textile industry was the Isère's most important industrial employer. Textiles, essentially the silk industry, accounted for one of every nine jobs in the economy of the Isère.

Farming or herding was the most important occupation for men, being the daily task of one of every two active men.[5] Textiles were the most important employer of women, occupying some 23,000, or one of four active women. But one should take care not to conclude that agriculture was the domain of men and industry the province of women. Textiles did employ one in eighteen active men, which is no small proportion. And textiles, along with tanning and glovemaking, employed more men than mining, more men than iron foundries and metalworking, even more men than construction. Outside of agriculture, the textile industry was the major employer of labor, male or female.[6]

But it was women's presence that set the textile industry apart and made industry in the Isère an overwhelmingly female activity. One factory manager, speaking of the general character of the labor

4. Paul Leroy-Beaulieu, "Les Ouvrières de la Fabrique," *Revue des Deux Mondes* 97 (1872): 637.

5. Calculations derived from figures reported in Direction du Travail, *Résultats statistiques* (1896), p. 23.

6. All statistics are from ibid. Of course, these tables must be used with caution. Many individuals were active in both industry and agriculture. A person's response could, without deception, vary from season to season. And of course the census taker's only source of information on occupation is the respondent. For a national overview see Marie-Hélène Zylberberg-Hocquard and Evelyn Diebolt's introduction to Aline Valette, *Femmes et travail au XIXe siècle* (Paris, 1984), pp. 38–40.

pool, commented that "in our region, more women than men work [in factories and workshops]." Soon other forces came into play. Women's wage labor became so important to household income that it subverted the conventional preference of a son to a daughter. By the 1870s, women's income was so important that, according to the factory manager, "parents prefer daughters to sons."[7] Perhaps never before had prejudices so deeply embedded in culture been so rapidly uprooted. Simple calculation of household interests radically readjusted women's "worth" and esteem within peasant society and culture.

The Factory System

The scene is such a familiar one that it barely needs a description—the nineteenth-century city surrounded by its "industrial belt." One need only mention the words "Industrial Revolution" and the mind immediately conjures up a Dickensian vision of workers tramping down cobblestone streets under a coal-blackened sky. The setting is unquestionably urban. Where else would employers find an adequate concentration of labor? Yet the entrepreneurs who constructed the Isère's textile factories did not choose the cities. The selection of a desirable site for a textile mill inevitably involved a compromise, since the two most important factors of production, labor and power, were not always to be found in the same location. And after all, the experience of the silk merchants with urban workers had now become a driving force.[8] The need for water power sent the textile entrepreneurs into the countryside looking for a suitable site on a river for the establishment of a factory and water wheel.

The silk industry handled its "artisan problem" by leaving it behind in the city of Lyon. But now a new problem arose: How to industrialize outside of the urban context? The answer was an un-

---

7. AN, C 3021, June 1871, Grand Lemps.
8. Fernand Rude, *L'Insurrection lyonnaise de novembre 1931* (Paris, 1944), and Robert Bezucha, *The Lyon Uprising of 1834* (Cambridge, Mass.: 1974), cover the artisan problem for the silk industry of Lyon.

usual mixture of factory and village, agriculture and industry.[9] Indeed, the combination brings to mind some of features of the model communities of Charles Fourier and Robert Owen, where the sharing of time between agricultural and industrial labor had a prominent place because it was believed it would have a salutary effect on the workers' health and sense of well-being. The point was not lost on contemporaries, who, even if they failed to draw explicit connections between textile villages and the utopians' model communities, nevertheless shared the utopians' romantic belief that, on the whole, rural life was more healthful than urban. Ardouin-Dumazet lavished praise on such a combination and saw in it a response to all of the unpleasant consequences of urban industry.

The larger mills certainly could not rely on the local population alone. Renage's Montessuy et Chomer plant needed 800 workers to operate at maximum efficiency—more than Renage, with some 2,500 souls in 1901, could supply. Many workers made the daily trek to the factory from farms within the commune of Renage, as Ardouin-Dumazet duly reported. But others were recruited from a much greater distance. For them a daily commute would be tedious. The factory owners found a novel solution: they built workers' dormitories. Housed there for the workweek, these workers were spared the tedious and time-consuming daily travel that might have ended by discouraging them from working at all.

The idea of dormitories was first tried in the silk industry in the 1830s, in the department of the Ain, in the town of Jujurieux. As the industry continued its move from Lyon, *façonniers* bent on building large mills imitated the idea of providing temporary housing to a vast rural labor force. At Renage resident workers were housed in buildings at the plant itself. Similar arrangements existed at Voiron, St-Nicholas-de-Macherin, St-Geoire-en-Valdaine, St-Siméon-de-Bressieux, and Coublevie.[10] Such dormitories ex-

9. As Charles Tilly has noted, "urbanization and proletarianization were interdependent processes": "Did the Cake of Custom Break?" in *Consciousness and Class Experience in Nineteenth-Century Europe,* ed. John Merriman [New York, 1979], p. 25). The novelty surrounding the urbanization/proletarianization linkage in the Isère is one of scale, not of kind—the process operated within reduced dimensions.

10. See Dominique Vanoli, "Les Ouvrières enfermées: Les Couvents soyeux," in

tended the range within which workers could be recruited. Without them the local labor supply would have been dangerously small, giving workers, in their relative scarcity, great leverage on wages and working conditions.

The dormitory system left another problem unsolved—that of transportation, for many workers had to be moved over considerable distances. The solution was to transport workers either by train, for which the factory owners concluded a special agreement with local railway operators, or by special wagons called *galères*. The *galères* fetched the workers on Sunday evening and returned them to their homes at the end of the workweek, on Saturday afternoon. The term *galère* refers literally to the galley ships rowed by slaves during ancient times; it was still used as a punishment in France under the old regime.[11] By the late eighteenth century it simply meant "hard labor." In late twentieth-century slang, *galère* refers to any kind of drudgery, however banal. The use of the word by the silkworkers in a period when it conveyed an idea closer to its original meaning strongly suggests their feelings about these vehicles, which marked the beginning and end of their week-long experience of work and separation from their families.

There was no uniform arrangement for the payment of these transport services. Some factories deducted the costs of transporting and housing the workers from their wages. At other factories, such as Renage, the employers absorbed these costs. One might surmise that the differences in this practice derived from the relative conditions of labor supply. Whatever the case, housing and transportation were necessary if the silk industry were to succeed in its strategy of locating its mills far from a concentrated labor pool.[12]

Recruiting a labor force meant more than simply providing shel-

---

Révoltes Logiques, Spring–Summer 1976, pp. 19–40; Abel Chatelain, "Les Usines-internats et migrations féminines dans la région lyonnaise," *Revue d'Histoire Economique et Sociale* 48 (1970): 373–394. See also Lucie Baud, "Les Tisseuses de soie de la région de Vizille," *Mouvement Socialiste* 2 (June 1908): 422; reprinted with foreword by Michelle Perrot as "Le Témoignage de Lucie Baud, ouvrière en soie," *Mouvement Social* 105 (December 1978): 139–146.

11. For an instance of galley punishment under the old regime see Robert Darnton, "Philosophy under the Cloak," in *Revolution in Print,* ed. Robert Darnton and D. Roche, pp. 27–49 (Berkeley, 1989).

12. On the factory at Renage see AN, C 3021, Renage, Montessuy, et Chomer. On the factory in the Ain see Leroy-Beaulieu, "Ouvrières de la Fabrique," p. 651.

ter and transportation. Other necessities, including food, linens, beds, and dormitory supervision and management, had to be provided. Food was generally the responsibility of the workers themselves; in most places workers brought their own weekly provisions. At some facilities, such as Renage, the workers' provisions were supplemented twice daily with a soup provided by the employer. Many factories sold supplies in a canteen. Beds were provided as a matter of routine but linens and blankets usually were the responsibility of the individual worker. This patchwork system was complicated by payroll deductions at some factories, which in 1906 ranged between 18 and 19 francs each month for meals and lodging. In one dormitory mill in Voiron, the owner charged workers a franc a day for meals.[13] At some factories whose owners assumed the personal maintenance costs of the workers, presumably wages were correspondingly lower. One contemporary observer has pointed out that, though in most cases the nominal earnings of "boarding" and "commuting" workers were identical, the wages of the boarding worker were not entirely at her disposal. Under one arrangement wages were divided into three parts: one part was held to cover boarding costs; another part was given immediately to the worker to pay for clothing, laundry, and recreation; a third part was retained by the establishment, apparently interest-free, until the worker's termination date.[14] Such a system depended for its success, of course, on careful and exact accounting and absolute confidence and trust between employer and worker; it also offered the employer an opportunity for abuse and an obvious tool for coercion.

Façonniers exercised discipline in other subtle ways. Supervision presented an especially thorny problem to the employers, and one of the most popular solutions among mill owners was to invite members of religious orders to supervise dormitories and kitchens. This practice was particularly common in the employment of younger women. Employers maintained that recruitment of young workers, whose parents' approval was needed, was facilitated by the reassuring presence of nuns. Parents whose children were about to leave home for the first time felt comforted, it was argued, by the

13. "Nos grèves," *L'Ouvrière Textile*, 1 April 1906, p. 3, and 1 July 1906, p. 4.
14. Leroy-Beaulieu, "Ouvrières de la Fabrique," p. 650.

knowledge that their son's or daughter's moral well-being was being looked after by members of religious orders. When one mill owner sent his director to Italy to recruit workers, he also sent along a priest.[15]

As the case of Châteauvilain showed, such religious supervision meshed neatly with the church's new missionary vision of France's workers. For the church, which by the late nineteenth century was painfully aware of its failure to cultivate workers' spirituality, this was an opportunity to reach and proselytize workers bound in place and hemmed in by the routine of mill and dormitory. For employers, religious personnel constituted an inexpensive cohort of supervisors uniquely equipped to exercise a moralizing discipline and control. A contemporary critic anticipated Foucaultian categories with the remark that the members of religious orders created a refined form of exploitation by "surveilling" the workers' "every act and gesture."[16] Dominique Vanoli cites the remarks of a priest who, though not assigned to a dormitory in the Isère, expressed what was probably commonly understood to be among the aims of the religious dormitory supervisor: "Beside his profoundly Christian wife, the husband will not long remain a staunch Socialist."[17]

The practice of using members of religious orders as supervisors was common at the larger mills, where dormitories were also more common. Of course, this situation would change after the 1901 law on associations and congregations led to the suppression of most such orders. The Sisters of the Good Shepherd looked after the workers at the Durand Frères mill at Vizille; at Renage it was the Sisters of St. Vincent de Paul. Workers' resentment of the practice seems to have been just as widespread. When textile workers in the village of La Frette went on strike in 1901, one of their demands was "that there be no supervision by religious in the workshop." Under pressure from the women themselves, regulations eased in the years between 1900 and 1914. At the conclusion of a strike in 1906, one factory owner tried to lure back workers who had re-

15. See Chatelain, "Usines-internats," pp. 380–381, and Joseph Jouanny, *Le Tissage de la soie en Bas-Dauphiné* (Grenoble, 1931), p. 55. On the recruitment of workers from Italy see Baud, "Témoignage," p. 144.

16. "Nos grèves," *L'Ouvrière Textile*, 1 April 1906, p. 3.

17. See the *pièce justicative* in Louis Reybaud, *Etudes sur le régime des manufactures* (Paris, 1859), cited in Vanoli, "Ouvrières enfermées," pp. 20–21.

turned to their farms with the promise of reformed dormitory regulations. He sent the workers a letter assuring them that they would be free to leave the factory/dormitory compound outside of working hours, provided they returned by 9 P.M.[18]

Living conditions in dormitories often left much to be desired. Eyewitness accounts, some of them anonymous, describe conditions fully equal to those chronicled by Friedrich Engels and other nineteenth-century critics of the conditions of the working class. Lucie Baud is one of the few textile workers of the Isère whose words and thoughts are still available to us. She had a broad perspective on the industry because of her personal experience at several mills; her mobility was due in part to frequent dismissals. Her fiery spirit made her a natural leader, a role that put her employment at risk. Her leadership of a strike at a mill in Vizille ultimately cost her her job and nearly got her blacklisted with other mill operators in the Isère. Her pride and outspokenness aroused the anger and scorn of mill owners. In one confrontation with the mill operator Duplan, only the intervention of the mayor stopped her from punching Duplan after he had dismissed her as "nothing but a little woman."[19] After Vizille, Baud found work at Voiron. She later set out to describe her experience at Vizille,

> this Permezel factory. Some of the women slept there. The dormitories were disease-ridden. Sheets and blankets were changed only twice a year and formerly they were changed only once a year. During the spring and summer the women could try to wash the sheets themselves in order to rid them of insects.[20]

18. The same letter also promised to provide lodging, linens, heat, and light without charge—an offer that suggests that these items had been charged to workers previously. See "Nos grèves," *L'Ouvrière Textile*, 1 July 1906, p. 4. On conditions at Vizille see ADI, 53 M, 16, special commissioner prefect, 23 July 1879. For Renage see AN, C 3021, Renage. For the strike at La Frette see ADI, 166 M, 5, 25 September 1901. In Voiron workers complained about pressure to join the Catholic workers' group Notre-Dame de l'Usine (Our Lady of the Mill)—a slightly different approach. On Voiron see *Droit du Peuple*, 19 April 1906, p. 3. On Notre-Dame de l'Usine see Claude Willard, "Les Attaques contre Notre-Dame de l'Usine," *Mouvement Social* 57 (1966): 203–209, and Patricia Hilden, *Working Women and Socialist Politics in France, 1880–1914* (Oxford, 1986), pp. 114–115.

19. "L'Action syndicale," *L'Ouvrière Textile*, 1 May 1905, p. 4.

20. Baud, "Tisseuses de soie," p. 422.

A labor inspector confirmed the essentials of her account and commented on the ease with which diseases could spread in the crowded and poorly ventilated rooms.[21] Jeanne Bouvier's experience of a mill dormitory in the department of the Ain was comparable: ". . . we were served soup morning and evening, but what a soup! Dogs refused to eat it it was so bad. Our beds were equal, but equally deplorable." Such conditions were not universal. Bouvier described much better conditions in a factory dormitory where

> we were well housed. The beds were good and clean; the blankets were changed every month. I was always happy to go to bed in a clean bed; like at my mother's house. The dormitory was well lighted, heated in winter, with a locker for each worker. I appreciated this organization very much.[22]

Even so, there were trade-offs. The workday at this mill started at five and continued until eight in the evening. The remarks of Jeanne Bouvier and Lucie Baud are instructive not only because they tell us about actual conditions but also because the bitterness of their language tells us how many women felt about dormitory conditions at their worst.

Despite concerns about the moral well-being of workers, so evident in the rhetoric deployed during worker recruitment and in defense of nun/supervisors, sleeping conditions in some dormitories suggested that cost rather than moral considerations drove decisions about the workers' accommodations. In 1849 the prefect of the Isère expressed grave moral reservations about the dormitory system, citing in particular the custom of sleeping two and three workers to a bed. Over fifty years later striking workers at St-Jean-de-Chépy voiced identical criticisms.[23]

Work Conditions: Wages

Despite the fact that the existence of an international market for silk fabric tended to impose limits on silk prices, it can

---

21. The labor inspector was Justin Godart. His comments may be found in *Travailleurs et métiers lyonnais* (Lyon, 1909), p. 391.

22. Jeanne Bouvier, *Mes Mémoires* (Poitiers, 1936), pp. 29, 31.

23. A synopsis of the prefectoral report is in Elie Reynier, *La Soie en Vivarais* (Paris, 1921), p. 206. For details of the strike at St-Jean-de-Chépy see *Droit du Peuple*, 7 April 1906, p. 2.

hardly be said that these circumstances imposed a uniformity of wages and terms of employment upon the industry. In fact, such things varied considerably from region to region and even from establishment to establishment, suggesting that nothing like a regional labor market existed. This might well have been a consequence of peasant/workers' limited mobility.[24]

The absence of a true regional labor market and variations in productivity owing to differences in loom technology nullify any possible statement about conditions in the "typical factory." Moreover, most textile workers were paid a piece rate, so wages varied with skill and effort. What level of effort could be sustained over eleven hours a day, six days a week? Demand for goods made of silk varied seasonally and water-powered mills were generally inactive during the low-water period of the summer months. Thus the workers lived through periods of feast and famine.[25] For how many days during how many months of the year did the average worker actually work? No information on these essential matters exists.

The method of payment presents other difficulties. In nearly all of the textile mills of the Isère the system of piecework, or payment according to the rate of production—francs per meters woven— was carried over from the Lyon Fabrique. Though all workers were compensated at the same piece rate, not every worker could weave the same volume of material in a day. A merely average day's productivity for one worker might be another worker's extraordinarily productive day. And, as the workers themselves sometimes complained, not all workers received the same quality of raw materials. The potential for abuse was tremendous. Evidence suggests that supervisors used their control over the distribution of raw materials to support pliable and deferential workers and to punish militants. Striking workers often charged that supervisors played favorites, giving the best available raw materials to cooperative workers and shoddy materials to troublesome ones. One can easily imagine the consequences: the worker with the shoddy materials must work slowly; her progress is impeded or interrupted by breaking thread while the favored worker makes smooth progress. Given high-

---

24. On the theme of labor markets see William Reddy, *The Rise of Market Culture* (Cambridge, 1984). See also the review by Rondo Cameron in *American Historical Review* 90 (1985): 1209–1210.

25. Not to mention alternation between peasant and proletarian identities.

quality materials, she works rapidly and is more productive.[26] Because the workers are paid a piece rate, these differences in productivity are reflected in their pay.

Finally, there were productivity incentives, known as premiums. Piece rates in themselves constitute a form of productivity incentive: the more a worker produces, the more she makes. Piece rates by their very nature compensate according to a measure of merit. But factory operators often offered additional premiums to encourage their laborers. If an order needed to be filled by a certain date, on short notice, or if demand for silk fabric was unseasonably high, owners and manager would offer to pay workers a few extra centimes. They hoped that the prospect of higher earnings would encourage productivity and reward promptness, diligence, and extra hours of work. The premiums were lifted once the quotas had been met. Operators favored the use of premiums because they allowed greater flexibility in productivity and cost management. In effect, premiums allowed managers to tailor the workers' wages to fluctuations in demand, at least within a limited margin. In this sense, premiums operated like bonuses in that they offered a real sense of a higher standard of living. Unlike bonuses, however, premiums were added to the piece rate and paid as part of wages. This practice created the impression, utterly deceptive, that the underlying rate of pay has ratcheted upward. The workers, of course, tended to view premiums as more or less permanent increases in the piece rate, especially when premiums were in effect for months at a time. When premiums were eliminated, workers frequently responded as they would to a pay cut—by going out on strike.

Bearing in mind these limitations, we can construct and assess long-term trends in wages. Prefects of the Isère regularly asked their subprefects to report quarterly on prevailing wage rates in their jurisdiction. The subprefects diligently reported these wage rates. Women's average daily wages under the Second Empire hovered about 1.50 francs. During the Long Depression from the late 1870s through the early 1890s they remained near 2 francs a day, though they episodically and abruptly fell below that figure. Only after

---

26. In 1898, workers at Voiron went on strike to protest the poor or uneven quality of the materials and demanded payment of 2.75 per day as the just form of compensation under the circumstances. See ADI, 166 M, 4, telegram, mayor of Voiron to prefect, 16 August 1898.

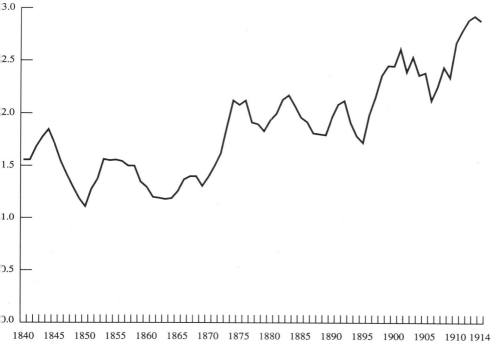

Figure 1 Average daily wage of female silkworkers, 1840–1911. (Archives Départementales de l'Isère, 163 M, 1; 166 M, 2; 138 M, 10–16; Statistique des grèves.)

1910 did average daily earnings approach 3 francs a day (see Figure 1).

How good were these wages? Marie-Hélène Zylberberg-Hocquard and Evelyn Diebolt, working from figures gathered by the Office du Travail for the twenty years before 1914, calculate that the average wag for women in the provinces in this period was 2.10 per day, while one could speak of a "good" wage for a woman only at 3 francs or above.[27] Women in the textile industry of the Isère earned a better-than-average wage for provincial France but fell short of the "good day's wage." In most parts of the Isère, and judging strictly by wage rates, textile mill jobs were the very best available to women; that is, they were the most remunerative.

Men's wages parallel women's but at much higher levels—160 to

27. Valette, *Femmes et travail,* p. 39.

200 percent above those of women. When women earned 3 francs a day, men earned at least 5. While women's earnings easily represented a crucial part of the income of their households, in households where both men and women worked for wages there could be no question whose wages were primary and whose were "supplemental." The difference reinforced existing unequal power relations between men and women. Men could feel reassured that there was no risk that women in the textile industry would earn more than men.

The trends seen in Figure 1 reflect a situation in which workers were made to feel market fluctuations directly. *Façonniers* immediately passed through to workers the effects of variations in demand, of competition (as often with other *façonniers* as with foreign producers), of disruptions in international markets. Note the sharp decline in wages during the mid-century crisis, the American Civil War, and the Long Depression. To those households that earned at least part of their keep from wage labor in the silk industry, these were indeed dark years. The rural silk industry was the very model of a lean, flexible, and responsive producer. For that very reason it was also the very model of a brutally direct employer.

The Rhythm of Production

Thus the nature of the marketplace and the profits of the *façonniers* favored a flexible system of wages and production. The intensity of silk production also tended to fluctuate according to natural rhythms that determined the rhythm of the market. In the world of apparel, silk was a seasonal fabric. Production, therefore, tended to be seasonal too. Production began to peak in late fall, extended through the winter, and tapered off toward summer. The extreme swings in these seasonal fluctuations could be attenuated somewhat by new production techniques, such as printing and dying after weaving, which allowed manufacturers to store finished products ready for sale at season's peak. But such attempts to develop a constant rate of supply in the face of seasonal fluctuations in demand were never completely successful.

The seasonal character of silk production persisted mostly because it was reinforced by immutable natural forces: the rise and fall of the rivers that powered the mills and the rise and fall of the availability of peasant labor. Farm hands who were expendable during the winter months could hardly be spared during the harvest. Many factories depended upon the assistance of large contingents of winter workers. In June 1873, when a factory owner at Bourgoin remarked that his workers were unemployed for the moment, he quickly added that there was no reason for alarm "because printed fabrics are worn in the spring and made in the winter." The rhythm of the fashion industry complemented the rhythm of the fields. In 1912 Ardouin-Dumazet described the same cycle of alternation between industry and agriculture in romantic terms: "These factories must bend to the needs of the countryside. The factories partially empty at sowing time and during the grape harvest. This is a great inconvenience for the factory operators but it has a marvelous curative effect on the workers."[28] This remark suggests that employers needed workers more than workers needed work because employers were unable to compel workers to stay at their looms when the harvest called.

A similar point was made by a factory operator at Moirans when he noted that "industry is merely a prop to small-scale farming. A father sends his daughter to the mill in order to [be able to] round out his little plot of land or pay his mortgage." In the opinion of an employer at Grand Lemps, however, one can be less certain for whom the need was greater: the worker or the mill owner. Agricultural work was something to be taken up when unemployment struck the textile worker. When laid off, most workers "occupy themselves by working in the fields." Roughly the same image of the proper balance between farm and factory was expressed by the prefect of the Isère in 1873. "The unemployed worker in the Isère finds farmwork more easily than does his counterpart in the

28. On Bourgoin see AN, C 3021. Ardouin-Dumazet's comments can be found in *Les Petites Industries rurales* (Paris, 1912), pp. 93–94. Ardouin-Dumazet's work exemplifies a genre of French literature on industry and agriculture in this period which tends to idealize rural life and extols the mixture of agriculture and industry both as a limit to the growth of cities (by nature unhealthful) and as a brake on the rural exodus. See also Jouanny, *Tissage de la soie*. Here romanticism has reconciled itself with the need for industry but not with the decline of the peasantry, an attitude that received official support under Vichy.

Rhône."[29] The principle difference being, of course, that the textile industry in the Rhône was concentrated in Lyon.

Undoubtedly the balance between agriculture and industry varied from year to year and from farm to farm. In some years employers might have to make sacrifices to attract workers. These would have been years good for both agriculture and industry—rare, to be sure, at the end of the nineteenth century. Conversely, if crops failed or if glutted markets depressed agricultural prices and reduced farm income, the peasant household's need for extra income could be a matter of utmost urgency for the future of the farm. If industry in these years was having difficulty finding buyers for its products and had to cut back production, the resulting cash shortfall could have been disastrous for farmers.

Such was the case around 1875, when the phylloxera crisis reached the Isère and ruined peasants who had depended on vineyards for their cash income. In those years it was said that the silk industry found plenty of laborers willing to work for very little, such was their need.[30] In some parts of the Isère, particularly in areas of small-scale farming and high population densities, well-being depended upon the unlikely combination of both healthy industry and prosperous agriculture. As a consequence, these areas could be hard hit by a sudden downturn in either sector, as we shall see.

Hours

Like so many other features of rural industrial population, the workday schedule varied from factory to factory. The earliest records of the daily work schedules in these factories dates back to 1853, that is, to a date immediately after France's first attempts, under the short-lived Second Republic, to establish national standards of industrial working conditions. In 1853 eighteen factory owners in the arrondissement of St-Marcellin complained

29. For industry at Moirans see AN, C 3021. The same dossier contains observations from Grand Lemps and the comments of the prefect.
30. For the consequences of the phylloxera infestation for the textile industry and more see Paule Bernard, "Un Exemple d'industrie dispersée en milieu rural," *RGA* 40 (1952): 141–142.

about attempts to reduce the length of the work day. The object of their protest was a plan to enforce the law of 9 September 1848, which limited the workday in the provinces to twelve hours. They described a typical workday schedule in their letter of complaint addressed to the prefect of the Isère: "Work in our shops has always started at four in the morning with a break at seven-thirty; resumption of work at eight, rest at eleven, resumption at noon, rest at three-thirty, resumption at four, closing time at eight in the evening."[31] The factory owners asserted that these hours caused no harm to the workers and cited in support of their claim the fact that they had *always* operated with these hours. Moreover, they argued, the peasants-turned-workers thought nothing of working these hours: these were farmer's hours.

Of course even farmers kept such hours only during seasonal peaks, not year round. Farmers' hours were daylight hours, and they worked the long days of summer because the harvest required them to do so; to work such hours during the industry's peak demand period of winter was something else again. And factory owners and managers would have to be more creative in cities, where these same hours were the norm and where the specious argument based on a peasant's habits could not be invoked. In the arrondissement of Vienne, for example, the standard workday was only one-half hour shorter, and the long day was just as much resented. In fact, as if collectively to add their voices to the debate, silkworkers staged the first known strike in the department of the Isère over this issue—in 1853. On the first of February some fifty women went out on strike at a factory at St-Symphorien-d'Ozon. In apparent reference to the law of 1848, these women charged that their employer was violating the law—a law they believed had freed them from work before five in the morning or after seven in the evening. While they may not have understood the letter of the 1848 decree, they clearly appreciated its intent: they should not have to work longer than twelve hours a day. Before the strike they had worked from 4:00 A.M. until 7:30 in the evening.[32] Even a legal maximum workday of twelve hours was hard to enforce.

---

31. ADI, 162 M, 3, "Protestation adressée par dix-huit industriels au préfet de l'Isère."
32. Ibid., mayor of St-Symphorien-d'Ozon to subprefect, 1 February 1853.

Despite such efforts on the part of workers, courageous in the political and social context of the early Empire, the law of 1848 remained a dead letter. The best evidence is the fact that the length of the typical workday schedule seems not to have changed very much in subsequent years. In 1864 the subprefect at St-Marcellin reported that it was the custom in his arrondissement for workers to start their workday at five in the morning and finish at eight in the evening with two hours out for meals—a thirteen-hour workday. By all evidence similar schedules were still in force in some factories in the department of the Isère at the beginning of the Third Republic. Workers in Voiron went on strike in 1876, complaining that they could not make a living on their piece rates even though they started at 4:00 in the morning and worked until 8:30 in the evening—on Saturdays work started an hour earlier.[33] This seems to have been far from an isolated case. In 1890 work inspectors cited owners of textile mills at Ste-Blandine, St-Bueil, and St-Nicholas-de-Macherin for violations of the twelve-hour workday, still the French industry standard, though by then outdated in comparison with most other European countries. Employers expected workers to conform to schedules calling for as many as thirteen and one-half hours at the factory, exclusive of breaks.[34] The fact that labor inspectors cited the owners of these mills at least shows that the laws were not altogether ignored, but the considerable interval between these incidents tells us all we need to know about the priority accorded to the enforcement of labor law under the Empire and the early years of the Third Republic.

New protective legislation, high on the Socialist legislative agenda, ameliorated the situation, although Socialists took their inspiration from conventional notions of gender roles. Jules Guesde, guiding light of the nominally Marxist Parti Socialiste de France, contrasted the image of the woman worker, "this monstrosity of

33. ADI, 166 M, 1. Undated petition from workers to prefect.
34. For St-Marcellin see ADI, 162 M, 3, subprefect to prefect, 1 February 1864. The same dossier contains the report of the Service d'Inspection's investigations of 1890. Inspector Beauquis's report to the Conseil Général de l'Isère, whose members included mill owners, shows the work of an extremely diligent man faced with an insuperable task: to ensure the observance of the labor codes in a part of the country where industrial facilities were widely scattered. See also AN, F 22, 166, report, 1901, Isère, "Travail dans l'industrie."

capitalist civilization," with that of the "mother, reproductress of the species"—apparently the Socialist ideal. For Guesde, protective legislation seems to have been an interim step toward an ideal state in which the *ouvrière,* the woman worker, no longer existed.[35] Laws protecting women and children were passed by the legislature in 1892 and 1893; in 1899 work inspectors cited 260 violations of these laws.[36] The law of 30 March 1900 extended the provisions of the 1892 law to all categories of workers, including men, who had been omitted from previous legislation, provided that they were working at a facility that employed women and children. Still, as late as 1905 women accused employers of demanding workdays in excess of fourteen and fifteen hours. The subprefect of Vienne found evidence to substantiate such charges. Indeed, in one case he verified an allegation that the mill in question had operated until eleven at night, an indication of a workday totaling perhaps sixteen hours, exclusive of breaks.[37]

The Millerand law of 1899 limited women's workdays to a maximum of ten hours. Legislation and enforcement were quite distinct matters, however, and by all appearances this maximum was often breached. The reason? Uneven enforcement. Lack of enforcement was common first of all because the dispersal of the textile industry made regular inspection tours difficult. And inspection was made doubly difficult by understaffing—responsibility for inspection was assigned to a single individual. This person was supposed to enforce health and safety codes in some 1,547 subject establishments; the labor laws, after all, did not apply only to the silk industry.

35. See "La Journée de huit heures," *L'Ouvrière Textile,* 1 March 1904, p. 1. Mary Lynn Stewart has persuasively argued that special legislation for women served, among other things, to defend male-dominated occupations. See *Women, Work, and the French State* (Kingston, Ont., 1989).

36. Early parliamentary reports on conditions in factories and mills glossed over the issue of work conditions. According to Deputy Leurent's testimony in 1873, "les manufactures aujourd'hui sont presque des monuments. Toutes les constructions nouvelles ont dû être faites en vue de l'installation de ces immenses métiers. Ce sont donc des locaux spacieux où il y a peu d'ouvriers et surtout beaucoup de broches. L'air y est très sain; on peut y passer des journées entières sans éprouver aucune incommodité": *Journal Officiel de la République Française,* 23 January 1873, p. 477.

37. See ibid. Allegations of fourteen- and fifteen-hour workdays can be found in ADI, 162 M, 5, subprefect (Vienne) to prefect, 4 December 1905. A summary of protective legislation can be found in Assemblée Nationale, *Commission d'enquête sur l'industrie textile: Procès-verbaux* (Paris, 1906), 3:35.

Finally, labor laws remained unenforced because some factory owners and managers sought to circumvent them.

In other cases they winked at violations they did not themselves encourage, or allowed them to occur by inattention. For example, some factories were open for periods longer than the legally permitted workday. By not imposing fixed hours of entry and exit, the factories were, in effect, offering open-ended shifts. In this nineteenth-century version of flextime, a worker could start at six in the morning and quit at three in the afternoon if she chose, though one suspects that such an unproductive worker might be discouraged from returning. Likewise, a worker could start when the factory doors opened at four in the morning and work until closing time at eight. Such a violation would go unnoticed among all the comings and goings of personnel, unless the worker herself complained. Less benign techniques to encourage extralegal hours included requiring take-home work or asking for "volunteers" for supplementary hours. Though the ten-hour workday was made the legal maximum for women in 1899, those who worked fewer than fourteen hours at factories at Les Echelles and Entre-deux-Guiers reportedly were given shoddy materials and branded as slackers.[38]

These circumventions of the law were rationalized in several ways. It was sometimes claimed (for example, by the subprefect of St-Marcellin) that the workers had no grounds for complaint because they knew the hours and conditions of employment when they asked to be hired. Others used moral arguments, maintaining that a reduction in work time would mean more leisure, and more leisure could only lead to temptation and immoral behavior. Certainly the more honest justification (and certainly just as mistaken) was that a reduction of the workday from fourteen to twelve (later ten) hours would render the French silk producer uncompetitive against foreign producers.[39]

38. The absence of regular hours as an impediment to the enforcement of labor laws was the subject of a letter from the prefect of the Isère to the minister of commerce, 23 February 1884. See AN, F 12, 4658. The practice of requiring homework was reported in "Travail des femmes," *Ralliement,* 27 February 1893. The alleged violations at Les Echelles and Entre-deux-Guiers were the cause of a strike there in 1906. The charges were printed in *Droit du Peuple,* 29 February 1906.

39. The argument that the workers sought to have known how long they were expected to work when they signed on was made by the subprefect at St-Marcellin. See subprefect to prefect, 9 December 1864, in ADI, 162 M, 3. Concerns about the

Most damaging of all to enforcement was the letter of the law itself. In fact, factory owners and managers could require long workdays and still be within the law. A section of the law of 2 November 1892 allowed certain industries (textiles among them) to overlook legal limits to the duration of the workday provided they secured the approval of the labor inspector. The law left the details of this section to be worked out by the minister of commerce, who ruled on 7 May 1900 that such special dispensations for seasonal industries could be granted for as many as sixty days out of the year. On these occasions the workday could be extended up to twelve hours for women and for workers under the age of eighteen. At the same time the minister ruled that laws providing for the *repos hebdomadaire*—Sunday rest—could be suspended for as many as fifteen Sundays during the year, again with the approval of the work inspector.[40] The arithmetic is simple: The dispensations allowed by the minister of commerce permitted textile manufacturers to operate twelve hours a day, seven days a week, for two months each year. In a seasonal industry this was perhaps all that was needed to cover peak production demands. Even so, violations persisted.

Violations did not always reflect the ill will of factory operators or the inattention of inspectors. Workers were sometimes implicated—driven by the logic of piecework—in their own exploitation. Attempts to reduce the length of the workday were sometimes resisted by the workers themselves. In the Ardèche in 1894, workers at twenty-two mills went out on strike against the law that limited hours. Paradoxically, workers at seventeen of these mills had struck a year earlier to compel the application of the law. The problem was that the Millerand law contained no provision for wage adjustments to compensate for wages lost to a legally mandated shorter workday. In an industry dominated by piece rates, a shortened workday meant a reduction in pay. The prospect of losing one or

---

moral consequences of a shorter workday were expressed by a factory owner at Moirans (AN, C 3021). Fears of competitive pressure were expressed by the prefect of the Isère in a letter of 10 February 1855 (ADI, 162 M, 3). Similar fears about competitive disadvantages produced by labor legislation were expressed in 1904: Assemblée Nationale, *Commission d'enquête,* 2:10, 35–36.

40. Assemblée Nationale, *Commission d'enquête,* 2:36. For an example of this practice in the Isère see Victor Renard, "Maître chez soi," *L'Ouvrière Textile,* 1 May 1905, p. 1.

two hours of weaving time each day, hence up to twelve hours' wages each week, was not very popular with workers whose full income was essential to their households. A shortened workday, however well intentioned, would be cast as a victory for workers only when their accustomed income was maintained.

The practical consequences of such lengthy workdays for the workers and their families are brought home when one recalls that many workers lived at a considerable distance from the mill where they worked. A work inspector reporting on a strike at Voiron in 1884 forcefully described the utter drudgery of this life:

> Of the seven hundred workers employed by Messieurs [the factory owners] three hundred sleep at the factory dormitories. . . . The other workers are from neighboring villages and have to travel three or four kilometers to return home at night. They reach home by nine for supper and leave again at four o'clock in the morning. This leaves them, at most, six hours of sleep.[41]

This routine was not unusual, the inspector added. It was the common experience of workers throughout the Isère. Henriette Bonnevie, the fifty-five-year-old worker who died in the incident at Châteauvilain, lived in Biol, a village at least seven kilometers from the mill.[42]

Work in the textile mills seemed to offer few real choices. As we shall see, peasants-turned-workers became deeply enmeshed in industrial labor—for many there was no question of backing out—and as long as remuneration was a function of productivity, of piece rates, legislation limiting the number of hours worked was definitely a mixed blessing. The remaining question was how much of a living was really left after a worker had spent her day earning it. For workers who chose not to have wages withheld for room and board, the part of the day not absorbed in work itself was consumed by the trek to work and the trek home. These nineteenth-century forebears of the commuter trapped in the eternal cycle of *métro, boulot, dodo* consumed their "leisure time"—grimly defined as time not spent at work or asleep—simply getting from farm to factory and back again.[43]

41. AN, F 12, 4658, "Rapport sur les grèves de Paviot et Voiron," 25 February 1884.
42. See "La Persécution jusqu'au sang," in *La Croix*, 11–12 April 1886, p. 1.
43. *Métro, boulot, dodo* = subway, job, sleep.

5

A Barrier against
the Rural Exodus?
Some Demographic Consequences
of Rural Industry

Despite the efforts of Gustave Courbet and Jean-François Millet, and of Emile Guillaumin and Pierre-Jakez Hélias, it was Edward A. Ross, an American sociologist, who supplied the most telling, not to mention amusing, evocation of the twilight years of rural society. When Ross discussed rural depopulation in the turn-of-the-century United States, he had no use for sentimental language. For Ross, depopulated towns were "fished-out ponds, populated chiefly by bull-heads and suckers." Those who remained were too stubborn or too foolish to leave.[1] Towns and cities took the best of the rural populace, not the worst—a fact to be celebrated, not deplored. Depopulation was transparently a good thing because it revealed a dynamic society, one that was willing to take risks, one in which talent followed opportunity. The World We Have Lost did not merit sentimental evocations. Better to say that it had simply outlived its usefulness.

So much for American matter-of-factness. The French used gloomier and more romantic language to mark the passing of peasant society. Of course, French culture evinced a preference for the rustic well before the rural exodus. It was already clearly in evidence in the eighteenth-century fascination with the authentic rustic virtues, exemplified by the cult of Ben Franklin. These senti-

1. E. A. Ross, "Folk Depletion as a Cause of Rural Decline," *Publications of the American Sociological Society* 2 (1917): 21–30.

ments made their way into the political culture of France after 1870 and have been exploited ever since—and not only by the right.[2] The humiliating defeat in the Franco-Prussian War became a symbol of France's political and spiritual decline.[3] Thus while rural depopulation was perhaps by strict scientific standards a sign of progress—agricultural yields allowed a distribution of labor out of the agricultural sector—in France rural depopulation was identified as a "problem" and cited as evidence of the nation's persistent weakness.

By the eve of World War I the *clocher*—the church bell tower that dominated the rural horizon—had become a symbol of *la France profonde*.[4] The future of France depended upon the preservation of a way of life linked to the countryside. The *clocher* stood in symbolic contrast to decadence, as much moral as military, invariably seen as a function of city life. Victor Ardouin-Dumazet, a French traveler and chronicler, declared that stopping the erosion of population from the countryside is "the most serious social problem of the present hour."[5] Employing language and concepts that were to receive official sanction under the Vichy regime—and that lose some of their cloying sentimentality in translation—he warned that "if we do not succeed in bringing back to the shadow of the native bell tower some of those who have forsaken it . . . the debilitation of the French race will accelerate until it becomes a calamity of the utterly shocking proportions of the great epidemics of the Middle Ages."[6] To Ardouin-Dumazet there was something essentially rural

2. French syndicalism also allocated an exalted status to rural life. See Jeremy Jennings, *Syndicalism in France: A Study of Ideas* (New York, 1990), pp. 51–53, 83–84.

3. On French responses to national defeat after 1870 see Allan Mitchell, *The German Influence in France after 1870* (Chapel Hill, N.C., 1979) and *Victors and Vanquished* (Chapel Hill, N.C., 1984).

4. It still is. The dominant motif of François Mitterrand's *Force tranquille* campaign of 1981 was a hilltop village dominated by a church tower silhouetted against a sky of blue, white, and red. It was perhaps the symbolic equivalent of the Main Street, U.S.A., motif used so effectively by the Reagan/Bush campaigns.

5. Victor-Eugène Ardouin-Dumazet, *Les Petites Industries rurales* (Paris, 1912), p. 1.

6. Ibid. The original language reads: "Si l'on ne réussit pas ramener à l'ombre du clocher natal une partie de ceux qui l'ont abandonné . . . l'affaiblissement de la race française s'accroîtra davantage et prendra le caractère d'une calamité autrement effroyable que les grandes épidemies du moyen age." On Vichy policy and attempts to halt rural depopulation, see Robert Paxton, *Vichy France* (New York, 1972).

about the French "race," and the vitality of the French nation depended upon maintaining close contact with the land.

But by the time Ardouin-Dumazet wrote of this national peril, much of the putative damage had already been done. *L'exode rural* had been the outstanding demographic feature of post-1850 France. The picturesque term "rural exodus" was as extravagant as Ardouin-Dumazet's language, for there is no evidence that anyone saw the "exodus" as any kind of escape from bondage, and the city was far from fitting most contemporary definitions of the Promised Land. Like the original exodus, however, this one seemed to involve the fate of an entire people. World War I would only hasten an uprooting that had been under way for more than two generations. And if it took compulsory education and the unifying experience of military service to turn peasants into Frenchmen, the experience of rural industry meant that peasants, who according to Eugen Weber's famous formula had perhaps not yet become Frenchmen, were nonetheless ceasing to be peasants at an alarming rate in the late nineteenth century.[7] For most of rural France, the entire second half of the century seemed to be a period of decline. After two centuries of gradual population increase, the countryside began a retreat from the demographic high ground of mid-century—a retreat that continues to the present day. These were the general features of the rural exodus in nineteenth-century France. But what features were

7. The literature on the history of population changes in France in the nineteenth century is not so vast as one might think, given the importance of demography as a kind of historical substratum in *Annales*-style social history. Charles-Marie Pouthas's *Population française au XIXᵉ siècle* (Paris, 1971) is comprehensive but so riddled with errors that his conclusions are cast into doubt. See Paul G. Spagnoli, "The Demographic Work of Charles Pouthas," in *Historical Methods Newsletter* 4 (1971): 126–140. Vols. 3 and 4 of *Histoire de la population française* (Paris, 1988), under the direction of Jacques Dupâquier, has provided the systematic treatment the topic deserves. See also Philippe Pinchemel, *Structures sociales et dépopulation rurale dans les campagnes picardes de 1836 à 1936* (Paris, 1957); André Armengaud, *La Population française au XIXᵉ siècle* (Paris, 1971); and Abel Chatelain, *Les Migrations temporaires en France, 1800–1970* (Paris, 1970), as well as Chatelain's articles on related subjects in *Etudes Rhodaniennes* and *Revue de Géographie Alpine*. The Centre National de Recherche Scientifique is providing some of the raw material for careful population study in the multivolume *Paroisses et communes de France*, ed. Jean-Pierre Bardet and Jacques Dupâquier. On the transformation of French peasants, see Eugen Weber, *Peasants into Frenchmen* (Stanford, 1976). The ambiguities in Weber's formula are highlighted in Charles Tilly's "Did the Cake of Custom Break?" in *Consciousness and Class Experience in Nineteenth-Century Europe*, ed. John Merriman, pp. 17–44 (New York, 1979).

unique to the department of the Isère and what was the connection between the exodus and the silk industry? Was Ardouin-Dumazet's vision of the silk industry as a barrier to rural depopulation, even as a stimulus to rural *re*population, borne out? Or did rural industry simply postpone an inevitable demographic decay into "decadence"?

L'Exode rural and Its Causes

The most important precondition for the onset of the rural exodus at mid-century was overpopulation—the progressive overburdening of rural resources through gradual increases in population. In an economic sector that is technologically static, there are few chances to bring about the dramatic improvements in productivity necessary to support the burden of increasing numbers. When population grows, limited available resources must be apportioned accordingly. When resources are stretched thin, the smallest disturbance can precipitate a crisis. Overpopulation, like scarcity, is a relative term; but when it leads to precipitant action, it has reached an absolute condition.

Even as the population of rural France increased over the first half of the nineteenth century, the problem of rural overpopulation was aggravated by the reduction of options traditionally available to the rural poor. According to customs prevailing in prerevolutionary France, peasants could supplement meager resources by taking advantage of traditional rights of access to community land and, under certain circumstances, private land as well. Under the regimes of the postrevolutionary era the right of gleaning and the right to common pasture had suffered various assaults, and their suppression shifted control of rural resources away from the poor at a time when their numbers were increasing. Given the limits imposed upon political expression by the regime of Louis-Napoléon Bonaparte, the poor rural citizen had little political recourse. With political protest specifically excluded, the rural poor could act out their discontent only in quiet ways. As Michel Augé-Laribé put it, the rural exodus was "a form of strike, individual and unremitting."[8]

8. Michel Augé-Laribé, *La Politique agricole de la France de 1880 à 1940*

Laws dictating partible inheritance constrained each generation, at least in theory, to dole out property in equal parts to descendants. Unless the law were circumvented in some way, the family farm would be divided among survivors; the result could be not shared wealth but shared misery.[9] New households would form, and meager quantities of land would be expected to support them. With the passage of each generation, these smaller parcels of land became increasingly inadequate to meet the needs of those who depended upon them. Even the limited aims of subsistence agriculture could not be achieved. The insufficiency of the yields of these microparcels forced the pursuit of other forms of income, the taking on of *un travail d'appoint*—a part-time job.[10] Some peasants turned to day labor on neighboring farms to make up the difference.

Not all of the alternatives, however, were within agriculture. Larger populations could be supported on the land if alternative resources beyond agriculture were available. These second incomes undoubtedly supported many small farms whose returns were below what would otherwise have been the practical threshold. Typical of these rural industries of early nineteenth-century France were lace and ribbon making and hemp weaving on a piecework basis.[11] Such work generally did not require skills beyond those generally

---

(Paris, 1950), p. 102, quoted in Pierre Barral, "Aspects régionaux de l'agrarisme français avant 1930," *Mouvement Social* 67 (April–June 1969): 10.

9. For a treatment of the impact of egalitarian revolutionary legislation on family and inheritance see Margaret H. Darrow, *Revolution in the House: Family, Class, and Inheritance in Southern France, 1775–1825* (Princeton, 1989).

10. This phenomenon has been remarked by many observers. Among the earliest was Turgot.

> The natural division of inheritances causes what is hardly sufficient for a single family to be divided among five or six children, each of these shares being frequently subdivided further. . . .
> If possible, they rent out their little property, which is insufficient even for their most essential needs, and turn to crafts, to trades, to commerce, to domestic service. . . . It is by their labor that these new heads of households—disinherited, so to speak, by the land—manage to subsist. They belong principally to the wage-earning class. The class of landed proprietors to which they cling only by a few rods of land . . . can lay only very slight claim to them. ("Memorandum on Local Government" [1774], in *The Old Regime and the French Revolution*, ed. K. M. Baker [Chicago, 1988], pp. 105–106)

11. On ribbon making and more in an urban setting see Elinor Ann Accampo, *Industrialization, Family Life, and Class Relations* (Berkeley, 1989).

available to members of rural households. Income from these cottage industries complemented the income of agricultural laborers or smallholders whose agricultural income met the greater part of the family's subsistence needs.

Cottage industries were especially important in areas where agriculture was unusually poor or in mountainous regions or both; but they existed elsewhere, including the Bas-Dauphiné, where the average parcel on comparatively productive land was too small for a single household. Rural industries could significantly reduce the minimum quantity of land required to support a household. They allowed the persistence of marginal farms in the early nineteenth century; their subsequent decline meant the loss of a major prop to high rural population densities. The supplementary income provided by cottage industries lulled otherwise marginal peasant producers into a sense of security that now was sometimes brutally revealed to be false. Imperceptibly they had come to rely more and more on these resources over which they had no real control. When these cottage industries began to collapse under the weight of the mid-century crisis, peasants were fully exposed to the precarious position of the marginal peasant household. "Cottage industry, [and] the tiny textile and metallurgical factories scattered throughout the valleys stopped one by one [and with them the] sources of supplementary income disappeared," argues Maurice Agulhon.[12] The result was the collapse of the population in communities where, in the absence of such nonagricultural pursuits, the population had achieved a density that was ultimately unsustainable within the limits of current agricultural technology and methods. Whether because of a more restrictive treatment of common property, an unwise inheritance law, or the decay of rural industry, the abrupt readjustment of population to resources was the principal feature of the rural exodus.[13]

The permanent migration from the countryside was manifest in complaints, first registered after mid-century, of a shortage of agricultural laborers. In extreme cases, especially in areas of cereal

12. Maurice Agulhon et al., *Apogée et crise de la civilisation paysanne de 1789 à 1914* (Paris, 1976), p. 399. For a discussion of the mutual affinity of rural industry and certain village types, see Pinchemel, *Structures sociales*, 82–86.

13. For a summary of the features of the *exode rurale* see André Armengaud, *La Population française au XIXe siècle* (Paris, 1971), pp. 67–68.

production, the decline in the number of workers available for the harvest was estimated to be on the order of 50 percent between 1861 and 1879. This claim was typically accompanied by complaints about the need to pay higher wages for such laborers. And, the loss was not limited to grain-producing areas. Sixty-five French departments (more than two of every three) lost population between 1851 and 1866. The loss was greatest in the more "backward" parts of France, in the Massif Central, in Brittany, and in the Vendée region—a reflection of the absence of industry or large cities to absorb the floating population in these areas.[14] Communes with populations of fewer than 2,000 were often the hardest hit.[15] The attraction of the city and the wages one might earn there may also be blamed for the exodus, if we may judge by the departments that posted net population gains during this period: the Seine (Paris), Bouches-du-Rhône (Marseille), Rhône (Lyon), Gironde (Bordeaux), Nord (Lille-Roubaix-Tourcoing), Seine-et-Oise (Paris), and Hérault (Montpellier).[16] The attraction of the cities, however, can be exaggerated. Where in the industrial city of the nineteenth century, one might ask with Engels, can one read the fulfillment of the Promised Land?

The Exodus in the Isère

At mid-century the population of the countryside in the Isère, as in the rest of rural France, had outstripped the limits of the rural economy. In addition to natural population increases, the Isère had had a positive immigration balance between 1836 and 1851: toward the end of the first half of the nineteenth century, the department attracted more than 15,000 more new residents than it

14. Although "floating population" typically indicates persons without a settled place of residence, I use the term here in a somewhat broader sense to include all those subject to the forces that drove the rural exodus.

15. Agulhon et al., *Apogée et crise*, pp. 221–223.

16. Jean Pitié, *Exode rural et migrations intérieures en France* (Poitiers, 1971), p. 147. On the attraction of the cities see Jean-Marie Mayeur, *Les Débuts de la Troisième République* (Paris, 1973), p. 57. Jean Garavel disputes the contention that the attractiveness of city life had anything to do with the *exode rural*, a slightly different point. "Ce n'est point l'attrait prétendu des villes," he argues; rather, it is the shortage of work in the countryside: *Les Paysans de Morette* (Paris, 1948), p. 2.

lost to other departments.[17] Rural population had reached all-time records; so had population densities.[18] In fact, the population density of some of the department's rural cantons was greater than that of the Nord, at that time France's most densely populated department. La Tour-du-Pin, for example, had more than 99 persons to the square kilometer; the canton of Morestel, "without any settlements of significant size," had more than 200 inhabitants to the square kilometer.[19]

Such high population densities were achieved by one of two means: *morcellement* and *défrichement*. The more common was *morcellement*, the division of the land into smaller parcels. Of course, "small" is a relative term especially when the subject is land, because the yield is determined as much by the quality of the land as by its quantity. Thus it is difficult to determine by size alone whether a parcel will provide a minimal existence to a household. In some parts of the Isère eight hectares was the bare minimum; elsewhere it was a single hectare.[20]

Défrichement, or land clearance—what economists call extensive agriculture—was sometimes worth the effort. But such efforts were usually expended on land commonly regarded as little suited to cultivation, or at least to the kind of cultivation that was practiced on them. Yields were generally poor on such lands. In the Bas-Dauphiné this procedure was limited largely to the hillsides where such wooded areas as still existed in the sixteenth century had finally been cleared away.[21] The practice increased the number of small property owners, though the quality of the land and the size of the yield left the tenants vulnerable to the slightest harvest shortfall. In either case, the net effect was an increase in the class of peasants who were barely able to subsist on the produce of their

17. Pitié, *Exode rural*, p. 109.

18. Louis Champier, "L'Equilibre économique du Bas-Dauphiné septentrional de la fin du XVIIᵉ siècle au milieu du XIXᵉ," *Evocations*, October 1949, p. 490. See also Pierre Barral, *Le Département de l'Isère sous la Troisième République* (Paris, 1962), p. 40.

19. Edmond Esmonin and Henri Blet, eds., *La Révolution de 1848* (Grenoble, 1949), p. ix. Only one commune in the canton of La Tour-du-Pin had more than 2,000 inhabitants at mid-century (Les Avenières, with 4,200).

20. Paule Bernard, "Un Exemple d'industrie dispersée en milieu rural," *RGA* 40 (1952): 137.

21. Ibid., p. 136.

land in the best of times. Population simply outstripped the productivity of the land.

In the worst of times a harvest shortfall could force the dislocation of hundreds of people. Such problems could be compounded when they coincided with changes in trade policy. Perhaps the worst of these crises occurred in the 1860s, when the liberal trade policies of Louis-Napoleon allowed foreign grains to enter the domestic French market at competitive prices. As a result, foreign wheat could be imported at Marseille for less than it cost to grow it in the Bas-Dauphiné. Peasants were doubly injured: not only as farmers but as farmworkers too. The many peasants who worked as members of harvest teams on the larger estates were customarily paid in kind. When agricultural prices were depressed, their labor was ill paid. These developments cast a shadow over the marginal peasant whose fate was linked to the economic success of large landowners. At the prices imposed by the arrival of cheap foreign grain, some large-scale agriculture was no longer profitable; day laborers who depended on large agriculture suffered too.[22] At the same time, that other prop to the marginal farm, rural weaving, also came under pressure. Hemp combing and weaving, the avocations of choice for the marginal peasant of the Isère before midcentury, were losing their market to cotton fabrics produced elsewhere in France.

Such events served to expand and to accelerate developments that would probably have taken place anyway, though in a less abrupt fashion. Even where small agriculture did not have the crutch of seasonal labor, the exodus got under way about the same time. Jean Garavel dates the rural exodus from the 1850s and notes a marked acceleration in the 1860s.[23] The Isère was among the hardest hit. It was among a handful of departments to lose more than 20,000 inhabitants between the censuses of 1851 and 1866, erasing most

22. Champier, "Equilibre économique," pp. 496–497. Even worse for the long-term prospects of such peasants, the economic future of these larger farms looked more and more doubtful. Champier is exaggerating somewhat when he argues categorically that large-scale agriculture was no longer profitable, because wheat production on large farms continued in the fertile plains of the Bas-Dauphiné after this period, though under changed circumstances. See Jean Ginet, "La Main d'oeuvre agricole saisonnière dans le Bas-Dauphiné," *RGA* 21 (1933): 337–339.

23. Garavel, *Paysans de Morette*, p. 40. Garavel also notes the importance of World War I to the acceleration of rural depopulation.

of the net population gain of nearly 30,000 posted between 1836 and 1851.[24] The economy of the Isère and the population it sustained had reached a Malthusian ceiling. Densities were at levels that made some population displacement inevitable—inevitable, that is, except in those privileged areas that received a major new stimulus to the rural economy in the form of a burgeoning silk industry.

The Demographic Consequences of Rural Industry: The Big Picture

"At one time," Pierre Barral comments, "the countryside was filled with 'little people.'"[25] In other words, the rural exodus was as much a social phenomenon as a demographic one. Those who left were not the well-to-do. They were the little people of the countryside: the small farmers, the majority of whom worked only a few hectares, and their hired hands. At the price of very hard work these people could live honestly during a favorable conjuncture, but only with difficulty during a period of crisis. Confronted with such problems, households had only two alternatives: they could find work or they could leave.

Most historians agree that peasants regarded outmigration as a last resort, but they disagree about the effectiveness of rural industry as a barrier to outmigration. Some historians attribute to rural industry the power to inhibit the rural exodus by providing supplementary resources to a propertyless or smallholding peasantry; others see rural industrial employment, and the temporary migrations it sometimes entails, as a mere prelude to a more permanent

24. The other departments were the Orne, Meuse, Meurthe, Haute Saône, and Eure: Pitié, *Exode rural*, p. 113. Population loss in the Isère continued unabated for the next 100 years. Only the high-technology boom of the 1950s brought the population back to what it had been a century before. See ADI, 123 M, 3, 6, 8, 10, 51, 53–55, 57, 60; Bernard Bonnin et al., *Paroisses et communes de France*, vol. 38 (Paris, 1983).

25. Barral, *Départment de l'Isère*, p. 106. For a study of the demographic effects of rural industry in the Vosges, see Louis Gachon, "Le Partage d'activités entre l'agriculture et l'industrie dans les familles paysannes de la montagne des Vosges," *Revue Géographique de Lyon* 27 (1952): 45–46. For an overview see Daniel Courgeau, *Study on the Dynamics, Evolution, and Consequences of Migrations*, vol. 2 of *Three Centuries of Spatial Mobility in France* (Paris, 1983).

move—as if temporary work in rural industry merely provided training and acclimated the worker to the idea of change.[26] Abel Chatelain, who made a life's work of the study of the phenomenon, offers a more subtle view. According to Chatelain, rural industry and temporary migration depended heavily on other historical circumstances. He tended to see the late nineteenth and early twentieth centuries as a period when rural industry was insufficient to inhibit the rural exodus. This period thus contrasts with the period before mid-century, when "temporary migration [was] a welcome break on the exodus threat," and the period since the middle of the twentieth century, when the automobile and the bus have potentiated a new round of industrial decentralization and a revived temporary migration.[27] Chatelain's view is predicated on the assumption that rural industry was in decline by mid-century almost everywhere in France, and that this decline was itself one of the precipitants of the late nineteenth-century exodus. In other words, after 1850 and until the automobile, there was no sanctuary against outmigration.

While this scenario works well for France as a whole, it manifestly does not apply to the rural silk industry, which remained a vital economic force in the Isère throughout the nineteenth century. Indeed, with the spread of rural industry, an economy that had been based largely on agriculture now took on a significant industrial dimension. The resultant binary economy, dependent on both industry and agriculture, was also insulated, to a degree, from the vagaries of either.[28] Because the potential labor pool was dispersed in this rural milieu, and because water power was plentiful and widely distributed, entrepreneurs preferred small-scale establishments and created dozens of factories. They took care, in a territorial fashion worthy of natural rivals, to maintain a respectable distance between themselves. This strategy soon had noticeable

26. For a statement of these issues see Armengaud, *Population française*, p. 69.

27. Abel Chatelain, "Les Usines-internats et migrations féminines dans la région lyonnaise," *Revue d'Histoire Economique et Sociale* 48, no. 3 (1970): 375–376.

28. On the binary economy in the twentieth century see Harvey Franklin, "The Worker Peasant in Europe," in *Peasants and Peasant Societies*, ed. Teodor Shanin, pp. 98–102 (Aylesbury, 1976).

social effects at the levels of both the individual household and the region, where the industrial stimulus imposed a drag on the pace of the rural exodus and sometimes even reversed it. The insinuation of the silk industry into existing patterns of rural life minimized and localized the demographic manifestations of change in significant ways.

The silk industry *was* a genuine barrier against rural depopulation, at least in the short run. A study of the cumulative population change in all of the 560-odd municipalities of the Isère shows the extent of the rural exodus. The median population change between mid-century and the eve of World War I was on the order of *minus* 30 percent.[29] In other words, the typical commune in the Isère in 1911 was smaller by one-third than it had been in 1846. A population of this size would have ably supported Ardouin-Dumazet's assertions about trends, if not his sentiments. The experience of textile communes, however, was markedly different.[30]

Figure 2 shows that the textile industry effectively limited the loss of population. Before 1900 the textile communes were largely untouched by the rural exodus. In fact, during periods when the textile industry grew, the populations of the textile communes increased. Only after 1900 are there signs of loss, for reasons explicable by the history of the silk industry, but even in 1911 the textile communes, collectively speaking, are no smaller than they had been before mid-century. In a department that suffered rural depopulation like few others, the rural silk industry provided an effective oasis.

29. This figure is calculated from census data in ADI, 123 M, 3, 6, 8, 10, 51, 53–55, 57, 60; and Bonnin et al., *Paroisses et communes de France*, vols. 38 and 69.

30. How does one identify textile communes? This question is more difficult to answer than it may first appear. The impact of the textile industry doubtless extended beyond the administrative limits of the commune so that any measure relying exclusively on the population figures of the communes with mills will undoubtedly fail to measure the impact of the industry on the surrounding communities. Second, there was some expansion but also considerable consolidation in the textile industry between 1846 and 1911. Many "textile communes" in 1866 were no longer so designated a generation later. I therefore chose for this analysis the thirty-two communes that were centers of the textile industry in 1866 and remained so through subsequent decades. I then used the demographic contour map discussed below to describe the impact of industry on the surrounding areas. For a list of textile centers see ADI, 138 M, 16; 162 M, 3–5.

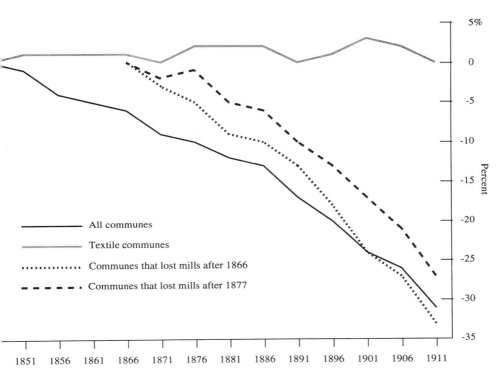

Figure 2   Cumulative median population change in textile communes, 1846–1911. (Archives Départementales de l'Isère, 123 M, 3, 6, 8, 10, 51, 53–55, 57, 60; and Bernard Bonnin, et al., *Paroisses et communes de France*, vols. 38 and 69 [Paris: Centre National de Recherche Scientifique, 1983].)

The effects of deindustrialization could be rapid and brutal. Communes that lost textile mills lost almost as many people as communes that had never felt the stimulus of the textile industry. Rural industry was indeed an effective barrier to depopulation as long as it lasted. Its salutary demographic effects often extended well beyond the mill towns themselves.

The Contours of Rural Industry: An Exercise in Historical Demography

The wages of many workers who stayed from Monday through Saturday in factory dormitories went directly home, to help support the household. This fact alone ensures that the impact of the industry was felt well beyond the limits of the textile commune.

Moreover, the impact of any business is rarely limited to its own work force. New industry in the Isère had a broad impact on services and transport, for example. Growth in one sector prompted growth in other areas, so that the relationship between employment and population, in growth as in decline, rapidly became mutually reinforcing. New industry meant not only employees but also a new café and probably a new bakery and other new businesses. It meant greater demand for transport facilities and for hands to operate and maintain them, and for workers to expedite the shipment of raw materials and finished products. It could bring new clients to merchants and impose new burdens on schools. Every worker employed by the textile mills increased the burden on the infrastructure, on local goods and services. A textile mill meant a more diverse and prosperous local economy. Since the textile industry was scattered throughout the rural Isère, the effects were widely distributed, creating broad belts of economic growth and prosperity. Around these belts were areas without industry—communities often marked by crisis and population decline.

One way to measure this broad impact is to examine population in a new way. Prosperity is a draw. It has its own specific gravity. The movements of households that sought work in the mills produced secondary movements of population to fill the need for expanded services, and so on.

Map 2 differs from standard contour maps in that it shows not changes in elevation but changes in the region's demographic contours. Within the contour lines are areas of population growth; outside them are areas of decline. From this demographic contour map one may make inferences about the relationship between population and economy.[31]

The Franco-Prussian War deepened the cultural and political pessimism so well expressed by Ardouin-Dumazet. Between the conclusions of the war and the onset of the Long Depression, the silk industry of the Isère enjoyed a period of unprecedented prosperity.

31. E. A. Wrigley, *Population in History* (New York, 1969), p. 99, proposes the use of contour-mapping techniques to explore economic regions.

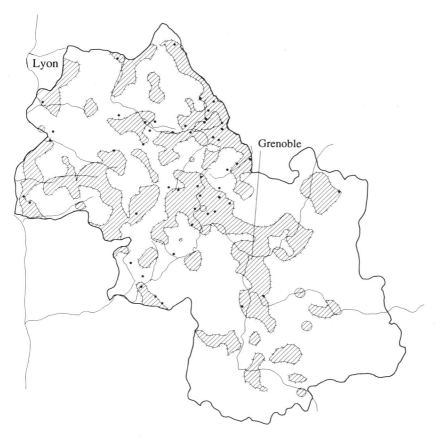

Map 2   Demographic contours of the Isère, 1872–1876

Map 2 shows the population of the Isère during a period of vigorous growth—unprecedented growth for the silk industry—in the
early 1870s. The contours reveal several broad zones of population growth and, by inference, broad-based prosperity: a Vizille-
Grenoble-Voiron axis, a broad littoral along the Rhône, and many
areas beside the waterways in the interior of the department. Many
of these areas have no major economic activity outside of farming
and the textile industry. Between the small agriculture for which
these regions are known and the prosperity of the silk industry,
these regions held their populations and, in fact, drew on the populations of less fortunate surrounding regions. In these areas the
rural exodus was arrested, even reversed.

Conversely, the Alpine regions in the southeastern portion of the department show broad population loss. Here the rural exodus continued without interruption. In fact, these villages were tributaries to the villages of industrial growth. Limited regional migration sometimes substituted for definitive rural exodus. The impact of the textile industry and of its related economic activity was quite widespread. Employing the language of Le Roy Ladurie in connection with Languedoc, we might call this the first phase of an economic and demographic "respiration."[32]

If prosperity looks like nothing so much as a broadly distributed growth, how might one visualize the demographic impact of economic recession? After 1870 the textile industry experienced two long economic cycles, two periods of prosperity followed by recession. The first cycle began with the short boom after the Franco-Prussian War; wages rose sharply as demand for labor increased. The effect on local populations is seen in Map 2. After the expansion of the early 1870s came the broader downturn marking the beginning of the Long Depression, which extended through the 1880s. A measure of prosperity returned in the mid- to late 1890s, the Bell Epoque. For the silk industry, however, this recovery soon faltered under the weight of foreign competition, especially from German and Swiss producers and the closing of markets, principally the lucrative American market, behind tariff walls. By the first decade of the twentieth century, the silk industry in France was suffering; much of the rural Isère was suffering with it.

The effect is seen in Map 3. Once again, population shifts reveal the contours of economic distress. Gone are the broad regions of growth identified in the boom of the 1870s. The Vizille-Grenoble-Voiron industrial axis has been broken, as has the line along the Rhône littoral and the zones of prosperity around the textile communes beside the interior waterways. This was the second part of the demographic "respiration." The difficulties of the textile industry prompted individuals and entire households to vote with their feet. The population that had been drawn to the rural textile centers was now being driven away by the silk industry's obvious distress. Some people seem to have gone back to farms; during the bleak years for the silk industry there are signs of population

32. E. Le Roy Ladurie, *The Peasants of Languedoc* (Paris, 1966).

Map 3   Demographic contours of the Isère, 1901–1911

growth in regions adjacent to the mills. But many simply left. For them the rural exodus, that "form of strike, individual and unremitting," had resumed. The rural exodus had not been evaded, only postponed.

Prosperity and Crisis

These are the outlines of demographic history of the textile industry. Surely not all of the population movement of these years can be attributed to the phases of prosperity and decline in the textile industry; the area in which the silk industry was concentrated adjoined some of the more prosperous agricultural areas. But the silk industry was the Isère's major industrial employer and its mills exercised a powerful attraction on the vast "floating population" set free by the persistent difficulties of small agriculture. The secondary effects of rural industry also stimulated growth in related and service businesses and magnified the impact of rural textiles. Between 1870 and 1911, the economy of the Isère was mercurial; it did not experience a relentless decline.

Thus the rural exodus was far from a linear process, a purge of the rural population, or a stripping of peasant society of its marginal elements. An organic metaphor for the decay of peasant society would be apt; peasant society even late in the nineteenth century was a complex organism, living symbiotically with rural industry. The rural exodus was symptomatic of the decay of peasant society from its apogee just before mid-century. It proceeded in a cyclical fashion as peasants were drawn into rural industry, only to be expelled later; rural depopulation proceeded through a series of respiration-like movements, spread out over generations. Rural industry inserted a pause in this decline but failed to arrest it. As peasant society was coming to an end, rural industry momentarily gave it new life or, more darkly, prolonged its mortal contractions.

Peasants almost certainly did not share Ardouin-Dumazet's dark cultural pessimism, springing as it did from a conservative Catholic and bourgeois milieu. In their culture the worst possible outcome was the *dépaysement* of the *paysan*. Most members of rural society seem to have much preferred to make an uncertain living from resources cobbled together, a marginal existence drawn from industry and agriculture, than to face the great uncertainty that the definitive exodus represented. Part of the value of rural industry for the peasantry, a value very much a part of the wages they earned, was derived from the promise of a future short of a definitive departure from the land, the abandonment of familiar surroundings and a familiar way of life. Consciously or not, rural industry thrived and quite literally capitalized on these fears and uncertainties when it conformed to the highly distributed nature of the French population in the nineteenth century. In this fashion, small firm size represented a rational, indeed shrewd, adaptation to the opportunities offered by the business environment in France, insofar as the distribution of labor shaped that environment.[33] Mill managers profited from the peasants' preference for wage work, however poorly paid, as an alternative to a definitive departure from the countryside. This strategy paid dividends in the cities, where artisans felt cowed into accepting wage scales determined in part by those that prevailed in the nearby countryside.[34]

The textile industry emerged as a major economic, social, and cultural force after mid-century. It reinforced the rural household just at the moment when resources had been stretched to the limit and hard times were forcing peasants to leave the countryside for the city. The textile industry brought the promise of prosperity to a rural economy stretched to its limits. As a luxury commodity, however, silk was subject to abrupt changes in consumer tastes. Contractions and consolidations were inevitable in an industry vulnerable to a notably fickle and mercurial market. The textile industry in the nineteenth century could not withstand a collapse of consumer confidence, nor could it be sustained during periods of political or economic crisis. And like other businesses, it could not always withstand the challenge of competition.

By the twentieth century, competition forced the French silk merchants to make cutbacks, which often led to strikes, consolidations, short hours, short weeks, layoffs, and plant closings. Income closely tied to the silk industry, then, was not reliable, and whenever the industry was forced abruptly to retrench and consolidate, the rural exodus resumed. The crisis of the silk industry and its workers struck at the very heart of the many rural households that had been lured into the rural binary economy and were now rudely being forced back onto their residual agricultural resources. Businesses reliant on workers as clients suffered, too. Communities that lost rural industry experienced decline every bit as devastating as they would have experienced had rural industry never appeared at all. For these communities, the textile industry merely inserted a pause

33. Nye, "Firm Size and Economic Backwardness," p. 668.
34. On the urban artisans' reaction to competition from rural weavers see Laurent Bonnevay, *Les Ouvrières lyonnaises à domicile* (Paris, 1896), and Robert Bezucha, *The Lyon Uprising of 1834* (Cambridge, Mass., 1974).

in what appears in retrospect to have been an inevitable decline. Moreover, the decline was perhaps all the more brutal for having been postponed. Hard times brought new waves of emigration. The rural exodus resumed with a vengeance.

6

A Working Class
Formed in the
State of Nature?

In a global economic sense industry and agriculture
lived symbiotically; on a human scale they sometimes meshed poorly. The patterns of industrial labor and agricultural labor did not
neatly coincide. Families separated each day, men going to the fields
and women to the factories. When women lived at the mill—most
of these women were young and unmarried—the family was re-
united only weekly, between Saturday evening and Sunday evening.
Women who lived close to the mill returned home daily, but given
the length of the workday in the mills, they returned very late in the
day. Since the peak season in the mills coincided with days of short
daylight, workers often returned well after dark. Thus though the
rhythms of the land and the loom were complementary, they took
peasants and workers, women and men, in different directions.

A Glimpse Inside the
Worker/Peasant Household

These work rhythms and the composition of rural
households reveal much about the complex strategies that guided

This chapter draws on material in my "Peasants, Population, and Industry in
France," *Journal of Interdisciplinary History* 22 (Autumn 1991): 177–200, and in
my "Visualizing Population in History: The Example of Population and Rural
Industry in Southeastern France," *Historical Methods* 24 (Summer 1991): 101–
109.

these households. Archival sources sometimes give up their secrets reluctantly. What follows is an attempt to pry information about the peasant/worker household from census lists. Three cantons of the Isère are represented in the sample: Pont-de-Beauvoisin, St-Geoire-en-Valdaine, and Virieu. I selected them because they are contiguous and because the importance of the silk industry varied considerably among them. The silk industry was very important in St-Geoire and was moderately important in Pont-de-Beauvoisin; it had little presence in Virieu, a canton of rather prosperous farms.[1] I defined as a "textile household" any household in which a silk-worker resided. My systematic sample contained more than 7,000 persons belonging to more than 2,400 households, including 615 textile households.[2]

A distinct picture of the textile household emerged from this exercise. First of all, textile households tended to be larger than the sample mean. Whereas the normal household contained 3.72 persons, textile households had 4.22 persons. This larger household size is all the more interesting in that the textile household was far less likely than the sample household to contain unrelated individuals—to employ a servant or apprentice, for example: 14 percent of all sample households but only 3 percent of textile households had servants. In fact, unrelated individuals, whether servants or lodgers, were present in every fifth household in the sample population but in only every tenth textile household.

This finding eliminates the possibility that the larger size of textile households was due to lodgers or servants. Larger textile households were a consequence of larger families and larger coresident kin groups. Households headed by a widowed or unmarried person represented about one in four textile households, versus more than one in three for the population as a whole. Textile households

---

1. The sample included every fifth household. The coded variables included age, occupation, relation, and sex. Occupational categories including farmer, worker, artisan, shopkeeper, civil servant, personal services, professional services, business professional, and rentier. Relational categories included head of household, spouse, offspring, parent, other kin, servant, lodger. For examples of categories and coding see Tamara K. Hareven, *Family Time and Industrial Time* (Cambridge, 1978), and Margo Anderson Conk, *The United States Census and Labor Force Change* (Ann Arbor, Mich., 1980).

2. Source censuses are ADI, 123 M, 61, Pont-de-Beauvoisin; 62, St-Geoire; 64, Virieu.

consisted of several persons who were related to one another, frequently headed by a married couple.

If the larger size of textile households can be explained by a greater number of relatives per household, which relatives were they? Descendants and collateral kin were more common in textile households than in others. Elderly parents were less common (4 percent of textile households vs. 7 percent in the sample) and kin and offspring were more so. This finding helps to explain why the average age in the textile household was lower. The mean age was a year less in textile households than in the sample, even though the heads of textile households were older (51 years vs. 50). This difference is undoubtedly a function of the number of offspring who remained in the household (2 offspring per textile household vs. 1.5 in the sample), even though they enjoyed the relative independence that came with employment and income. Fully 54 percent of offspring residing in textile households were employed (vs. 35 percent in the sample) and of course the presence of working young adults in the textile household tends to lower the mean age. The fact that younger working family members tended to stay with their parents' household rather than start their own suggests that wage income did not always lead to early marriage.

In fact, the employment rate for all adults (individuals aged 20 and over) was higher in textile households (62 percent vs. 51 percent). There were more working adults (2.1) and more working family members of all ages (2.5) in textile households than in the sample households (1.6 and 1.7, respectively). In a quite literal way, textile households were working households, households in which most members worked.

Half of the women in the sample between the ages of 14 and 53 worked. This figure compares with 90 percent employment for men in the same age groups. Although women of all ages and life situations worked, peak employment came in the early twenties (19 to 23 years; see Figures 3 and 4), when two women in three worked; men's employment rate for the same years was 88 percent. Men's peak employment years came later, between the ages of 34 and 38, when employment ran at virtually 100 percent (see Figure 4).

Although the number of women in the work force declined steadily with age, work remained an important feature of many women's lives. Many continued to work after marriage and even after they

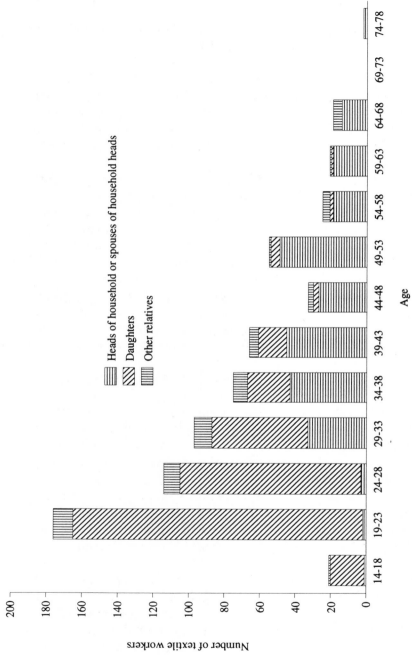

Figure 3 Number of female textile workers in St-Geoire, Pont-de-Beauvoisin, and Virieu, 1896. (Archives Départementales de l'Isère, 123 M, 61, 62, 64).

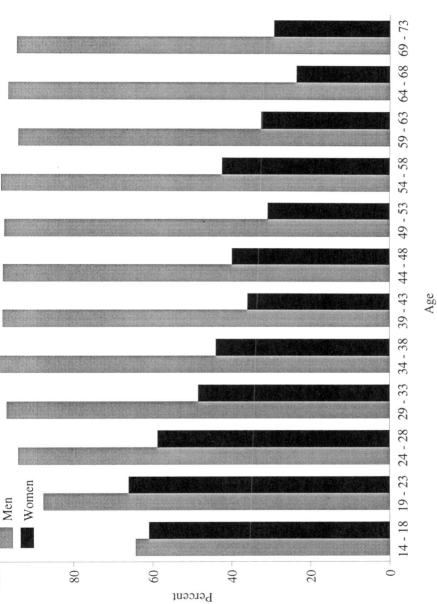

Figure 4 Rates of participation in labor force by men and women, 1896, by age group. (Archives Départementales de l'Isère, 123 M, 61, 62, 64.)

bore children. Forty-five percent of women over the age of 14 in the entire sample worked, and the number of women in the labor force was generally higher than one in three in the later age groups. Many women, it seems, continued to work until their children were old enough to take their places as wage earners. The decisive break in the employment history of many women—but not all—came with the maturity of their offspring.

It should come as no surprise, then, that the survey produced evidence of a considerable number of working mothers, giving substance to our image of women's work in the nineteenth century as far from exclusively premarital or prefamilial, at least for the popular classes of the countryside. Overall 16 percent of households sampled contained a working mother. In textile households the figure was much higher, nearly double: 29 percent of textile households included a working mother.

Many of these women were single parents. Nine percent of textile households were headed by a woman who combined the roles of textile worker, mother, and head of household. The figure does not include kin (sisters, aunts, nieces, or sisters-in-law) who were working mothers, nor does it include daughters who bore *enfants naturels,* whose numbers were not insignificant. What does this finding say about the fragmentation of peasant-worker households? Is it possible that frequent and long separations of couples led to permanent separation? The census lists do not carry that kind of information but the record is suggestive.

The age distribution of textile workers reveals that the largest categories of women workers consisted of the young and single. Unmarried women made up the majority of textile workers in age groups extending through the age of 33. Beyond that age, however, married women dominate the numbers. The typical female silk-worker was married by her late thirties.

Women's employment in the silk industry of the Isère tends to confirm what Louise Tilly and Joan Scott called the "family life-cycle stage model," though with significant differences.[3] More than half of the young women employed in the textile mills in their teens and early twenties continued to work in the mills when they reached marriage age. Perhaps a third of them continued to work in

3. Louise Tilly and Joan Scott, *Women, Work, and Family* (New York, 1978).

the mills through their thirties and forties. For these workers, the relevant family cycle seems to have been the arrival of *their* children at working age. It is likely, in fact, that these figures show us two distinct populations, the young single women who worked in the large mills and boarded at the factory dormitory and the older, often married women who worked in the smaller mills closer to home.

Anecdotal evidence from Vizille confirms these observations about the persistence of married women at work and about their mobility. At the conclusion of a bitter strike undertaken by 210 women, only 100 remained. The majority had simply left Vizille to find work elsewhere. Who had departed? Which women had remained? The triage was simple. Those women who remained were place-bound mothers who could not, like the other women, go to find work in other locations.[4]

The high rate of employment (more than one member in two) in textile households shows how important the earnings of each household member could be. Young people worked in order to contribute to the household into which they had been born. After they married and established their own independent households, they continued to work. Gender-based wage differentials perpetuated, through the force of a skewed economic rationality, the presumption that parental responsibilities fell naturally to women, for if one parent were to quit work to look after children, obviously it should be the lesser paid. But many mothers of young children worked too, presumably because in working and marginal peasant households they had no alternative. Finally, most but by no means all left the mills when their children were old enough to replace them.

In many textile households, then, marriage and children did not signal an end to the years of work. Rather, they gave new meaning and importance to the work of all able household members. Given the rationale of the peasant household, it seems more likely that the *maturity* of children, rather than their arrival, may have been a signal to exit the active labor force. Once they reached the age of 14, sometimes 13, the children went to work and contributed

4. "L'Action syndicale," *L'Ouvrière textile*, 1 June 1905, p. 4 ("ce sont les mères de famille rivées au pays").

Table 2.   Occupations of heads of textile households and of other sample households, 1896

Occupation	Textile households		Other households	
	Number	Percent	Number	Percent
Not currently employed	37	6%	148	8%
Farmer	280	46	929	50
Worker	213	35	298	16
Artisan	59	10	178	10
Shopkeeper	9	1	96	5
Government services	7	1	70	4
Personal services	6	1	37	2
Professional	0	0	20	1
Business professional	0	0	25	1
Rentier	0	0	45	2
All occupations	615	100%	1,846	99%

Source: Archives Départementales de l'Isère, 123 M, 61, 62, 64.

something to the household, just as their parents had contributed to their own family income when they were young. But even so, the record makes it abundantly clear that many women worked throughout their lifetimes.[5]

What was the social background of the textile worker? The question is difficult to answer unequivocally, except by the arbitrary use of the occupation of the head of household, usually male, as a guide. For the sample population, the most common social background, as measured by the occupation of the head of household, was in agriculture. "Farmers" headed half of all households in the sample (see Table 2), as might be expected in a rural department such as the Isère.[6] Workers, artisans, and shopkeepers were also fairly common categories for heads of households. A minority of household heads made their living in the liberal professions (1 percent), business (1 percent), or as rentiers (2 percent).

5. For a similar discussion of women workers in the adjacent department of the Ain, see Raymond A. Jonas, "Politics in Rural France: The Example of the Ain" (master's thesis, University of California, Davis, 1980), pp. 54–58. In the Ain the figures were somewhat higher; a full 50 percent of the women textile workers in the town of Serrières-de-Briord were married with families. That figure strongly suggests that proximity was a crucial factor. When the mill was local, women continued to work.

6. This category includes *cultivateurs, fermiers,* and *proprietaires-cultivateurs,* as well as *journaliers* and *domestiques-agricoles.* Vagaries in reporting make it difficult to treat these designations as reliable indications of discrete categories.

The 615 textile households present a slightly different picture. First of all, farmers are still the most important category among heads of textile households (46 percent vs. 50 percent for the general population). "Worker" was the second most common category, and of course some of these people worked in the textile industry. This finding suggests a different order of departure from the countryside than the one suggested by Charles Tilly.[7] Industrial workers could be among the most tenacious in their resistance to the rural exodus. Taken together, peasant and worker backgrounds accounted for four-fifths (81 percent) of textile households; the only other significant groups were the artisans (10 percent) and the unemployed (6 percent). Heads of textile households are peasants, workers, and artisans, or between jobs.

We can flesh out this argument by turning to some case studies of individual households in other parts of the Bas-Dauphiné. The evidence confirms that work in the silk industry was not casual. Jeanne Bouvier's father was a barrel and vat maker. Phylloxera ruined the winemaking business and drove her father out of business.[8] At the age of 11 Jeanne began what would be a lifetime of labor in textile mills. An examination of the 1896 *liste nominative* for the commune of St.-Jean-de-Moirans reveals a wide variety of household strategies. Information gleaned from the census rolls of 1896 reveals cases such as that of Pierre Bois, who at 47 was a *journalier,* an agricultural day laborer, and ranked as head of household. His wife, 44-year-old Marie Bois (née Chollet), worked in a silk mill with their daughter of 16, also named Marie. Their two other daughters, at 12 and 7, had not yet started to work.

Joseph Brosse (50) was also a farmer, though, unlike Pierre Bois, he owned the land he worked with his son Joseph (20). Annette (50), his wife, was a silkworker, as were their 18-year-old daughter, Marie, and their 14-year-old son, Louis. Their neighbor Antoine Perrin was a farmer too; his wife, Rosalie, looked after the farm and household (*ménagère*) and cared for their 12-year-old daughter, Alice, while their son, Marius (19), and daughter Josephine (16) worked in the textile factory. In yet another household, six women (five French, one Italian) aged from 29 to 60 all worked as textile

7. See Charles Tilly, "Did the Cake of Custom Break?" in *Consciousness and Class Experience in Nineteenth-Century Europe,* ed. John Merriman (New York, 1979), p. 37.
8. Jeanne Bouvier, *Mes Mémoires* (Poitiers, 1936), p. 23.

hands. Finally, we have Joseph and Françoise Hubert, a retired couple, who were supported by their daughter and son-in-law, both 29 and both silkworkers.[9]

The *listes nominatives* of two other communes, neither a textile town, permits an assessment of the range of the textile industry's recruitment. Do household strategies differ significantly in communes not directly affected by textile manufacture? The arbitrary choice of the villages of Sardieu and Sillans, both in the heart of the textile region of the Bas-Dauphiné but not "host communes," suggests that the textile industry drew upon a vast collection of communities.[10] The censuses reveal several households with members whose occupation was "silkworker," an indication that the silk industry did indeed have a long reach.

What conclusions can be drawn from this information? Though age (or life-cycle stage) clearly was a factor in women's employment in the rural Isère, work certainly was not restricted to young, unmarried women. Women of all ages worked, not just in occupations consonant with the role of "household manager" and not only in jobs involving "familiar" work. They worked as members of their natal family and continued to work when their own children were very young. They worked to support households that sometimes included aged parents, other kin, and in-laws.

There is no evidence to suggest that textile workers were motivated by anything more or less than the needs of the rural household. The accumulation of a dowry, for example, rarely appears as a factor. That is the point of one factory owner's comment that "here the working woman [*tisseuse*] is a great help to her family. A few years ago, misery reigned in many of these households; now they are happy."[11] The textile industry broadened the economic basis of the rural household. In effect, the textile industry introduced a binary economy, half industrial, half agricultural, into the countryside. The peasant-worker was part of an equation that meant solvency for marginal peasant households. Work in the textile industry made the difference between income adequate to maintain a household and the rural exodus.

9. ADI, 123 M, 53, St-Jean-de-Moirans.
10. Ibid., 54. They had the additional advantage of being placed consecutively in the *carton*.
11. AN, C 3021, Moirans.

Women, Work, and the Peasant-Worker
Family: Evidence of Another Kind

Parents had special concerns as workers; employers had to consider the needs of parents, typically mothers, if they were to retain them. Many did. At Moirans, for example, a mill owner instituted flexible hours to accommodate working mothers. "Every effort is made to accommodate working mothers [*femmes de ménage*]," he wrote. "They leave the mill before [the others] and return after the appointed times."[12] This was not altruism at work but shrewd business sense. The apprenticeship of a textile worker might last six months. Employers tried to accommodate the special needs of married women and working mothers in order to retain these trained and skilled workers.[13]

Savvy employers offered some form of child care for working parents. At Renage the factory operator reported that "in some factories crèches and nursery schools have been instituted to take and protect young children while their parents work. When work is over, the children are returned to their parents." Sometimes mothers of very small children could not be accommodated. "Grand Lemps has a crèche," wrote the owner of another facility, "but children under the age of three are not admitted." Similar accommodations existed at Moirans, where the "nursery schools accept children from a very young age." Thanks to inquiries conducted under the Radicals into the role and influence of the religious in the textile factories, we know that in at least "two factories in the canton of Rives, there [were] nuns attached to the establishment, . . . occupied solely with the supervision of the workers' children."[14]

The three women workers in ten who were also mothers may well have been the most important workers the mill owners had. The number of factories that offered child-care facilities and flexible hours suggests that mill owners valued the labor of seasoned, reliable, disciplined workers.

12. Ibid.
13. It was the practice of C. J. Bonnet, for example, to require one-year apprenticeships and to compensate accordingly. See Louis Reybaud, *Etudes sur le régime des manufactures* (Paris, 1859), pp. 198–203.
14. For Renage, Grand Lemps, and Moirans see AN, C 3021. The information on the factories in the canton of Rives is in AN, BB 18, 1902, 9 July 1892.

It also suggests how little real choice peasant women had about their work. If we assume that they would prefer to return to farming, the fact that they continued at the mills tells us that they had little choice. According to Emile Guerry, Catholic priest, organizer for the Catholic *syndicats libres,* and advocate of the provision of care for the children of employed parents, women certainly did not prefer to continue working in the textile industry after marriage— something intuition might suggest, given work conditions there— but few of them had any choice in the matter. "It is correct," he argued,

> that the rural worker . . . hopes to leave the factory by marrying. But in most cases she is put into the factory when she leaves school and she knows quite well that, the economic conditions of life being what they are, she will have to stay in the factory, even married, even as the mother of a family.[15]

In a sense, rural industry reinforced rather than undermined the interdependence of husband and wife.[16] But it often irrevocably changed the locus of women's work. Moreover, when a peasant woman entered the factory and her household began to depend on her wages, she found it very difficult to withdraw from the industrial labor force.

Even so, her lower wages reinforced the idea that her contribution was secondary rather than primary, supplemental rather than central. A woman's earnings were rarely so great as to threaten the basis of patriarchal authority. By this mechanism, the relationship of dependence established between rural industry and the peasant household economy respected traditional relations of authority between wife and husband. It should also be pointed out, however, that the combination of wage labor and farming made a crucial difference in the options available to women. Many working women in the cities were driven to prostitution because the gendered

15. In his efforts to attract workers, Guerry fashioned his Catholic syndical platform around his perception of workers' needs. His campaign to draw workers away from the socialist unions earned him the financial backing of some mill owners. The *syndicats libres* ultimately failed. See Emile Guerry, *Les Syndicats libres féminins de l'Isère* (Grenoble, 1921), p. iii.

16. See Antony Copley, *Sexual Moralities in France, 1780–1980* (London, 1989).

differentiation of wages gave them less than a living wage.[17] It is likely that some silkworkers in the textile villages of the Isère also supplemented their wages in this way; not all textile workers shared the combined resources of a household.

The shift toward greater dependence on industrial income was almost imperceptibly slow. For most peasant households these sacrifices and compromises were preferable to leaving the countryside altogether. Observers who were inclined toward a favorable assessment of the impact of the textile industry on rural society depicted the relationship between agriculture and industry as symbiotic rather than parasitic. Joseph Jouanny, like Ardouin-Dumazet, described it in strictly positive terms:

> [as soon as] a factory is erected nearby—and they are lacking nowhere— . . . the mother and the daughter get themselves hired: the father stays on the farm and works by himself; if he needs help, he hires a helper. Meals are summary: soup and vegetables; the man must get his meals for himself, but what satisfaction to receive 500 to 600 francs free and clear every other week.
> Thus two forms of activity live in complete harmony.[18]

Other observers painted a much bleaker picture. For them, rural industry did not avoid the moral and social problems associated with urban industry. Those problems survived the move from the city to the country intact. In Voiron, for example, the center of rural textiles in the Bas-Dauphiné, the new working conditions were thought to have an unhealthy moral effect on workers. Using language that recalls the descriptions of the urban *classes laborieuses, classes dangereuses,* the police of Voiron complained that "morals leave a great deal to be desired" and that "cases of drunkenness are quite frequent."[19] Big-city problems in a small-town world.

But not only the spirit suffered and not only morals degenerated. The physical effects of textile labor in the nineteenth century generally are well documented and the textile industry was not an excep-

17. See Claire Auzias and Annik Houel, *La Grève des ovalistes* (Paris, 1982), pp. 143–149.
18. Joseph Jouanny, *Le Tissage de soie en Bas-Dauphiné* (Grenoble, 1931), p. 20.
19. ADI, 55 M, 3, Commissariat de Police de Voiron, March 1881.

tional case. In the Isère one of the consequences of life as a textile worker was the likelihood of early death. Yvonne Le Jeune studied these questions in depth and noted the alarming mortality rates of young people and adults in Voiron: ". . . how can we explain this if not by reference to the very poor hygienic conditions and excessive hours of work. Thus, in 1901, during the period when the factory dominated the life of Voiron, mortality was highest among workers between the ages of 30 and 39."[20] Textile work in the countryside, like textile work in the city, was hard on the body and was undoubtedly responsible for the premature deaths of many rural workers. Plainly put, the urban or rural context of industry was unlikely to have any measurable influence on the moral or medical status of workers.

What about the consequences of industrialization on the reproductive habits of the peasantry? The legendary Malthusianism of the French peasantry had its cause and justification in the realization that the productivity of the peasantry was likely to exceed the productivity of the land. The attempt to raise a family larger than the land could support was folly, as was any attempt to marry and begin a family without securing adequate resources in land. Thus, much to the chagrin of conservative observers who ardently desired more robust reproductive habits among the peasantry, scarce resources in land served as an effective check on two important determinants of population growth: new household constitution and reproduction. But the availability of industrial wages removed this constraint on household constitution and family size, at least in theory. Households that could be described only as marginal in comparison with the traditional measures of independence and self-sufficiency in rural society suddenly became viable with the addition of income from industrial employment. Did the availability of industrial resources alter the fertility patterns and rate of household constitution among peasants in the Isère?

Some observers certainly thought so, and commented approv-

---

20. Yvonne Le Jeune, "Structure professionnelle d'une petite ville industrielle du Bas-Dauphiné: Voiron," *RGA* 42 (1954): 720. Poor health was also often a consequence of employment in the Isère's other major rural industry, glovemaking. In 1872 a government inquiry revealed that "la santé et le taille des jeunes filles sont souvent éprouvés par la position sur leurs machines à coudre." See ADI, 162 M, 3, Enquête sur les conditions du travail en France, Theys, 1872.

ingly on the trend. Jouanny praised what he regarded as the positive demographic consequences of rural industry on the Bas-Dauphiné. Jouanny, who promoted the idea that rural industry could spare France the evils of urbanization, was enthusiastic about the population patterns revealed by communes that benefited from rural industry. He cites the commune of Abrets, "where everyone weaves silk—[there is] one loom for every three inhabitants—we see [that] the number of inhabitants has increased to 1,831 in 1926 as opposed to 1,203 in 1831."[21] Jouanny did not investigate the causes of this 50 percent increase in population, but he clearly believed that it was due to the beneficial effects of rural industry on the lusty sexual appetites of peasants; the silk industry was undoing the Malthusianism of the French and bringing back the large peasant families of yore.

There is some evidence to support this claim. In the cantons of Virieu, St-Geoire, and Pont-de-Beauvoisin, the number of children in textile households averaged just 2.04[22]—hardly a *famille nombreuse,* but it must be admitted that the sample as a whole showed 1.6 offspring per household. Evidence that textile households maximized income through larger families? Not likely; these figures are probably related to other factors: the fact that children in textile households tended to stay in the parents' household longer (the average age of offspring was higher in textile households than in the sample) and the fact that, given the relative youth of the textile working population, these were households in which women were more likely to be of childbearing age—hence the higher aggregate figure for the textile household group. Finally, we should recognize that the number of offspring per household is not commensurate with any scientific measurement of natality. Anecdotal evidence suggests that textile households were not notably prolific. Writing in response to a question about the number of children in workers' families in his commune, an official at Moirans noted that in general couples had two children. Large families were rare. Most important, the respondent could see no evidence of any change in these habits: "This state of things is not likely to change."[23]

21. Jouanny, *Tissage de soie,* p. 122.
22. ADI, 123 M, 61, Pont-de-Beauvoisin; 62, St-Geoire; 64, Virieu.
23. AN, C 3021, Moirans.

Population growth around textile centers is more likely to have come from migration than from natural increase. In fact, the migration patterns fostered by the textile industry, since they tended to be gender-specific, could have a deleterious effect on fertility. Voiron, the center of the Isère's textile industry, was incapable of reproducing itself. Working conditions were so poor in the textile industry there that the mortality rate of female workers in their later reproductive years was high, a sure impediment to population maintenance. Yet the low rate of reproduction in Voiron was not entirely attributable to health and work conditions. The employment opportunities for women so far outstripped those for men that the male/female ratio at Voiron was badly out of balance. Such circumstances are simply not conducive to a high birth rate. Factory owners promoted the establishment of "male" industries in order to restore gender balance to the population. The combination of gender imbalance and poor health conditions for women in their reproductive years created a disequilibrium in natality/mortality ratios that persisted for a century. As a consequence, only a constant migration stream could maintain the town's population.[24] In Voiron, at least, there is no evidence that the silk industry promoted reproduction of the population. On the contrary, it hindered it. In this sense, the relationship between the textile industry and the peasantry was not symbiotic but parasitic.

The same probably applied to smaller towns and villages, though with less force. In the first years of the Third Republic, a factory owner at Renage, a commune of 2,290 in 1891, described fertility patterns similar to those discovered in Voiron. No natural increase here; population growth was entirely due to the afflux produced by the rural exodus: ". . . there is growth of the population, not by the growth of families—deaths and births balance each other—but by the arrival at the industrial centers of large families from the surrounding communes who have nothing but their labor to nourish them."[25] The silk industry got its workers not from the higher fertility rates of its employees but from temporary and permanent migrations from the failing and failed peasant households of the countryside.

24. Le Jeune, "Structure professionnelle," p. 732. On related issues in another context see Gay L. Gullickson, *Spinners and Weavers of Aufray* (New York, 1986).
25. AN, C 3021, Montessuy et Chomer. Maps 3 and 4 of course show similar patterns.

The textile industry served as a magnet to the marginal peasant households. It relied on a shift of rural population resources from the hinterland to the industrial commune—rural textiles thwarted the rural exodus by providing an intermediate step. When the Bouvier farm was hit by the phylloxera crisis, Jeanne went to work in the mill. She was "proud to bring the product of my labor to my mother."[26] Rather than quit the farm for the city, marginal peasant households could remain in the countryside either by establishing a new residence in the industrial commune or by making a daily or weekly commute.

With these two points we are touching on perhaps the most important demographic consequences of the binary economy. When a primarily agricultural economy acquires a substantial industrial base, it may create more attractive conditions for the establishment of households, and at the very least it creates conditions conducive to the preservation of the more marginal households among the existing ones. That is why many nineteenth- and twentieth-century observers, in promoting a cultural and political agenda, praised the "ruralization" of industry: they believed it would halt the stagnation of the rural economy and reverse the decline of the (conservative, devout) peasantry. They were right on the first point: industry gave the rural economy a boost. We can only imagine what the *exode rural* might have been like had it not been for the presence of rural industries. But on the second point they were probably wrong. If we conceive of the peasantry as a specific form of economic organization characterized by little division of labor, by scarce land-based resources, and by relative independence from market relations with the outside, we can see that the arrival of rural industry could only further erode the "peasant-ness" of the local economy.[27]

---

26. Bouvier, *Mes Mémoires*, p. 25.

27. On theories of the peasantry as a form of economic organization see Henri Mendras, *Sociétés paysannes* (Paris, 1976), pp. 39–55, and the following works from Teodor Shanin, ed., *Peasants and Peasant Societies* (Aylesbury, 1976): Basile Kerblay, "Chayanov and the Theory of Peasantry as a Specific Type of Economy," pp. 150–161; Boguslaw Galeski, "Sociological Problems of the Occupation of Farmers," pp. 180–201; Daniel Thorner, "Peasant Economy as a Category in Economic History," pp. 202–218; and Evgenii Preobrazhensky, "Peasantry and the Political Economy of the Early Stages of Industrialization," pp. 219–227. Of course, all paths of inquiry on this subject lead back to A. V. Chayanov, *The Theory of Peasant Society* (Homewood, Il., 1966; first published 1920).

The decision to maintain a household on resources derived from both industry and agriculture is usually irrevocable. Once this line is crossed, there is little chance of going back, and the peasant household becomes enmeshed in a variety of contacts with the outside world.[28] The addition of income from rural industry had the effect of preserving the rural household, no longer peasant strictly speaking, thus sparing it the rural exodus at the price of facilitating the erosion of its primary dependence on the land. In fact, industry was a kind of Trojan horse: once incorporated within peasant society, it corrupted from within.

Its effects proved durable, too, because it touched the young. The new silk industry attracted young peasants, quite naturally, for it was the young who made up the insecure and the underemployed. For these young peasants, and through them, the industrial experience introduced important cultural changes in rural society: the culture of workplace and wages. Factory labor, however unpleasant in some respects, offered the undeniable appeal of frequent and varied human contacts at the workplace. For peasants accustomed to life in relative isolation, this bond of labor in common, which could readily be converted into a form of solidarity, exercised a powerful attraction. Wages seduce. They teach the power of money and whet the appetite for consumer goods. The bond of friendship and solidarity formed in labor and the attraction of money left workers with a wider sense of the world and its possibilities. As young people changed in such a fashion, many undoubtedly found that they no longer fitted comfortably within the narrow confines of village society. In time many shared in the creation of households that remained wedded, culturally as well as in direct and tangible ways, to the larger world.

This observation also suggests a line of inquiry into the links between rural industry and the emergence of a rural Socialist electorate. Generational differences in experience may well have prepared the change in political orientation. If so, the Socialist voters of the Isère were younger voters whose social and political outlook owed as much to textile labor as to agriculture. Textile work was not exclusively adolescent experience, but it was an occupation in

28. On this feature of the binary economy see Harvey Franklin, "The Worker Peasant in Europe," in Shanin, *Peasants and Peasant Societies*, p. 101. Mendras makes a similar point in *Sociétés paysannes*, p. 11.

which young people dominated, perhaps by as much as two to one. Textile work may have saved these young peasants from the disaster of the rural exodus, but the trade-off was rural proletarianization and incorporation into an emerging industrial culture based on workplace solidarity, wages, and commodity consumption: they would survive the crisis of the peasantry and remain in the country-side not because of their meager resources in land but by virtue of membership, theirs or their spouses', in an emerging rural indus-trial working class.

Village and Mill: An Urban Experience and a Gendered Sociability

Not all of the changes brought by rural industry worked with such subtlety. While industrial wage labor served gently to wean the peasant household from a stricter dependence on agricul-ture, the transition at the workplace was more abrupt. The features of daily working life were clearly different from those of the peasant once one entered the factory gates. There workers found a new working world created for them, a world unlike anything they had experienced before. Managers, rather than the workers themselves, determined the pace of work. Management also specified and stan-dardized work procedures; the looms themselves dictated the requi-site movements of the body for hours on end. The possibilities for individual initiative were narrowly circumscribed by the division of labor and a hierarchy of rank. Rural workers enjoyed a greater measure of independence by virtue of their land; it was much easier for a peasant day laborer to walk away from an unpleasant fore-man, especially around harvesttime, than for a factory worker to do so. But it was working for oneself at one's own pace that consti-tuted the allure of peasant life; and it was this feature of peasant life that textile labor in the factories most directly assaulted.

The context of work changed too, and not only for the workers. Even in the countryside, work became urbanized—or at least vil-lage life took on some of the features of urban life. For even though rural industry inhibited urbanization as a grand process, rural in-dustry fostered the transformation of towns, villages, and even hamlets into micro-urbs. The median textile commune had a regular population of about 1,500, well below the 2,000 recognized as the boundary between urban and rural communes.[29] The population captured by the official census, however, greatly underrepresented the workday population. The effective population of the industrial villages was inflated by dozens, sometimes hundreds, with the arrival of the mill hands. The 600 workers in Coublevie's mill transformed the village of at most 1,500 souls when they arrived for work. During its daylight hours, at least, Coublevie was "urban." Workers produced a similar effect on Charavine, whose population of 960 grew by nearly one-third when over 300 workers arrived to begin their day. In such villages and hamlets, population increased and decreased with tidal regularity—a gravity and rhythm determined by the mill, its size, and its schedule.

Thus even if textile villages typically fell short of the "urban" classification, they duplicated city life in some important respects, including social diversity. Unlike the many villages that became increasingly and more uniformly peasant after the onset of the rural exodus at mid-century, textile villages remained socially diverse. In textile villages, as many as one household in two was a textile household; here, then, was a rural proletariat in intimate contact with peasant society.[30]

Yet another distinctive feature of the textile town was that of gender, for it was an overwhelmingly feminine proletariat that set the tone for village life. True, men's labor force participation rates were higher than women's, but the most important occupational category for men was agriculture. In crude terms, men's work took them into the fields, while women's work brought them together at the mill. This gendering effect was most pronounced in mill towns and villages, which of course drew heavily each day on the population of women living in the surrounding countryside. Textile towns and villages were the mirror images of masculinized garrison towns and port cities. Women became accustomed to dominating public spaces with their numbers and their voices, a fact with significant consequences during strikes.

29. The median case in 1891 was Coublevie, with 1,540 persons: ADI, 123 M, 6, and AN, F 7, 12785.

30. ADI, 123 M, 61, 62, 64. As Table 2 indicates, of the 2,400 households in the cantons of Pont-de-Beauvoisin, St-Geoire-en-Valdaine, and Virieu, 615 were textile households, or one in four. The ratios were as high as one textile household for every two households in villages and towns containing mills.

Many village residents not directly linked to the textile industry owed their livelihood to it. Shopkeepers depended on the patronage of textile workers and their families and understood well enough that their fate was tied to that of the industry and the women who worked in it. The mills attracted new social elements to the village by acting as magnets for the unemployed and underemployed labor force of the surrounding countryside. The mills introduced a new element into peasant society: a landless migrant population; a homeless population too, if only temporarily. Whatever the proportions of this floating population of the countryside, because of its migratory nature it served as the critical leavening agent in worker militancy: partly because these people depended fully on their industrial wages and so felt deprivation more acutely, partly because they felt the keen insecurity that comes with moving from job to job. Lucie Baud, one of the Isère's premier militants in the early Third Republic, was one such worker. Baud started her career in Vizille. After she was fired for her leadership role in strikes there, she found work in Voiron. If she maintained local ties, we are unaware of them; she seems to have gone wherever opportunity and the promise of work led her—and where her reputation had not preceded her.[31] It is difficult to conceive of the textile industry's multifactory strikes breaking out and spreading without the benefit of the interfactory contacts established by mobile workers such as Lucie Baud.

In all, the textile industry made these villages anything but socially uniform, the exclusive domain of kulaks, bullheads, and complacent middle peasants. It introduced the peasantry to a community parallel to and only partially overlapping that of the village community—the community of the mill workers. It lent an urban atmosphere to the village as dozens, perhaps hundreds of persons enlivened the village with their conversation, their activities, their arguments, their mere presence on their way to work, at mealtime, and on the way home. Some days, particularly paydays, workers lingered and spent significant sums in local businesses—a fact workers exploited when they asked merchants for their support during strikes.

These effects were not limited to the people who lived in what

---

31. Lucie Baud's story, as written by herself, is summarized in "Les Tisseuses de soie de la région de Vizille," *Mouvement Socialiste* 2 (June 1908): 418–425.

urban demographers call the "agglomerated settlement"—in plain English, the village proper. The extent of the textile industry's impact was limited only by its reach. Many families, even those located outside the villages of the Bas-Dauphiné, felt its impact through the experiences of their mothers and daughters, wives and friends, employed in the new industry. Textile mills created a vigorous hybrid social tissue, richer and more vascular—hardier too, for a time—than that traditionally associated with insular and inbred peasant society. If peasant society is typically closed and suspicious of outsiders, this feature was the first to be trodden down by the coming and going of the women of the mills.

Working Class or Peasantry?

But who were these people? After the subtle and the abrupt changes the arrival of the textile mills brought to the peasants of the Isère, were they still a peasantry? Or had these communities been stripped of their peasant identity?

One way of approaching this question is to examine where these people lived. If we found that the vast majority of textile workers were listed as legal residents of communes with fewer than 2,000 inhabitants, that would tell us something about their background. As we have seen, however, the reach of the textile industry was vast. To draw up a recruitment map of the industry one would have to consult the *liste nominative* for each commune in the department, in itself a problematic procedure and in any case a task beyond the means of a single researcher.

Alternatively, we may make the assumption that most textile mill owners recruited locally, that most of the workers of a mill resided in the same commune. This might seem like an especially promising approach for larger communes such as Voiron, where the population was large enough to constitute an adequate labor pool. Unfortunately, the evidence does not permit such an assumption. There are accounts of thousands of textile workers in Voiron simply packing up and going home to the farm during a strike against a particularly stubborn employer. This is, in fact, one of the most interesting features of worker-employer relations in rural departments such as the Isère. Workers could rely on their rural resources during protracted negotiations with their employers. Unlike their urban counterparts who could draw only upon their *syndicat,* their strike fund, and their resolve, rural workers always had the choice simply to go home.

Most urban workers would break before going three months without pay. But in the rural context, the penalty for stubbornness was not nearly so high. This was the case even for workers outside the textile industry. The 200 men and 100 women and minors at the Bergès paper factory at Lancey exploited the agricultural alternative during their three-month strike in 1904.[32] But we can make the same point with examples drawn from the history of the textile industry. Voltaire would have loved the 180 workers at the textile factories at St-Bueil and Voissant who, when they went on strike in 1903, "bus[ied] themselves cultivating their gardens," a perfectly Candidean image.[33] A protracted strike at a factory where rural workers were boarded, as at Vinay in 1906, put the owner to the added expense of sending workers home.[34] Are we then permitted to assume that workers in the smaller towns were "more peasant" than workers in larger towns?

Pierre Léon has suggested as much. As early as 1848, Léon observed, "a distinction can be made between workers who remain rural or semirural and those of the towns and cities. The former, in general owners of a small parcel of land, manage to get by somehow."[35] During a strike in Vif in October 1882, only 50 of 120 workers stayed to demonstrate and parade through town; "the others went to the vineyards for the harvest." In March of the same year, when the subprefect at St-Marcellin advised striking workers at La Sône to go back to work, they retorted that they preferred "to work in the fields, where they claim they will get a more remunerative wage."[36] Workers in places even as large as Voiron apparently benefited from significant contacts with the land as late as the 1890s. Workers at the Permezel factory became so frustrated in their negotiations during a strike in the summer of 1896 that they

32. ADI, 166 M, 8, January–March 1904.
33. See ibid., 7 April 1903.
34. AN, F 7, 12785, 24 August 1906.
35. Pierre Léon, *La Naissance de la grande industrie en Dauphiné* (Paris, 1954), 2:750–751.
36. ADI, 166 M, 2, Gendarmerie Nationale à Vif, 9 October 1882; sub-prefect of St-Marcellin to prefect, 1 March 1882.

decided simply to leave Voiron altogether. In his report to the prefect, the reporting police agent noted that

> three hundred strikers, residents of nearby communes, began leaving for home yesterday and today without claiming their pay. Some refused to accept their pay even when it was offered to them, saying that they didn't need it. This leads one to suppose that they don't intend to return until after the harvest.[37]

Workers who could walk away from paychecks were in an envious position indeed. They obviously retained important ties with the countryside.

Over time the trend undoubtedly was toward more tenuous ties with farming as households came more and more to rely on wages. This conclusion is corroborated by evidence drawn from incidents a decade later in Voiron. It is clear that by that time many workers could be termed purely proletarian. At the peak of the general strike in 1906 the *commissaire spécial* noted that "the general strike includes twenty-three factories employing a total of 3,600 workers. . . . Of these perhaps 1,500 live in the country."[38] Even in smaller towns the labor force seems to have had its strictly proletarian component. During a strike in 1892 in Vinay, a town of some 2,500 persons, some workers went home to their farms while others sought work elsewhere. According to contemporary accounts, a distinction had to be made between those who had local contacts and those who did not. "Those who have no interests in Vinay," noted *Le Droit du Peuple,* "get themselves hired elsewhere, in other centers of silk production.[39] Many workers thus depended wholly on their wages and in that sense were truly proletarians.

They were also highly mobile. Unable to return to farming in the event of a strike, landless workers tried to find work at the next mill upstream. With no local ties and no farming interests to look after, they moved from mill to mill, contributing to the creation of a de facto regional wage. As they moved about, they also established interfactory contacts, and acted as leavening agents for worker militancy.[40] Employers understood the connection and tried to limit

37. Ibid., 3, 2 July 1896.
38. See AN, F 7, 12785, 22? March 1906.
39. *Droit du Peuple,* 17 August 1892.
40. Some strikers at St-Jean-de-Chepy simply found work elsewhere. See ibid., 14 July 1906: ". . . nombre de demandes d'usines proches ont été faites aux ouvrières qui bientôt accepteront les avantages qui leur sont offerts."

their workers' mobility. In 1882, when two mill owners in Moirans acted upon a reciprocal agreement not to hire each other's workers for three months after termination of employment, workers went on strike to break the agreement.[41] In an industry presenting such a dense matrix of work opportunities, mobility was one way workers could test wage elasticity. As they played one mill off against another, they established contacts, promoted communication, and fostered militancy.

Regional mobility had always been a feature of rural life in the Isère, where hemp combers and harvest teams moved from job to job. In this sense, going off to work in the textile mills was not a complete break with the home town in the same way that going off to make a living in Paris, Lyon, or even Grenoble might have been. Some workers undoubtedly were constantly on the move, going from place to place in search of steady work in the fashion of migrant agricultural workers; others returned to a rural home at the end of the day or the end of the week. One must bear in mind that "rural" is not always sociologically equivalent to "peasant," and despite its consequences for rural and peasant society in the Isère, work in the textile factory was an alternative to the definitive exodus, not a strict equivalent.[42]

These women differed in a crucial way from the peasant-miners studied by Rolande Trempé. The miners of Carmaux were both peasants and workers and, as Trempé describes them, they sometimes conformed poorly to industrial routine. Their commitment to mining made farming a secondary activity, but their interests in farming were substantial and made these men sometimes less assiduous and reliable as workers.[43] These two social identities were represented by two occupations carried out alternatively by the same individual—peasant-miners farmed before or after work at the mines. In the Isère, outside of peak seasons, the sexual division of labor made farming the principal occupation of men and textile work the occupation of women.[44] Many of these women could

---

41. ADI, 166 M, 2, subprefect of St-Marcellin to prefect, 15 March 1882.

42. On the fate of those who chose the option of the city, see Abel Chatelain, "La Formation de la population lyonnaise: Apports savoyards au XVIIIᵉ siècle," *Revue de Géographie de Lyon* 26 (1951): 345–350.

43. Rolande Trempé, *Les Mineurs de Carmaux* (Paris, 1971), 1:190–209.

44. Jeanne Bouvier described going back to the mill in the fall, after work in the fields was completed: *Mes Mémoires*, p. 29.

return to farming when they needed to do so, and they enjoyed considerable leverage when they did, but unlike the men who mined at Carmaux, these women were not constantly shifting between farming and textile work.

Thus, although one might be tempted to conclude that their dual identities made these peasant-workers somehow less willing to defend their interests as industrial workers, less receptive to the call to organize, from a tactical point of view it mattered little during a strike whether the women worked their fields or walked the picket line. In either case they were not available to the employer. The key question is whether they walked off the job with the other workers, not where they went after they did so. In walking off the job they showed a keen sense of their interests and their loyalty to one another as workers. Unlike the peasant-miners of Carmaux, these women were committed to full-time work in industry, and this commitment also explains why the silkworkers of the Isère were rarely indifferent to questions of organization.

In time the differences between labor in the rural silk industry and older forms of temporary regional rural migration became clear. Moreover, the status of peasant-workers was not fixed. There was a clear trend from a largely agriculturally based existence to one quite heavily dependent upon industrial income. Ultimately, any expectation workers entertained of returning to the peasant household economy of their parents and grandparents appeared more and more illusory. True, workers could leave the industrial work force temporarily, most notably during a strike, and rely exclusively on the traditional resources of the peasantry. But one can be justifiably skeptical of the bravado displayed by striking women who walked away from paychecks because they did not need the money. Such gestures were difficult in the short run—they entailed tangible sacrifices—and out of the question for the long run. Though resources in land gave rural textile workers greater flexibility in their confrontations with the *patron,* they could not defy him. Very few had the option simply to give up textile work and go back to the farm. They were committed to industrial labor, and sooner or later they would have to come to terms. In these moments peasants-turned-proletarians were made acutely aware of their changed status.

This changing state of affairs in the relation of peasant-workers to the land became more apparent with the passage of time and the language used to describe their status. Sources from the early Second Empire speak of textile work as *un appoint* for the peasants, a part-time occupation.[45] Agriculture had the preponderant weight. In the waning years of the Second Empire, the relation between industry and agriculture had reached a kind of equilibrium; according to Pierre Léon, one could talk of a special category of worker, "half peasant, half worker," still securely tied to the land.[46] The decisive shift in the balance between industry and agriculture probably occurred in the twilight years of the nineteenth century, as sources describing later periods suggest that textile workers derived little support from agricultural resources; by the 1920s, "agriculture [was] a secondary concern [for workers], the part-time job."[47] The commitment to farming went little beyond the cultivation of a "garden" and hiring oneself out for the harvest.

By the post-1945 period, most workers' land resources were truly residual; cultivation of the land was little more than a pastime. An observer noted, for example, that most of the 300 rural cobblers in the area around Izeaux and Sillans were "shoemakers from father to son, who [left] the factory in the evening to go cultivate the patch of land, the remains of an ancestral patrimony."[48] A similar observation had been made a few years earlier:

> [The worker] generally retains a large garden or a patch of land for his personal needs. Those who have cows are rare today. . . . Thus it is indirectly that industry at Izeaux has brought about the disappearance of small property [farming] such as existed fifty years ago.[49]

The same point was made about textile workers: ". . . in the old days, the number of worker-peasants was considerable. Nowadays the number is limited."[50]

45. In 1861: ADI, 53 M, 15.
46. Pierre Léon's "Les Grèves de 1867–1870 dans le départment de l'Isère," *Revue d'Histoire Moderne et Contemporaine* 1 (1954): 275.
47. G. A. Nicolas, *L'Organisation sociale de l'industrie du tissage de la soie* (Paris, 1923), p. 32.
48. Paule Bernard, "Un Exemple d'industrie dispersée en milieu rural," *RGA* 40 (1952): 149.
49. Charles Laffond, "L'Industrie de la chaussure à Izeaux," *RGA* 34 (1946): 84.
50. Robert Thiervoz, "L'Industrie en Valdaine et ses répercussions démographiques, sociales, et électorales," *RGA* 42 (1954): 94.

In the mid–nineteenth century, rural industry was part-time work for the peasant; it provided supplemental income to the marginal peasant household. By the postwar period, even in the smallest towns only the vestiges of many former peasant holdings remained, reduced to small gardens cultivated at odd hours. The great-grandsons and -granddaughters of peasants marched off to the factory or workshop on a schedule that permitted only casual, intermittent contact with the land. Only during the boom years after World War II was the transition from peasant to worker completed.

7

Public Order and
Public Opinion:
Workers, Family, Community

In April 1906, bands of angry women patrolled the roads linking the textile communities of Voiron and Paviot. A reporter for *La République de l'Isère*, sent to cover the weeks-old strike, conveyed the terror aroused by the women's aggressive mood and behavior. "We were on our way to Paviot. All along the way we encountered strikers who bore down on us with their eyes. The women, the very old side by side with the young, carried a variety of instruments, from walking sticks to clubs. All of them were thus armed, and their attitude was anything but reassuring." The eyewitness perceived the fury of these women, who not only refused to avert their eyes before the male gaze but fixed all passersby with a stare. "One had to witness today's events," the reporter added, "to understand their character and importance. This is no simple conflict between Labor and Capital."[1]

Nor did the women stop at threatening behavior. Later that day they encountered a young man escorting his sister to her job at the mill. She planned to defy the strike; he would serve as her protector. The women let the would-be strikebreaker go, but they completely overwhelmed her brother, restrained him, then stripped off his clothing. Having thus humiliated him, they whipped their naked victim before setting him free.

1. *République de l'Isère*, 18 April 1906.

145

Here is an incident in which women go beyond Michelle Perrot's archetype of the "rebellious woman of the people," mobilized typically by subsistence issues.[2] And if the editors and respectable readers of *La République de l'Isère* were shocked by the incident, how are we to interpret it? Violation in pantomime? Perhaps. Aggressive assertion of feminine public authority? Almost certainly. Expression of frustrations accumulated during an apparently interminable strike? Undoubtedly. In any event, this act of public humiliation demonstrated unmistakably that these women, not the authorities, had taken control of the public ways. Women had assumed the dominant public role.[3]

This incident, which occurred in the middle of a months-long multifactory strike, neatly epitomizes the consequences of the transformation of rural society by the ruralization of the silk industry. It put women in the public realm in uncustomary areas, in great numbers, and on public ways as a kind of embodiment of the public and community sentiment. It gave them, albeit unwittingly, a basis for understanding themselves and their place in the world—their identity both as women and as workers. Most of all the incident shows women redefining politics collectively through an expression of unmediated power, power neither tempered, diverted, nor diluted by institutional form or process. Their actions directly challenged male authority, symbolized by the protective brother, and demonstrated their own public power in a direct, even brutal way.

Revenge of the *Canuts?* Origins of Political Militancy, 1869–1906

The women policing the rural roads of 1906 represent the end point of a trajectory whose origins are in the 1830s. If

2. Michelle Perrot, "Les Femmes, le pouvoir, l'histoire," in *Une Histoire des femmes, est-elle possible?* ed. Perrot (Marseille, 1984), p. 210; on the gendered boundaries within public and private see pp. 213–214.

3. On the gendering of the public and the private see Rayna R. Reiter, "Men and Women in the South of France: Public and Private Domains," in *Toward an Anthropology of Women,* ed. Reiter, pp. 252–282 (New York, 1975); Mary O'Brien, *The Politics of Reproduction* (London, 1981), esp. pp. 95–113; Michelle Perrot, ed. *History of Private Life,* vol. 4 (Cambridge, Mass., 1990); Joan B. Landes, *Women and the Public Sphere in the Age of the French Revolution* (Ithaca, 1988). On themes of sexuality and public dominance see David M. Halperin, "Is There a History of Sexuality?" *History and Theory* 28 (1989): 257–273, esp. 260.

"indiscipline" was the downfall of the *canuts*—silk merchants would rather move the production of silk to the countryside than contend with the Lyon artisans on their terms—it was one of the rich ironies of the history of the silk industry that the daughters of the *canuts* would inherit the legacy of indiscipline, enriched by time, space, and numbers. In the 1830s and again after the events in Lyon in 1848, the silk merchants abandoned Lyon and the Lyon silk-workers and turned to rural workers in places such as the Isère. There, dispersed among the farms, hamlets, and villages, rural weavers labored in the service of the Fabrique. Domestic weavers' isolation was splendid for the merchants because it rendered them un-organizable, therefore without leverage or influence over the terms and conditions under which they sold their hours and their efforts.

The terms were reciprocal, however. Isolation also left the putting-out entrepreneur with limited influence over the domestic weaver. Domestic weavers could not be relied upon to work at a rate desired by the entrepreneur, especially at times of sowing and harvest. Work rhythms of the farm and the irregular habits of worker-peasants, with their daily and seasonal variations, seemed almost calculated to frustrate the *façonniers*. Entrepreneurs preferred farming to conform to the weaving routine rather than the other way around. They responded by centralizing weaving in factories, by introducing mills and mill routine to the countryside. This strategy solved the problem of control over the quality and quantity of production. But it created the conditions for the mobilization of rural workers.

Even gathered in factories rather than isolated on farms, workers in the Isère suffered from a sense of separation, because there were literally dozens of factories to organize and link. The silkworkers developed their own contacts and network of militants; they even managed to coordinate a kind of industrywide strike in 1884, though it ultimately failed. The successful organization of the workers of the Isère grew out of a decision taken by silkworkers in Lyon in 1903. Lyon workers, whose affiliations included the French Section of the Workers' International (SFIO), the *guesdiste* (and later SFIO) Union des Syndicats du Tissage Mécanique de la Région Lyonnaise, and the Lyon Labor Exchange, set out to organize the workers of the Isère. They aimed to give worker organization in the silk industry of the Lyon region dimensions that fully matched those of the industry itself.

Organized strike activity in the textile industry of the Isère can be traced back to the Second Empire, or further still if we consider the old independent textile center at Vienne.[4] It is not surprising that workers in the Isère were not nearly so actively and openly militant under the Empire as they would be under the more tolerant Third Republic. Like textile workers elsewhere and especially like women workers elsewhere, these silkworkers tended to be underrepresented on the strike rolls, the records of strikes, their causes, and their outcomes.[5] Only with the Third Republic, when women would account for nearly one in three strikes in the region's silk industry, did they come into their own as full partners in the militant workers' movement.[6]

Strike activity in the Isère textile industry was concentrated in three periods: the last years of the Second Empire; 1883–1884; and 1905–1906, the peak years in a long stretch of strike activity running from 1890 to 1914 (see Figure 5).[7] The reasons for the burst of strike activity at the end of the Second Empire are well known. The Cobden-Chevalier Treaty with England brought freer trade but also sharper competition for markets and sharpened relations between workers and employers. Strikes became legal in 1864. Workers, like almost everyone else, sensed the loosening of the regime's grip on power, on its ability to impose order. The "Liberal Empire," whatever its motivation, could be seen as a demonstration of the regime's sense of insecurity. Thus it comes as no surprise that the first record of a strike (how many incidents went unrecorded?) in the textile industry of the Isère bears a date from the Liberal Empire.

4. Vienne's wool industry antedated by decades the arrival of the rural silk industry, so the workers' formative political experiences and their political traditions were of another era. For this reason, references in the text to "the textile industry" are meant to imply the textile industry minus Vienne. For 1869 in Lyon see Claire Auzias and Annik Houel, *La Grève des ovalistes* (Paris, 1982), p. 139.

5. On the size and frequency of strikes under the Second Empire see AN, F 22, 234.

6. There were eighty-nine strikes in the Isère silk industry between 1890 and 1914. See ADI, 166 M, 1–10; Direction du Travail, *Statistique des grèves, 1893, 1894, 1895, 1897, 1899–1914* (Paris, 1894–1915). Dominique Vanoli writes that there were at least 300 strikes against silk firms in the entire Lyon region: "Les Ouvrières enfermées: Les Couvents soyeux," *Révolts Logiques*, Spring–Summer 1976, p. 20.

7. On strikes in all industries in the Isère see Yves Lequin, "Sources et méthodes de l'histoire des grèves dans la seconde moitié du XIXe siècle: L'Exemple de l'Isère (1848–1914)," *Cahiers d'Histoire* 12 (1967): 231.

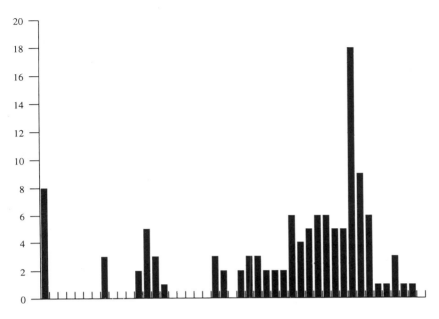

1870 1873 1876 1879 1882 1885 1888 1891 1894 1897 1900 1903 1906 1909 1912

Figure 5   Number of strikes per year in the Isère silk industry, 1870–1914.
(Archives Départementales de l'Isère, 166 M.)

The wool workers of Vienne, emboldened by changed political circumstances, went out on strike in 1868.

The silk industry, for its part, remained tranquil. Pierre Léon has noted that workers in this region and of this period often remained deeply respectful of their bosses. Habits of deference, one presumes, combined with repressive politics made the Empire an uneventful period for the silk industry, at least as far as strikes were concerned. The rural silk industry, still in its infancy, recorded its first strike in 1868. It lasted eight days and the laconic official record of the results notes only that it ended in "accord."[8]

By the 1880s, attitudes had changed and the textile workers of the Isère presented an entirely different picture in both the number of strikes and the number of workers on strike. Under the Third Republic, from the 1880s forward, the textile workers effectively

8. AN, F 22, 234; Pierre Léon, "Les Grèves de 1867–1870 dans le département de l'Isère," *Revue d'Histoire Moderne et Contemporaine* 1 (1954): 295.

assumed leadership of the workers' movement in the Isère, a turn of events no one would have dared to predict two generations earlier. This development was undoubtedly related to two circumstances: first, the collective maturation of the textile workers themselves, the development of a collective identity based on a set of shared experiences within the industry, and later the awakening of the working-class leadership in the department and the region to the importance of this constituency. These two tendencies, regional workers' identity and militant leadership, converged to produce the strike of the winter of 1905–1906, a strike of unprecedented breadth and impact.

The Spontaneous Industrywide Strike of 1884

Prosperity brought by the postwar boom meant that there were few strikes in the early years of the Third Republic: there had been only one strike under the Empire before its collapse and perhaps a dozen through the 1870s. The Long Depression settled in after 1874 and left its stamp on the 1880s; low profit margins and stagnant or declining prices would haunt the European economy from the late 1870s until the early 1890s. Since the silk industry produced a luxury commodity and was heavily dependent on sales to foreign markets, this was bad news indeed. The silk industry was among the first to feel the effects of the Long Depression, and its impact was communicated directly to workers in the form of wage cuts.[9] Uncoordinated strikes broke out in silk factories in several places in the Bas-Dauphiné in 1883, a year when unions, although not strikes, were still outlawed. In textile-producing villages as small as La Sône (730 inhabitants in 1891) and factory towns as large as Renage and Voiron (2,290 and 11,334, respectively) workers tried to win concessions from employers or to defend previous agreements by walking off the job for periods of from three to ten days. There were six strikes in silk factories between January and December 1883. Although most of the strikes were defensive, the principal issue was the cut in piece rates, and half of them ended in

9. For wages see ADI, 138 M, 10–16; 163 M, 1; 166 M, 2. For long-term trends see Fig. 1.

failure. Already anyone who cared to pay attention would have noted that a new spirit animated the countryside. Grenoble, with its larger population, its hundreds of workers, and its decades of craft traditions, had only one strike during the year. The initiative in the workers' movement had passed from the cities to the villages and towns; the somnolence of the textile workers under the Second Empire and the first decade of the Third Republic ended abruptly.

The events of 1884 only confirmed the trend. On 1 February 1884 the gendarmerie at the subprefecture of St-Marcellin dutifully reported that twenty-two workers at St-Jean-de-Moirans had ceased work. By the time this report had been filed, however, it had been rendered inaccurate. The number of striking workers had jumped to more than 300.[10] The strike was spreading.

The stoppage was essentially defensive. Under the extreme competitive pressure imposed by the Long Depression, mill owners tried to drive down costs by cutting piece rates and to increase production by extending hours. After a year of relentless decline in wages, the workers felt compelled to strike. They demanded an increase in wages and a standard workday.[11] Even by the standards of the period and even given the reputation of the textile industry, the workday was long: including breaks for meals, it extended from 4:30 A.M. until 10:00 P.M., and the number of hours actually worked routinely exceeded fifteen during the early summer months of 1883.[12] These conditions may well have been typical of the industry throughout the region, because the strike spread quickly to other mills, with no sign of planning or overall coordination.

Even as the strike spread, the police attempted to reassure the prefect with the prediction that the original strike at St-Jean-de-Moirans would soon collapse because "the strikers are mostly the workers from distant communes"; presumably the logistical problems confronting dispersed rural workers on strike doomed them to early failure. In a matter of days it was clear that the police had badly misjudged the workers and the situation. Rather than collapse in failure after a few days, the strike spread and soon included

10. The original report and the prefect's summary are in AN, F 12, 4658, 3 and 4 February 1884. See also Michelle Perrot, *Les Ouvriers en grève,* 2 vols. (Paris, 1974), 2:709.

11. On wages see AN, F 12, 4658, 4 February 1884.

12. Ibid., 17 February 1884.

thousands of workers. At its peak, as many as 3,000 workers were out on strike and nine factories stood idle.[13] This was the first sign that peasant-workers were, if anything, *more* tenacious than city workers because they could support themselves on their rural resources.

Though demands inevitably varied from mill to mill, strikers at all mills were united in demanding that wages must return to the rates that prevailed in 1880. The textile workers were still using the strike as a defensive weapon in response to a perceived wrong.[14] Careful examination of the sources makes clear the defensive nature of the strikes. The workers' demand for a raise of 8 centimes per meter, for instance, when they were prepared to accept an offer of 5 centimes, might lead one to believe that the strike was initiated to increase wages. But as the prefect pointed out in his report to the Ministry of Commerce, the workers' wages had been cut 10 centimes per meter over the previous year. Thus they had gone on strike in the hope of recovering perhaps half of the value of the wages they had lost.[15] But the strikers also had a bold idea: a regional pay scale. The notion of a *tarif*—a standard scale—had its origins in the silk industry of Lyon. By adopting regional working traditions and incorporating them in their strike demands, the workers had revealed an awareness of the industry's regional extent, its past, and their participation in it.[16]

The factory owners, in the midst of a prolonged period of market uncertainty, insisted that they were in no position to return to the scale offered in more prosperous times. This was not a disingenuous response, as the workers knew. Economic data from the period support their claim. The distress of the industry strengthened the resolve of the factory owners. Lacking planning and regional coordination, the silkworkers' strike ended in failure, despite the strike's unprecedented extent and duration. The defeat of 1884 put an end, temporarily, to the cherished idea of uniform conditions and pay

---

13. AN, F 22, 234. Police estimates and comments can be found in F 12, 4658, 17 and 23 February 1884. The prefect gave the same figure in his report of 23 February.

14. See Lequin, "Sources et méthodes," p. 229, and *Les Ouvriers de la région lyonnaise, 1848–1914*, 2 vols. (Lyon, 1977), 1:89.

15. See AN, F 12, 4658, 4 February 1884.

16. It was the prefect who reported the workers' demand for a *tarif:* ibid., 23 February 1884.

throughout the region's textile mills; the *tarif* would remain an ideal and the workers' wages would remain subject to the anarchy of the marketplace. The defeat of 1884 effectively extinguished the first flames of militancy among the silkworkers of the Isère.

Even so, the textile workers had demonstrated to the Lyonnais *patronat* and to themselves that the silkworkers' movement had developed a regional dimension that mirrored that of the silk industry itself. They had learned by the very speed with which the strike spread that proper conditions existed for the formation of a multifactory consensus on workers' issues—a vital precondition for a successful movement in an industry where isolation had consistently spelled failure. The events of 1884 showed for the first time that industrywide conditions had created an identity of interests among workers and a willingness to act.

The General Strike of 1906

Snow still blanketed much of the Isère when the general strike of 1906 broke out. It all started on 2 February at one of Voiron's smallest mills, with an employee roll of barely 200. Seven days later at Moirans, a town of some 3,000 persons, the workers' request for a raise of half a centime per meter was rejected by the management of the factories of M. M. Bouvard et Cie. The next day, at a workers' meeting called to discuss the employers' response, the Moirans workers decided not to return to work. A few days later the strike spread to the town of Vinay, 30 kilometers downstream. In that town of 2,600, 150 workers stopped work after their demand for a raise of 3 centimes per meter was rejected.[17] Within the space of ten days, strikes had idled hundreds, perhaps thousands of workers. With the addition of the strike at Vinay to those at Voiron and Moirans, the strike included workers in textile mills located all along an arc stretching over 33 kilometers (see Map 4).

The strike continued to spread. In the next three weeks, workers idled more than fifteen textile factories. In Voiron, the Isère's most important textile center, workers set up soup kitchens (*cantines populaires*), a sign of the preparedness for a long strike. Mean-

17. AN, F 7, 13819, 21 February 1906.

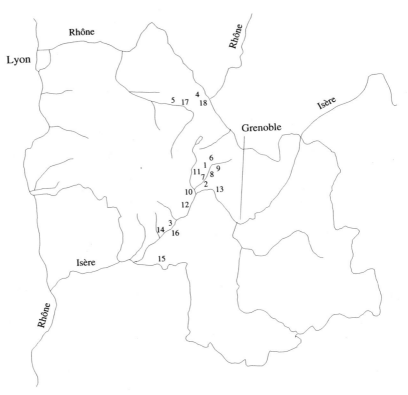

Map 4   Centers of silkworkers' strikes, 1906, in order of onset

while, workers in two factories (Bron and Permezel) at St-Jean-de-Moirans established unions.[18] It appeared that the strike would soon involve all the facilities in the rural textile industry.

Meanwhile, meetings had been arranged between representatives of the workers and representatives of the forty-five local textile employers. On 22 February a recently selected workers' delegation called the entire *corporation de la soierie* to convene in Voiron.[19] At the meeting the workers' delegation reported on the results of their contacts with the employers. The employers had agreed in principle to the workers' most cherished goal: a unified regional wage scale (*tarif*) for the silk industry. The workers' delegation in turn accepted the employers' stipulation that the unified scale

18. *Droit du Peuple*, 23 February 1906.
19. Ibid., 21 February 1906.

would have to be accepted by two-thirds of the mill owners within the orbit of the Lyon Fabrique to be binding. The mill owners and managers did not wish to be hampered by uneven application of the contract. Perhaps they proposed the stipulation as a means of shifting the responsibility for any eventual failure of the *tarif* onto the shoulders of mill operators elsewhere in the Lyon region. The thought undoubtedly occurred to them. In any case, in a show of good faith the employers agreed to abide by the scale until they had had an opportunity to meet with other industry employers, discuss the proposal, and vote on it. Under the terms of the agreement, the regional mill owners' meeting or *congrès* was to take place as soon as possible and in any case before 15 April.[20]

The workers agreed to return to work pending the outcome of the vote. If the other employers in the industry failed to agree to a unified scale, then the employers who had signed the agreement would no longer be bound by it and would be free to pay any wage they deemed appropriate. The workers' delegation and the employers' association held additional meetings in which the two parties elaborated on the basic agreement. The workers were to receive a 15 percent increase in wages pending the employers' *congrès* in April, and the agreement was to be binding on all forty-five employers in the association.[21] On these terms, and pending the outcome of the *congrès,* the strike was officially concluded on 26 February, an apparent victory for the workers and their tactic of carefully orchestrated strikes.

The agreement collapsed. A factory owner in Voiron refused to grant the interim raise provided for in the agreement—in his case, 2 centimes. The silkworkers saw this move as a provocation to resume the strike.[22] Once one of the owners was paying less than the others, the agreement was bound to crumble, if not out of employers' solidarity, then out of a desire to remain competitive. The workers met to decide on a common response. On 17 March they voted to strike the establishments of all of the signatories of the original agreement, beginning the following Monday.[23]

20. Ibid., 23 February 1906.
21. Ibid., 26 February 1906. The Socialists' newspaper stated that the owners of forty-two factories were members. The owners themselves put the figure at forty-five, the figure adopted here. See AN, F 7, 12785, 30 March 1906.
22. AN, F 7, 12785, 31 March 1906.
23. *Droit du Peuple,* 18 March 1906.

The owners, meanwhile, had adopted a new attitude toward a regionwide *tarif* and the congress called to approve it. In a departure from the negotiated position—a departure that validates the workers' charge that the owners were to blame for the breakdown of the agreement—the owners backed away from their earlier agreement to pay the new tarif. A handbill posted on 30 March read: "Wage rates in Voiron cannot be raised until such time as the mill owners' congress . . . has adopted a standard rate."[24] The workers were furious. These were not the terms of the original agreement. The workers had already voted to begin a strike that would turn out to be larger, longer, and more devastating than any in the history of the region.

The strike ultimately extended beyond the forty-five factories affiliated with the employers' association. At one time the factories involved stretched from Chatte, on the Isère downstream of St-Marcellin, to Entre-deux-Guiers, about 23 kilometers from Chambéry. Altogether the area involved was over 70 kilometers in diameter.[25] As many as 3,000 workers in all parts of the Bas-Dauphiné were involved at the strike's peak.

Before the strike ended it had inspired demonstrations and meetings attended by as many as 2,000, according to friendly witnesses. It routinely featured demonstrations of 300 and 400 persons, and occasionally 600. By April, with no end in sight, the Ministry of the Interior was being regularly informed of events. By 20 April the situation seemed serious enough to warrant the dispatch of soldiers to protect life, property, and the right to work. The end of the strike, on 30 May, could do nothing for the ill feelings on all sides and the enduring harm done to the industry in the region.[26] Moreover, the long and bitter strike served as a point of departure for the transformation of political attitudes in the Isère.

24. AN, F 7, 12785, 30 March 1906.

25. On Entre-Deux-Guiers see *Droit du Peuple,* 29 February 1906. The strike at Chatte is interesting also for its demand for an equal wage "pour tout ouvrière habile, italienne ou française": ibid., 28 March 1906.

26. AN, F 7, 12785, includes a large dossier of correspondence between the prefect of the Isère, the Ministry of the Interior, and various special delegates. Demonstrations are regularly described in *Droit du Peuple* as well as by official sources. The crowd of 2,000 is described in *L'Humanité,* 23 March 1906, in AN, F 7, 13819.

"Stirring This Human Flock"

Factory owners are fond of saying that strikes are fomented by "outsiders," implying that, had it not been for some force external to the employer-worker relationship, the workers would not have gone on strike. Such statements have such a self-serving air about them that historians usually discount them. In 1906, however, the employers were at least half right.

As it turned out, workers in the Isère had a great deal of help from outsiders. This fact is in itself remarkable, because union leaders and militants agreed with employers on at least one thing: that women made docile workers and were therefore poor prospects for union organization.[27] Union leaders sometimes too readily assumed that women were short-term workers and therefore lacked interest in the long-term goals that make such organizations worthwhile. And, of course, some union leaders saw men and women as locked in bitter competition for work. They argued that women's lower wages undercut men's wages, depressing wages for all and driving the working class to ruin. Far from attempting to recruit women, some union leaders would have been happy to see them leave the job market altogether.

Such notions were inappropriate in the Isère. For these women, jobs in the silk mills were not stopgaps. Nor did their husbands share union leaders' enthusiasm for the withdrawal of women from the labor force. Interdependence within the peasant household—interdependence that linked industry and agriculture in the binary economy—bound men and women in a common fate. Women's choice of industrial labor rather than farm labor, driven by the fundamental weakness of peasant agriculture, was durable. Consequently, so was their commitment to organization.

By the eve of World War I, women workers in the Isère were better organized, both proportionally and in absolute numbers,

---

27. Emma Couriau, a dues-paying member of the typesetters' union employed at union scale, was refused membership in the Lyon branch of the typesetters' union because of her sex. For details on this and related issues see Madeleine Guilbert, *Les Femmes et l'organisation syndicale avant 1914* (Paris, 1966), p. 63; and Charles Sowerwine, "Workers and Women in France before 1914: The Debate over the Couriau Affair," *Journal of Modern History* 55 (1983): 411–441.

than their male counterparts. In fact, it was a matter of some embarrassment to the leadership of the Confédération Général du Travail (CGT) that workers in the metallurgical industry, the best organized of the "male" industries in the department, had a lower membership rate than women in the textile industry. A police agent in attendance at the 1913 departmental congress of trade unions noted the palpable embarrassment of delegates confronted with irrefutable evidence of the feminization of syndicalism in the Isère: "Workers in the Isère, except for the women in the textile industry, are resistant to union organization. . . . The metalworkers' unions, the most important one [sic], includes only about one in ten [metal]workers." Some 5,000 workers paid the dues that allowed them to claim membership in one of the forty-one unions in existence in the Isère in 1913.[28]

Thus the outstanding difference between the regional strikes of 1884 and 1906 was union organization. The initiative came from Lyon, as part of the only possible satisfactory response to the deepening gloom surrounding the weavers there. The unsatisfactory outcome of their strike in 1903, along with the weakening of their position, led them and the Lyon Labor Exchange to conclude that they would have to organize rural workers if they wanted to control conditions in Lyon.[29] Weavers in Lyon tried several methods to compete with mechanized rural looms; some of these efforts were even subsidized. Gas-powered motors were tried and judged too costly.[30] The decline of the silk industry in Lyon accelerated in the 1880s and 1890s; what was left of the *canuts* found their bargaining position progressively undermined by rural weavers. From a total of 16,000 in 1889 the number of hand looms in Lyon slipped to fewer than 9,000 in 1900, a truly catastrophic decline of 44 percent in only eleven years.[31] Soon it was evident that the fate of silkworkers in Lyon and beyond, both male and female, depended on the development of a regional organization.

28. AN, F 7, 13604, 30 March and 5 April 1913. Monthly dues were 5 centimes for women, 10 centimes for men.

29. See ibid., 12785, 8 April 1906.

30. Joseph Jouanny relates that "an attempt to use compressed air was even more expensive. It was also impractical, given the inevitability of leaks in the tubes": *Le Tissage de la soie en Bas-Dauphiné* (Grenoble, 1931), p. 15.

31. Lequin, *Ouvriers de la région lyonnaise*, 1:87.

Its name was L'Union des Syndicats du Tissage Mécanique de la Région Lyonnaise.[32] The Union des Syndicats claimed affiliation with the Fédération Nationale Ouvrière de L'industrie Textile de France. The latter organization was led by Victor-Charles Renard, the son of a weaver and member of the former French Labor Party (Parti Ouvrier Français, or POF). Renard's organization, in turn, claimed affiliation with the CGT although, given the POF's notions about the proper relationship between unions and the party, the two organizations were not always on good terms.[33] Its goal was to influence wages and conditions throughout the region by bringing the entire regional textile labor force into its membership. Its Socialist affinities were explicit.

The Union des Syndicats offered several advantages to textile workers in the Isère. First of all, it provided continuity. The local, often emphemeral trade unions that antedated the Union des Syndicats often represented only workers of a single establishment. Leadership quality was thus a matter of locally available talent, and leadership continuity was often hampered by turnover as workers retired, quit, or were dismissed for their union activities.[34] Second, the regional union provided communications. Factory-based unions and their leaders were usually limited to ad hoc contacts with other workers in the region, if only because their obligations to work full-time prevented ongoing contacts. Only a full-time leadership could afford to travel and remain in regular personal contact with a widely dispersed work force. The Union des Syndicats had the resources to provide just this kind of full-time leadership, so it could also provide regular contacts between groups. In one four-month period in 1906, representatives of the Union des Syndicats visited and spoke at Voiron, Pont-en-Royans, Pont-de-Chepy, St-Jean-en-Royans, Vinay, St-Geoire-en-Valdaine, and Moirans, all of them important centers in the strike.[35] Third, the regional union could organize and draw upon a broader resource base. The Union des

---

32. See *Droit du Peuple,* 23 January 1906.

33. See AN, F 7, 13819, prefect of the Nord to Minister of the Interior, 14 December 1905.

34. See, e.g., Lucie Baud, "Les Tisseuses de soie de la région de Vizille," *Mouvement Socialiste* 2 (June 1908).

35. See *Droit du Peuple,* June–September 1906. These visits appear to have been fairly regular. *L'Ouvrière Textile* reported a similar round of visits in November and December 1909.

Syndicats supported strikers by collecting funds from those still on the job elsewhere.

Finally, the Union offered experience. Since its leaders were often themselves former textile workers who had participated in strikes, they understood the workers' concerns, and as they acquired experience in strikes and negotiations they became better skilled at these things than the average full-time worker might have been. This was the case, for example, with Charles Auda, the treasurer of the Union des Syndicats and delegate to the affiliated unions in the Isère. Auda, Italian by birth, had years of experience as a worker in the textile factories of the region, including the Bouchard mill at Chaley and the Lacroix mill at Charpennes, both in the department of the Ain.[36] He was enormously popular with workers in the Isère, earned their respect by his irreproachable conduct, and by all accounts was an unusually gifted and energetic individual. Even the *commissaire spécial* at Voiron felt obliged to concede that Auda had "a reputation as a diligent worker and his comportment and moral conduct had never been the subject of an unfavorable remark." This was high praise coming from a man who was undoubtedly not predisposed to like those who "profess revolutionary socialist opinions."[37] Auda had led Lyon strikers in 1903.

In fact, it is through the person of Charles Auda that we can most directly see the connection with the workers of Lyon. His connections with Lyon underline his role in the development and implementation of a regional strategy for silkworkers. Auda's Union des Syndicats worked out of the Lyon Labor Exchange, where, except for a period between 1903 and 1906 when they were challenged by the ultrarevolutionary *blanquistes,* the authority of the *guesdistes* was uncontested. Socialist control was again consolidated after 1906 when leadership at both the Labor Exchange and the local SFIO section were united in the hands of . . . Charles Auda.[38] Auda personified the ideal of the unity of Socialist politics and trade union practice in the years before 1914.

36. Auda's Italian background seems not to have been an issue in his relationship with the unions of the Isère, where resentment against workers from Italy lay just below the surface.

37. For the *commissaire spécial*'s assessments and other details on Auda see AN, F 7, 12785, 8 April 1906.

38. Lequin, *Ouvriers de la région lyonnaise,* 2:235, 310–311, 319.

Auda also embodied some of the contradictions of a union committed to the organization of women but dominated by men. No one worked harder than Auda to connect the silkworkers scattered across the Isère with one another and with the regionwide initiative centered on Lyon. Auda was tireless in his campaigns among workers in small towns and villages. He believed deeply, almost fanatically, in the goal of a single scale for silkworkers, a goal he saw as realizable only if workers of both sexes were organized. This laudable goal fell short, however, of a commitment to full equality for men and women.

Auda wanted to organize working women and improve their conditions but he believed, along with Jules Guesde, that women would best serve their own interests in the long run by returning to the home, so that their jobs could be filled by men. Both men and women could then live out their lives in the conventional gender roles. Auda's thinking on these subjects might not have been clear during the key organizational years of 1905–1906, but in 1909 he spoke in unmistakable terms to audiences in a series of textile villages. At La Sône in 1909 he described working women as slaves who had driven down wages and replaced men in the workshop. Men's unemployment was thus the fault of women.[39] In an address at Fures he blamed working women not only for men's lack of interest in unionism (in the Isère women were more easily recruited than men) but also for men's propensity to drink.[40] One searches in vain for an indication of how Auda's audience received such remarks. One cannot doubt Auda's commitment to women's labor organization, but that commitment, it seems, was driven by the idea that organization would erase the wage differential between men and women. Would it then abolish employers' preference for women workers?

Whatever its origins, Auda's vision of a patriarchal utopia squared poorly with the reality of many women's lives and choices.

---

39. See "Action syndicale, La Sône," *L'Ouvrière Textile*, 1 November 1909, p. 3: ". . . les hommes sont forcés de supporter le chômage; ils n'ont pas de travail à cause de la femme."

40. Ibid: ". . . [les] ouvriers préfère [sic] s'abrutir dans les cafés au lieu de s'organiser." He told a crowd at Les Abrets that "le but du syndicat est de rendre la mère de famille à son intérieur, afin qu'elle puisse élever ses enfants et tenir son ménage sainement."

Working full-time at raising a family was simply a luxury few could afford, as Auda must have known. Ironically, Auda was the one who "discovered" Lucie Baud, developed her native leadership ability, and exploited her symbolic value as the image of the militant, mature, and engaged silkworker. As a widow and mother of several children, Baud necessarily deviated sharply from Auda's ideal of the homemaker in a two-parent, single-income, male-provider family. As a woman of thirty-six years whose working life had begun at the age of twelve, Baud was the kind of silkworker who had the most to gain from union organization and coordination.[41] Unlike the young single women who could simply move on to another mill to escape low pay, harassment, or abusive treatment, place-bound married women and mothers such as Baud necessarily took a long-term perspective favorable to unionism. They had every reason to plant their feet and fight to make things better where they were. Baud's experience as a working woman and mother was instructive for younger women, who perhaps too readily assumed that they would turn their backs on the mills long before they reached Baud's age.

Baud's record as a militant was impeccable. She had founded the Workers' Union of Vizille and led it until her dismissal in 1905. She was an early convert to the necessity of regional organization. She readily accepted Auda's invitation to join the Union des Syndicats initiative, along with a core of militant workers selected from Moirans, Montalieu, Voiron, Allevard, and Vizille. Baud presided over the meeting called by Auda at the Labor Exchange in Lyon on 25 May 1905, at which the Union des Syndicats was founded.[42] If Auda spoke at this meeting on the subjects of women's work and men's unemployment, the record doesn't show it. One presumes that Baud, Auda, and the others formed the Union des Syndicats in order to pursue a goal they shared—that of bringing thousands of women silkworkers into a single regional organization.

In pursuit of this goal, they had the unyielding support of the Socialists and the newspaper of the Federation of the Isère, *Le Droit du Peuple*. The Isère Socialists placed organizing the women of the silk industry at the top of their agenda for 1906. As the party of the

---

41. For biographical details see Jean Maitron, ed., *Dictionnaire biographique du mouvement ouvrier français* (Paris, 1973), 10:225.
42. "Action syndicale," *L'Ouvrière Textile*, 1 July 1905, p. 3.

working class, the Socialists saw the silkworkers as part of their natural constituency. Even so, they expressed puzzlement at the evident absence of sustained militancy among the workers of the Isère's most important industry. What did the future hold if Socialists could not mobilize the workers of the silk industry? In the background lay concern about the party's dismal showing in the 1902 election, a showing that offered little hope for success any time soon. Evidently the Socialists planned to use the silkworkers' strikes to establish a presence and identity among silkworkers and their communities. Of course, there was nothing particularly novel or sinister about this strategy. Members of the International had used the 1869 strike of the *ovalistes* (stocking weavers) in Lyon to mobilize and win the allegiance of workers there.[43] The strategy can also be seen as the mirror image of the Catholic strategy, which saw the disciplined Catholic woman worker as the best insurance against the Socialist husband. The Isère was not notably devout; the Socialists there saw the militant woman worker as the surest way to break down the indifference of the apolitical husband.[44] Thus the programmatic and strategic priorities of the Federation of the Isère and the regional initiative of the Union des Syndicats converged on the women workers.

The new Socialist priority required a certain amount of fanfare. In a special front-page column of the New Year's edition of *Droit du Peuple,* its editor, Max Cance, identified the organization of the women of the textile industry as the Socialists' leading priority for 1906.

> More than 30,000 workers labor in the bosses' dungeons [*géhennes patronales*] of the textile industry of the department of the Isère, and unlikely as it may seem, and unhappily only too true, barely 2.5 percent of them are unionized.[45]

43. See Michelle Perrot's foreword to Auzias and Houel, *Grève des ovalistes.*
44. The Catholic perspective is reflected in the remarks of a priest attached to a mill outside the Isère: "Ils ont senti que c'était par la femme qu'il fallait commencer, que c'était par elle qu'il fallait combattre le socialisme et ses exécrables doctrines, et qu'à côté d'une femme profondment chrétienne, le mari ne serait pas longtemps un socialiste redoutable": *pièce justificative* in Louis Reybaud, *Etude dur le régime des manufactures* (Paris, 1859), cited in Vanoli, "Ouvrières enfermées," p. 21.
45. Cance's estimate appears to be accurate. The boom in membership came after the events of 1906.

This despite the fact that, if there is an industry in which wages are low, hours are long, . . . factory rules are strict, and women are subjected to controls more rigid than a prison, to indecent harassment from thugs and papa's boys, it is certainly the textile industry. We need to awaken this flock of sheep from their torpor, to make them aware of their own human dignity, and to inspire in them a higher conception of their productive value. . . . [It falls] to our comrades in the Socialist groups, to the workers' organizations, to undertake this work of moral uplift and the organization of this feminine proletariat.

Cance's editorial of 2 January 1906 constituted the Socialist agenda for 1906.

Cance was more than a little unfair. As the events of 1884 had shown, the textile workers were not helpless, careless of their dignity, or ignorant of workers' organizations. In the past, textile workers in towns such as La Sône, Renage, Voiron, and Paviot had far surpassed workers in places such as Vienne and Grenoble both in per capita hours on strike and in the sheer number of strikes. As the next few years would show, if the socialist movement had a heart and head in the Isère, they resided in the workers of the textile factories.[46] But the strike wave of 1884 was now over two decades old, beyond the memory of all but a few workers. The workers' movement in the Isère seemed to have lost all momentum, all semblance of militant élan.[47]

The Union des Syndicats:
Revenge of the *Canuts*

The decisive difference between the events of 1884 and those of 1906 was the commitment of the Union des Syndicats and

---

46. The only possible exception to this statement might be the workers of the city of Vienne. But Vienne's militancy was anarchosyndicalist, not socialist, a feature of working-class politics it seems to have adopted from native artisanal traditions. In fact, if such generalizations can fairly be made, it was the older generation of workers, male and connected to the old trades, that clung to the syndicalist tradition. Socialism would soon emerge as the politics of choice for the new generation of workers, who tended to be female, unskilled, and not yet disabused of their faith in the ideals of the Republic.

47. On the strikes in the 1880s see AN, F 22, 234.

the Socialist Federation of the Isère to guide, support, and concentrate their efforts on organizing the silkworkers. By 1906 the Socialists and the Union des Syndicats were prepared to cement their relationship with the working people of the Isère by directing their energies toward its largest single constituent group, the women of the textile mills. Under the terms of this entente, Socialist and union leaders would help the workers coordinate their actions. It led directly to the general strike of 1906.

The 1906 strike had as prologue a series of meetings held by members of the Union des Syndicats in the textile towns of the Isère. The idea of the entente, implicit in the foundation of the Union des Syndicats in May 1905, was first broached in a meeting held on 21 January 1906 at Voiron. Auda spoke of the importance of forming the entente, including all organized workers in the department, for unified action. The umbrella organization, of course, would be the Union des Syndicats. Auda held similar meetings in the other textile centers.[48] Eleven days after the meeting in Voiron, the union local there voted unanimously to initiate a series of planned industrial actions at individual factories in an effort to raise the general level of wages. Apparently the strategy was to press wage demands singly, but with the support of all of the organized factories—in short, to employ a strategy of divide and conquer.[49]

When the first strike broke out at the beginning of February, the Socialist daily carried an announcement of the strike followed by an appeal for aid: "Will the concerned workers [*travailleurs*] of Voiron fail to help those [*celles*] who struggle for their bread?" Within a week the appeal had gone out across the nation. The timing suggests vigilance and a well-coordinated response. The Fédération Nationale Ouvrière de l'Industrie Textile de France, the POF-sponsored umbrella organization for the Union des Syndicats, created a strike fund and asked that donations be sent to its headquarters in Roubaix. Meanwhile, representatives of the Union des Syndicats were meeting with textile workers in other towns in the Bas-Dauphiné. When employers at Moirans rejected a request

48. On Voiron and subsequent meetings see *Droit du Peuple*, 23 and 26 January 1906.
49. Ibid., 1 February 1906.

for a nominal raise, workers called for a meeting. The next day, with Auda presiding, they decided not to return to work. The strike was spreading rapidly. Within days the divide-and-conquer strategy had been abandoned in favor of a multifactory general strike.[50]

When a settlement was reached, everyone recognized the key role played by Auda and the Union des Syndicats. They had negotiated the settlement that put an end to the strikes, pending the employers' meeting. The Union des Syndicats was given a backhanded compliment in a clause of the contract stipulating that the Union des Syndicats would "immediately cease all agitation in the Voiron region among those who accept the minimum scale and shift its efforts to regions where the scale is lower."[51] It seems the Union des Syndicats had earned the respect not only of the silkworkers but of the employers' association as well.[52]

The Union des Syndicats, along with the Federation of the Isère, thus proved essential to the coordination of the workers' efforts. Together they provided the organizational linkages; they supplied a motivated and talented leadership capable of earning the workers' trust; they drew on national resources. Most important, they had a single clear goal, taken almost unchanged from the heyday of the industry at Lyon. That goal was the mobilization of the industry's labor force to force the standardization of working conditions throughout the industry.

This Socialist graft on an indigenous militant tradition took; it marked the beginning of Socialist political leadership in the textile region of the Isère. The strategy of reorienting and organizing politics around the militancy of the largest segment of the proletariat—the women of the textile industry—succeeded. The transition from

50. Ibid., 5, 11, and 15 February 1906.
51. Ibid., 23 February 1906. See also "Bonne foi patronale," *L'Ouvrière Textile,* 1 April 1906, p. 1.
52. It is interesting to note, too, that some of the language echoes that of the *canuts* of 1831 and 1834. The agreement was described to workers as offering the possibility of a "general wage scale to be paid in all factories, which will thus unify working conditions." The industrywide scale would also set limits to cutthroat competition among factory operators for orders from Lyon—competition carried out on the backs of workers through wage cuts. Was this why the agreement ultimately failed? Did Lyon see the *tarif* as a threat? For a summary of the negotiated agreement see *Droit du Peuple,* 23 February 1906. On the potential advantages for mill operators, see "Bonne foi patronale," *L'Ouvrière Textile,* 1 April 1906, p. 1.

1884 to 1906 shows how the Socialists took an elemental rebel-
liousness, shaped it, organized it, gave it a program and a name:
socialism.[53] The politics of the textile workers thrived on feelings of
solidarity and gave a political coloration to the great and small
moments of everyday life, from the village dance to a game of
boules. Fully seventy years after the revolts of the *canuts*, the extension of the Lyon silk industry led not to the defeat of Lyon's militant political tradition but to its transmission, suitably modernized
and adapted, to dozens of surrounding villages and towns.

Exploring the Boundaries of Public
Roles, Public Order, and Public Opinion:
Workers, Family, Community

The textile workers' strikes against the mill owners were
the kind of political apprenticeship they were intended to be. The
number and extent of the strikes, their duration, the workers' organizations, and, as we shall see, their increasing tactical sophistica-
tion showed that the workers had acquired a new repertoire of
tactics; the behavior of the mill owners and the role of political
authorities contained important political lessons. But nothing in
this situation leads us directly to conclude that the politics of anyone else in the department had to change as a result. After all, most
textile workers, being women, did not vote.

Yet these experiences and these events did not take place in per-
sonalized compartments of rural life. Rural industry was much too
important in too many lives for these events to have had only a
restricted effect. In textile communes, one household in two was
dependent on income from a textile worker. More generally, one
Bas-Dauphiné household in four depended on income from rural
textiles.[54] Surely many of these households would have been part of
the rural exodus without the income of rural industry. Indeed,
many women earned what was undoubtedly the greater portion of
their households' cash income, and people who depended on the
patronage of textile workers and their families knew well enough
that their fate was tied to that of the dominant local industry.

53. Though what was meant by "socialism" remains to be examined.
54. ADI, 123 M, 61, 62, 64.

These links are tangible. They are easily traced, grasped, enumerated. But there were other important ties, sentimental and otherwise. Any individual worker probably participated in at least three entities: her household, her *syndicat,* and the rural community. Some of these ties are no longer visible to the historian's eye. We have to be enterprising if we are to learn anything about how rural solidarity developed and how it was represented and conveyed. Above all, the efforts of the working women of the Isère should be seen as part of an attempt to appeal to what Mona Ozouf has called "the impersonal and anonymous tribunal of public opinion."[55] Women identified public support as a primary objective. In a sense, public opinion was the ultimate court of justice. Here was a forum with unlimited suffrage, one where each voice counted. The hearts and minds of family, friends, and neighbors became the objective in a campaign to turn public opinion in their favor.

Family Solidarity

In August 1906 the months-long strike had reached a crisis. The mill operators resolved to reopen the mills, even if they had to use strikebreakers. Strikers took up positions at the mill at six in the morning to guard against the entry of strikebreakers. Over the next two hours the crowd continued to grow, so that by 8 A.M., according to the account,

> all of Vinay is present. . . . Everyone: fathers, husbands, brothers of the workers are there to protect their daughters, wives, and sisters in case of an incident. . . . Finally a strikebreaker arrives escorted by gendarmes who guarantee the preservation of order. She [the strikebreaker] enters surrounded by the jeers of the workers and the population.[56]

The Vinay incident demonstrates how such incidents could emotionally involve an entire community.

The reporting of the Vinay incident also reveals the shrewd and

---

55. Mona Ozouf, "L'Opinion publique," in *The French Revolution and the Creation of Modern Political Culture,* ed. Keith Baker, 3 vols. (Oxford, 1987), 1:425. See also Roger Chartier, *The Cultural Origins of the French Revolution,* trans. Lydia Cochrane (Durham, N.C., 1991); and Jürgen Habermas, *The Structural Transformation of the Public Sphere,* trans. Thomas Burger and Frederick Laurence (Cambridge, Mass. 1989).

56. *Droit du Peuple,* 21 August 1906.

self-conscious way in which the Socialists represented the strike as built upon networks of neighbors and kin. These were sound political tactics, to be sure, and they fitted well with the Socialists' stated aim of organizing their political efforts around the women of the silk industry. They also corresponded to actual organizational features of the local unions. Textile workers made a point of organizing union activities as family activities. Workers' family members were welcome at meetings, for example. According to one source, in 1893 the Voiron Cercle des Travailleurs had more than 200 members. "The club gives them the opportunity to meet several times a week, especially on Sunday. . . . Every member has the right to bring family along."[57] The policy may have had its origins in the realization that if women workers were to join in, allowances would have to be made for the participation of families. In a society that largely did not question constructions of gender that charged women with the total care of children, union meetings would undoubtedly have suffered from high rates of absenteeism if members were not permitted to bring their families.[58]

But it wasn't only official business that was conducted *en famille*. There is evidence that the union frequently became the focus of village social life. At the conclusion of the 1906 strike, for example, the Voiron Cercle organized *"une grande fête d'union syndicale et de fraternité"* for the workers of the mills of Voiron and Moirans. The "fête" consisted of a Sunday picnic, and the organizers chose as an appropriate and convenient date the 14th of July. The announcement urged everyone to come and to "fraternize with these thousands of valiant and courageous women whose unprecedented victory derives from their energy and their solidarity."[59] Sometimes

57. See *Ralliement*, 12 February 1893. Socialists in the Isère contributed pieces to *Ralliement* before *Droit du Peuple* came into existence. The Cercle was the principal focus of activities for textile workers in Voiron; many workers' demonstrations began and ended there. *Droit du Peuple*, 14 June 1906, describes a collection taken up "among a group of workers from the factory of J. B. Martin, at the Cercle des Travailleurs."

58. The practice may not be as rare as we sometimes think. Madeleine Rebérioux has reported on a rural *groupe d'études sociales* whose membership policy and attitude toward the participation of family members was less restrictive: "Un Groupe de paysans socialistes de Saône-et-Loire à l'heure de l'unité (1905–1906)," *Mouvement Social* 56 (1966): 92.

59. The text translates poorly. The original reads: "On voudra venir fraterniser avec ces milliers de vaillantes femmes de coeur dont leur victoire due à l'énergie et à leur solidarité est un exemple sans précédent": *Droit du Peuple*, 3 July 1906.

the workers mixed business with pleasure, as in the "solidarity balls" of the textile union at Vinay. The events were organized as fund raisers and morale builders for the striking workers. Typically they included an evening of dancing to the tunes of "a top-flight musician who has agreed to lend his support to this union endeavor" and sometimes ended, as did the April ball, with the singing of the "Internationale des Tisseuses."[60] Admission was 50 centimes per person except for the workers themselves, who were admitted without charge. The invitation was extended to anyone "who would like to honor us with their presence and at the same time participate in the great work of worker solidarity."

A ball in October followed by a month a successful *"fête de famille"* held in a café and organized by the *syndicat*.[61] Four years later the textile union of the tiny village of La Sône (961 persons in 1911) adopted the solidarity-ball device in an event that echoed the banquet movement of the late July Monarchy, in which apparently innocuous public events served as political opportunities. The event in La Sône freely mixed fun and politics as the guest of honor, "Comrade Barret of Moirans," rose during dessert and "in a few well-chosen words reminded us of the benefits of union organization." During the festivities the union secretary took up a collection "for the cashiered railway workers." The collection produced "4 francs 25" and solid evidence that the rough handling of workers at the hands of Radical governments could earn the Radicals enemies in the smallest of French villages.[62]

Such incidents show how effectively the union used sponsored events to make important political distinctions as much as to publicize and politicize the silkworkers' cause. Of course, in a factory town, factory issues are always community issues; after all, the money these women earned went directly to support many local households. Under these circumstances, the "private" question of relations between employer and worker rapidly overgrew these limited boundaries and burst into the public sphere. Labor struggles

60. Ibid., 30 March 1906.

61. Ibid., 30 September 1906; 5 October 1906. At least three such balls were held in 1906.

62. Ibid., 12 November 1910. On the railroad workers and Radical policy toward trade unions generally, see Jacques Julliard, *Clemenceau briseur de grèves* (Paris, 1965).

became, by the nature of the rural household economy, struggles that demanded the allegiance and support of entire households. And once family interests and loyalties had been engaged, it was only a matter of time before factory issues developed into community issues as well. In this manner the industrial experience of the textile workers transformed the political attitudes of the rural communities of the Bas-Dauphiné.

This point is made most persuasively in a letter sent to the *Droit du Peuple* during the general strike of 1906. Written by someone in the commune of Sillans, not a "host" textile commune, the letter invokes the obligations of family and class in its call for support of the striking workers. Even though the strike touched Sillans only as a home town of textile workers, the author writes,

> the general strike of the Voiron textile industry attracts our attention because among these courageous silkworkers . . . are found our families and neighbors [*compatriotes*]: wives, sisters, and friends [amies], who are exiled each week in order to earn their means of existence. . . . It is now up to us, proletarians of both sexes, to do our duty. . . . Their cause is ours.[63]

The letter makes an explicit connection between local interests and the strike on the grounds that the strikers are "wives, sisters, and friends." Household economic interests mesh with sentimental familial ties.

It was only a matter of time before such incidents had political effects. It was exceedingly rare for strikes and other incidents in the rural textile mills *not* to spill over into local politics—especially when the factory owner was also the mayor.[64] Feelings often quickly overran the boundaries of the commune and communal politics. Workers and their families appealed directly to deputies and their republican sentiments to use their influence to settle industrial disputes. Workers wrote directly to the prefect or to their deputies seeking their intercession.

One such hopeful letter, bearing the official seal of the local union, was addressed to Deputy Gustave Rivet in 1884, during the

---

63. *Droit du Peuple*, 22 March 1906, p. 3.

64. ADI, 166 M, 1, 31 January 1891: "M. Brun est à la fois patron d'usine à soie et maire de Coublevie."

first major wave of strikes to hit the textile industry in the Third Republic: "We appeal to all of your republican sentiments and pray you to join your voice of authority with ours in order to halt an abuse that all honest people must condemn, and to uphold the law." The law in question was the one that limited the work day in the textile industry to twelve hours for women and minors. According to the workers, this limit was regularly exceeded by as many as two hours.

> We assure you that all of the strikes that have desolated our region have had as their goal—and there are thousands of signatures to attest to it—the reduction of the workday to twelve hours. . . .
> As for ourselves, we are firmly resolved no longer to permit our wives, our sons, and our daughters to lose in excessive labor the little health and strength remaining to them.

These individuals, apparently the husbands and fathers of the textile workers, trusted in their deputy's wisdom and good republican sense of fair play. They asked that Rivet "associate himself with our protest and bring it to the attention of the Government." In a charming variation on the traditional French closing, they asked Rivet to "accept with our gratitude the assurance of our most Republican sentiments!"[65]

Thus many workplace issues and household issues developed a political aspect. The deputy who ignored the pleas of these voters on behalf of their working wives, daughters, and mothers did so at the risk of losing considerable political support.[66]

Public officials, for their part, appreciated the importance of the relationship between the industrial politics of the textile workers and the political opinions of their families. The police were aware of the potentially undesirable political repercussions of the general

---

65. AN, F 12, 4658, undated letter received 20 February 1884.
66. It is not known what efforts, if any, Deputy Rivet made on behalf of the textile workers. The strikes of 1884 ended in failure. But ten years later the prefect successfully intervened in a strike when workers appealed to him. The workers' letter, dated 12 April 1894, began as follows:
> Les grévistes du P-de-V viennent vous remercier de tout coeur de votre grande bonté et de votre bienveillant appuit qui leurs a permis de s'entendre avec leur patrons. . . . Elles ont obtenu gain de cause sur les tarifs, avec promesse formelle qu'on ne les diminuirait plus. [ADI, 166 M, 3]

strike of 1906 and took care to communicate their concern to their superiors. In March of that year the *commissaire spécial* described for the Ministry of the Interior the scope of the strike and the breadth of support likely to exist among the general population. "The general strike [involves] twenty-three factories [employing] male and female workers . . . , and since they are women for the most part, they will most likely be supported by their husbands, brothers, or parents." In an earlier report the agent had taken care to point out that support for the striking workers extended beyond their immediate families to the general community, "which finds their demands just."[67] Since, in retrospect, the industrywide strike of 1906 looms as the formative event in the development of a Socialist constituency of the Isère, the assessment of the *commissaire spécial* must have been correct.

Solidarity beyond the Textile Households

Inevitably the café figured as a center of social and political life for textile workers. According to one source, "there is not a single hamlet that does not have its 'mill café.'" It was axiomatic that "when a mill went up, a café was set up forthwith."[68] The textile industry brought many features of urban life to the textile communes; factory cafés could be the centers of political activity— recall the workers who "drank, danced, and sang" at a local café after meeting with the mayor of Renage. The use of cafés as union headquarters in smaller towns and villages was probably commonplace, since small towns were less likely to be able to support a separate meeting place. That, at least, was the case for the 150 members (75 men, 75 women) of the Union Syndicale des Ouvriers Tullistes de St-Clair-de-la-Tour, who held their meetings at the Café

67. AN, F 7, 12785, 20? March and 13 March 1906.
68. Joseph Jouanny, *Tissage de la soie*, p. 131. Did leadership roles in local political groups go to these *cafétiers*? Claude Pennetier has noted that such small business owners often filled these roles because "their shop served as a rallying point and a meeting place for the membership." These people, "by their talents and their human contact skills, [formed] an elite part of rural society": "Le Socialisme dans les départements ruraux français: L'Exemple du Cher (1850–1921)" (thesis, Université de Paris I, n.d.), p. 223.

Vial.[69] And despite the ubiquity of cafés, some workers had to settle for a barn.[70] Nothing could prevent workers in the smallest of villages from creating a *cercle des travailleurs* if they were hell-bent on having one—La Murette had only 808 inhabitants in 1911 but somehow it created and supported its *cercle.*

Café owners rarely needed to be instructed in these matters. Almost literally they saw the coins go from the paymasters' purse onto their countertops. Most seemed to have contributed with hesitation to strike funds. The textile workers made direct and frequent appeals to other tradesmen, especially during strikes. Their message was simply that the shopkeepers ought to support the workers on whom their businesses depended. The appeal in 1906 was perhaps typical. It pointed out that

for the last six years wages have declined. . . .
    Is it possible for anyone to live, to raise a family, to conduct oneself honorably with such a wage? Of course not!
    Shopkeepers, . . . adequate wages for us represent more bread, more meat, more shoes, clothing, and items of all sorts. And for you it represents greater prosperity, well-being, and happiness.[71]

A handbill emphasized the consequences if the strike effort failed:

If the strike does not end under acceptable terms for the working class, it is certain that some of the silkworkers will leave our city to go work elsewhere. . . .
    Our interest therefore is to undertake every effort to retain the industry for our region; and for that we must help our silkworkers [*ouvrières tisseuses*] to obtain livable wages, so that they will stay in our region.
    When the worker [*ouvrière*] thrives, commerce thrives.[72]

Similar appeals and warnings went out during strikes at Vinay, Moirans, and Entre-Deux-Guiers. The most interesting is the ap-

69. AN, F 22, 67.
70. ADI, 166 M, 1, subprefect of St-Marcellin to prefect, 1 March 1882.
71. *Droit du Peuple,* 18 February 1906.
72. AN, F 7, 12785, 14 April 1906.

peal that addressed "all friends of Justice and Humanity: workers, shopkeepers, farmers, all must show their solidarity with these hundreds of discontented." But the message to the merchants was always the same: There can be no prosperity in town as long as the workers are on strike or are underpaid. And the workers had a point: most of these small businesses would have withered and died were it not for the business the textile workers represented. The establishment of some small businesses literally coincided with the establishment of a mill. The workers support small business, therefore small business should support the workers.[73] Many store owners saw the logic in the workers' argument and donated either cash or food for the workers' *cantines populaires*. Other merchants knew that, whatever their private views, a gesture of support was important. And the workers knew how to reinforce their argument by providing favorable publicity to those who gave and negative publicity to those who did not. Sometimes all it took was a simple notice in the newspaper, such as the one published at the request of the Vinay union: "Here is the list of businesses and individuals who have opened their pocketbooks for the striking workers. . . ."[74]

Above all, workers relied on one another for support. The largest contributions to strike funds often came from workers on the job at mills elsewhere. Workers in one factory made regular contributions in support of workers on strike at other factories, with the expectation of reciprocity, of course. During one strike the silkworkers at two mills agreed to contribute 1.5 francs a week to their striking sisters at another facility. This was a generous contribution, equal to perhaps a fifth of these workers' pay for the week. But the textile workers did not rely exclusively on the generosity of people whose occupation or business reputation inclined them in the workers' favor. They depended on altruism, too. The cause of the textile workers attracted the support of large segments of the rural population, particularly during the long strike of 1906. The police were aware of the substantial sums of money the workers were receiving from sympathizers, even from outside the department. A report to the prefect of police noted that "the workers' union receives funds

73. *Droit du Peuple*, 17 February, 4 and 8 March, 22 September 1906. Here we have additional evidence that the rural communes of the Isère were not the fished-out ponds typical of other parts of rural France.
74. Ibid., 30 March 1906.

from all sides, from individuals, from numerous collections, from help sent from other workers' unions in the Isère and from those in neighboring departments."[75]

Other sources tell us something more about these contributions. The unions raised money by staging community events, such as the popular solidarity balls and fêtes at Vinay and La Sône. In other communes, sympathizers raised money by holding *"une grande soirée artistique"* (Moirans) or a Sunday concert (Voiron).[76] Collections were routinely taken up at the annual congress of the Socialist Federation of the Isère. Citizeness Jane D'Helmay collected more than 15 francs for the unions of Vinay, St-Jean-en-Royans, and Fontaine at the 1906 congress.[77] Even unpolitical events could be turned to political uses. Not even *boules* was sacred. A collection was taken up after a game of *boules* at Moirans; the proceeds went to workers in the tiny village of St-Jean-de-Chépy.[78] Weddings could be politicized in the same way. Two francs 30 centimes were collected after a wedding in Bourgoin. At Charnècles the *garçon d'honneur* at the wedding of Xavier Chassignieux and Maria Budillon asked for donations outside the town hall. Altogether he collected 3 francs "for the benefit of the strikers of Voiron."[79]

Formal occasions could attract a crowd of possible donors, and any group event was likely to produce a few contributions. But the textile workers probably got most of their money by passing the hat, and for that no formal event was needed. The textile workers in the more distant rural communes, too remote to participate in the regular demonstrations in town, raised funds for their unions in this manner. Thus striking workers in the village of Sillans (1,035 residents in 1901) went from house to house and among workshops in 1906 to collect donations. According to contemporary accounts, "they [*elles*] received a warm reception from the population wherever they went. They never left a house or workshop without funds and encouragement."[80] Expressions of solidarity

75. AN, F 7, 12785, 8 April 1906.
76. *Droit du Peuple*, 13 May and 25 February 1906.
77. Ibid., 15 October 1906. The Socialist Fédération Textile was another important contributor. A donation of 100 francs was reported in ibid., 11 June 1906.
78. Ibid., 17 July 1906.
79. Ibid., 18 February and 6 April 1906.
80. Ibid., 28 March 1906. Sillans was not a textile center. It *was* the home of workers who were employed elsewhere and who were on strike. The note describes

and contributions to the strike fund arrived from concerned groups and individuals throughout the Bas-Dauphiné. One such group, "*le group socialiste d'Izeaux*," was proud to announce that "it had collected 3F10 for the striking workers."[81]

The workers did not always restrict their activities to areas where they were well known. Published lists of contributions reveal that individual textile workers traveled a circuit to gather donations, especially in support of fellow workers on strike. The lists published in *Le Droit du Peuple* on 28, 29, and 30 March 1906 are typical of dozens published during this period. Here are a few of the items:

> For striking workers:
> Collection taken at Vinay, 51 F
> Collection taken at Chirens, 2.50
> Collection taken at St-Beuil by Mme Ribaud, 76 F 25
> At St-Aupre by Mme Vagnon, 5 F 45
> Collection taken at the mill in St-Nicolas-en-Macherin, 105 F
> The Workers Club at La Murette [undisclosed amount]
> At the Café Chaney in Sermerons, 0.85
> After a speech by Citizen Brizon in Fontaine, 3 F
> From the Café Cochat in Voiron, 0.60

Besides revealing the breadth and geographical extent of support for the textile workers, the list gives us a peek into some of the forms of sociability common in the Isère.

These meetings and places, donations and fund drives speak volumes about the way rural industry transformed the culture of towns and villages. Would there have been a *cercle des travailleurs* in La Murette if it were not within walking distance of several textile mills? Or would the 525 residents of St-Nicholas-de-Macherin have produced over 100 francs for striking workers in other parts of the department had it not been for their own experiences, or those of their mothers, wives, sisters, and daughters, in their own textile factory? The textile industry built and depended

---

the people making the rounds as "*grévistes dévouées du pays*"—striking workers who were both local and devoted to the cause.

　81. Ibid. Izeaux was a village of approximately 1,700 after the turn of the century. It had a large number of peasant-workers engaged in shoemaking.

upon a vast network of rural workers, a network that ultimately provided the basis for a community of interests. Since today's worker may be tomorrow's striker, the workers' efforts to support one another fostered a consciousness of that community of interests. The textile industry had created a legion of rural industrial workers—and a legion of supporters, allies, and sympathizers—in the tiniest of rural hamlets.

Union Solidarity and Public Opinion

Community solidarity is not dependent exclusively upon spontaneous initiatives. The striking workers and their leaders knew that the outcome of their strike efforts depended in part upon winning the war of public opinion. They had to ensure that the larger community understood the issues in the strike and the position taken by the workers. If they failed to do so, they risked being forgotten, losing the community's support, and then it would be a simple thing for the plant to be reopened and the looms attended either by new workers or by renegades as discouraged workers trickled back. Then as now, the best way to achieve success in a political struggle was to maintain solidarity, and the best way to maintain a spirit of solidarity was to develop an effective symbolic repertoire—images, slogans, and music—and convey it effectively to the public.

Among the textile workers of the Isère, the demonstration was the method of choice for the deployment of the symbolic repertoire of solidarity. "Solidarity parades" were the most prominent features of the strikes of 1906; everyone writes about them. They figure in the reports of the police commissioner, of the prefect, and of journalists. But they did not originate with the events of 1906 (nor were they unique to the Isère, for that matter), and their content, particularly the imagery employed, changed significantly over the years. The technique undoubtedly had its origins in peasant folk customs, which relied heavily on ridicule, signs with clearly articulated or thinly veiled meanings, and "rough music." The aim was invariably to shape or express community sentiment, especially disapproval. One of the first incidents involving working women in the Isère began with the charivari at the home of the mill owner in Vizille. When the charivari failed, the women went on strike—an unusually clear instance of the transitional moment between the archaic and the modern.

The first evidence of a solidarity parade during a labor dispute dates from 1881, when a hundred striking textile workers marched through the town of Voiron. They marched in the evening. (Remnant of charivari? Or perhaps simply a matter of prudence—the better to preserve anonymity and avoid reprisal.) As they marched, they invoked the French revolutionary tradition by singing the "Marseillaise," two years after the "Marseillaise" had become France's national anthem. A year later some fifty silkworkers paraded through Vif in similar fashion, drawing the attention of the public and alarming the gendarmerie.[82]

The use of political symbols was not vain or empty; the women's goals were implicitly political, sometimes explicitly so. Though they could not vote, they never missed an opportunity to show that they had the support of people who could. Nor did they miss opportunities to invoke transcendent and universal language that at least implicitly included women. They also showed that they understood where political power lay. In St-Blaise-de-Buis, striking workers chose election eve for their march on the town hall. Fifty rowdy strikers marched from La Sône to the subprefecture at St-Marcellin singing the "Marseillaise," putting the government on notice and invoking its intervention. Most of these early demonstrations incorporated the tricolor flag as a symbol. In Renage in December 1882, 125 women textile workers formed into lines behind the tricolor flag and paraded through town to the town hall, where they demanded an audience with the mayor. Afterward, apparently loath to disperse while in such a boisterous mood, they occupied a local café. This demonstration sent ripples all the way to the top.[83]

82. ADI, 166 M, 1, 1 February 1877; 2, commissioner of police to prefect, 26 March 1881, and Gendarmerie Nationale to Vif, 9 October 1882. On revolutionary symbolism see Maurice Agulhon, *Marianne au Combat* (Paris, 1979); Mona Ozouf, *Festivals and the French Revolution* (Cambridge, Mass., 1988); Lynn Hunt, *Politics, Culture, and Class in the French Revolution* (Berkeley, 1984).

83. ADI, 166 M, 1, subprefect of St-Blaise-de-Buis to prefect, 29 August 1881; subprefect of St-Marcellin to prefect, 1 March 1882; prefect to Minister of Commerce, 15 December 1882. For contrast, see Rayna Reiter's description of Colpied (Haute Provence) in the postwar era: "Public places like the village square, the cafés and the mayor's office are the domain of men": "Men and Women in the South of France," p. 256.

After the turn of the century, the form of the solidarity parade remained but its symbolic content began to change. As Maurice Agulhon has noted, not before the 1880s—not until after the 16 May crisis—did the symbols of the Great Revolution, including the "Marseillaise," become conventional, part of the official national symbolic repertoire.[84] By then early enthusiasm for the Republic had dissipated. Republican politicians and administrators had failed to deliver what the Republic promised, which of course had assumed mythic proportions long before the Third Republic.[85] By the turn of the century, workers' expectations of the Third Republic had been dampened. They began to transfer these expectations to a yet-to-be realized "social republic," one that would fulfill yearnings for a republic with an explicit social content. The symbols employed by workers on parade changed appropriately. They turned to symbols that, unlike the tricolor, had not yet lost the power to shock. Every afternoon during their strike in July 1900, the workers of the Schwarzenbach factory marched in procession carrying the tricolor of the French Revolution side by side with the red flag of social revolution.[86] Red flag and tricolor together made a fitting symbolic expression of an ideal republic that was both democratic and social, one in which, presumably, women would more fully share.

The musical repertoire followed a similar trajectory; it too expanded after the turn of the century, when the "Internationale" displaced the "Marseillaise." This innovation belonged to workers at a textile factory at Vizille in 1902. After an unproductive meeting between the factory owner and a delegation of strikers, the strikers resolved at least to be heard in the streets. They formed a group and marched down the Grande Rue singing the "Internationale." A workers' march in Vif made different use of such "rough music." In January 1903 some fifty striking workers disrupted the work of strikebreakers by singing as they marched outside the mill. According to the prefect, the marching and singing so thoroughly intimidated the strikebreakers that gendarmes had to be called to escort

84. Agulhon, *Marianne au combat*, p. 151.
85. On Boulangist attempts to capitalize on these sentiments and Orléanist attempts to capitalize on Boulanger, see William D. Irvine, *The Boulanger Affair Reconsidered* (New York, 1989).
86. ADI, 166 M, 5, 6 July 1900.

them from the mill. The striking workers celebrated their victory by marching through the town of Vif "singing."[87]

By 1906, by which time the Federation of the Isère had made the organization of the silkworkers its highest priority, the deployment of political music and symbols—tricolor or red—had become commonplace among the workers at the mills. It was their way of providing a political context for their actions. After the successful resolution of a strike, the residents of Moirans were treated to a victory march by the workers of the Giraud-Bouvard factory:

> At one-thirty in the afternoon, the striking workers gathered at the center of town to go to the factory in a column; each of the women was wearing a red cockade, symbol of union and victory. The crowd that gathered along the route, as well as the workers of the other factories, gave them a lively round of applause.[88]

Such spectacles are not quickly forgotten in small towns.

The 1906 general strike offered numerous opportunities for such displays. Imagine the spectacle created by the 400 workers of Voiron who, beginning at six in the morning, marched behind a red flag past each of the silk factories in town singing the "Internationale" and the "Carmagnole." They then left Voiron for Paviot, the nearest commune with a textile mill, which had been closed in anticipation of their arrival, thanks to advance notice from the police. From Paviot they marched another six kilometers to St-Jean-de-Moirans, where again the silk factory had been closed on the advice of police. By this time their entourage included two brigades from the gendarmerie. Together—gendarmes and working women—they made their way back to Voiron, the women singing and whistling all the while. Three days later another group of women closed ranks for a march behind a red flag through the streets of Voiron before marching on the nearby commune of Coublevie. They memorialized the event by stopping for a group photograph on their way. They disbanded at the Voiron Cercle des Travailleurs.[89]

87. Ibid., 31 January 1903.
88. *Droit du Peuple*, 15 January 1906.
89. AN, F 7, 12785, 2 and 5 April 1906. See also the report for 13 April, which describes another event of this kind.

Equality in Difference?

Michelle Perrot has suggested that the patterns of women workers' militancy reflected their territory and a different conception of the world that came with it. Theirs was a world seen through communitarian lenses, a populist vision that incorporated town, village, or hamlet and that reflected women's wider and more frequent circulation in society among merchants, among neighbors, at the washplace, at market. Pierre Pierrard has made similar remarks about the locus of feminine sociability.[90]

More to the point was the fact that women, unlike men, remained outside the polity in one crucial sense—they lacked the vote. Maurice Agulhon has argued that political integration of peasants, as well as of workers, began with the "apprenticeship" of the Second Republic.[91] Concomitant with this political apprenticeship in the forms of modern political expression was a decline in prepolitical forms or, more precisely, preparliamentary and preelectoral forms of political action—the riot, the politically laden charivari, the armed march on the *chef-lieu*, on government offices. Peasants let go of "undisciplined" premodern political tactics when the acquired modern political forms. As peasants adopted and learned to exploit the formal political repertoire available to citizens in an age of mass politics, they abandoned the violent, emotional, episodic, and rebellious "politics" of the premodern world.[92] With a few notable exceptions, the history of the "traditional" peasant revolt ends in 1848; it is replaced by the history of peasant politics.[93]

90. Michelle Perrot, "Les Femmes et la class ouvrière," *Colloque de Vincennes*, 16 December 1978; Pierre Pierrard, *Histoire des curés de campagne de 1789 à nos jours* (Paris, 1986), pp. 215–218.

91. Maurice Agulhon, *1848* (Paris, 1973); see also Yves-Marie Bercé, *Croquants et nu-pieds* (Paris, 1972) and *Fête et Révolte* (Paris, 1976). For more on the signal importance of 1848 see William Sewell, *Work and Revolution in France* (Cambridge, 1980); for a comparative perspective on political integration see Guenther Roth, *The Social Democrats in Imperial Germany* (Totowa, N.J., 1963).

92. For perspectives on politics as a substitute for unregulated violence ("politics is war by other means") see Nancy C. M. Hartsock, "Prologue to a Feminist Critique of War and Politics," in *Women's Views of the Political World of Men*, ed. Judith Hicks Stiehm, pp. 121–150 (Dobbs Ferry, N.Y., 1982).

93. Eric Hobsbawm tended to attribute this shift from the prepolitical to the emergence of the industrial working class, at least in the urban context. See his *Primitive Rebels* (New York, 1959), p. 110.

And while Agulhon has used this distinction brilliantly to show how peasants acquired a rudimentary sense of the rule of law under the Second Republic, a fact that explains peasant quiescence during the workers' riot of the June Days of 1848 as well as it explains the "just revolt" of peasants against the 18th Brumaire of Louis-Napoléon Bonaparte in 1851, surely the apprenticeship of the Republic was incomplete.[94] Agulhon's argument ought to be used only to make sense of the conduct of men. For although textile work broke down the system that tended to relegate women to a private, domestic realm, women still lacked the legal basis for complete public expression. Working men could rely upon politicians and administrators to be mindful of their political power—all the more so as working men became more savvy about political organization. Women, however, did not enjoy active political citizenship; this part of the public realm remained closed to them. Is it any wonder, then, that women's tactics differed from those of men; that, given their liminal status, they worked the boundary between newer conventional forms and older undisciplined forms of political behavior?

Their language emphasized universals, which admitted of no gender distinctions, and their politics relied all the more heavily on the invocation of symbols that emphasized women's membership in polities (the nation, the public, the people, the proletariat) unrestricted by gender: the tricolor and the red flag, the "Marseillaise" and the "Internationale." There was also a darker side: the perpetuation of the more direct and brutal forms, violent intimidation or the threat of violence. The charivari of 1877 was one such episode.

There were others. Martine Segalen has commented on the profound fear generated in traditional society by the sight of women in numbers, whose appearance and power threaten patriarchal authority.[95] As some of these incidents suggest, women's presence in the public ways could be perceived as in keeping with the genre of the nineteenth-century demonstration, male or female. But such demonstrations by women possessed a latent power, a threat. Their very numbers and their presence in public places seemed calculated

---

94. See also Ted Margadant, *French Peasants in Revolt* (Princeton, 1980).

95. Martine Segalen, "The Family Cycle and Household Structure," in *Family and Sexuality in French History,* ed. Robert Wheaton and Tamara Hareven, pp. 253–271 (Philadelphia: University of Pennsylvania Press, 1980).

to test gender boundaries and challenge the boundaries of feminine confinement within the public realm. Groups of women marching and singing deeply disturbed the sense of a well-ordered society.

The sight of women in an agitated or excited state certainly perplexed public officials. Some official reactions bordered on the hysterical. In 1876 the mayor of Voiron wrote in alarm to the prefect: "I am deeply fearful that the continuation of this strike will lead these women, morally and physically overexcited [*femmes surexcitées moralement et matériellement*] by their leaders and by events, to deplorable extremes, and that it will be necessary to repress them severely. Advise promptly."[96] In this message, pretense of official bureaucratic detachment has been abandoned. Women who escaped a largely private and domestic role, women who acted aggressively in public ways, aroused fear.

The women who stripped and beat the strikebreaker's brother had armed themselves with clubs and switches and set out on the roads to confront renegades in a manner that recalls the October Days or the Amazons of 1793. The women evoked other memories of summary revolutionary justice through the modification of popular songs. The "Ça ira," which had been used so effectively to implicate the nobility in every threat to the Great Revolution, was turned against the mill owners in 1906. The striking women of 1906 sang of hanging the bourgeois and the bosses from lampposts:

> Ah, ça ira, ça ira!
> Les bourgeois à la lanterne.
> Ah, ça ira, ça ira!
> Les patrons, on les pendra.[97]

Did they intend to assimilate the mill owners to the prerevolutionary seigneurs, the new ruling class to the old?

Another group of striking women, also armed with clubs and sticks, marched through Voiron with the aim of sparking a true general strike—one in which all work would come to a stop. Their tactics were revealing. They burst into business establishments— retail merchants and workshops—proclaiming, "We are the parliamentarians!" These parliamentarians, just like the real ones it

96. ADI, 166 M, 1, mayor of Voiron to prefect, 2 February 1876.
97. *République de l'Isère*, 20 April 1906.

seemed, could do whatever they liked. In this horrifying masquer-ade, in their assumed identities as deputies, the women proclaimed a day off, then demanded that the workers celebrate the holiday by joining them on parade. These tactics manifested an acute sense of difference.[98] Here was an abrupt redefinition of the political, a symbolic coup d'état. Women's seizure of power, symbolized by their clubs and their appropriation of a parliamentary identity, seemed to call everything into question: male political authority as much as the authority of the employers.

Union organization helped to channel and discipline women's militancy, though it could not do so entirely—no more than it could in the case of men. Gender difference in conduct derived in part from a kind of sublimation that was itself driven by differential political integration.

The separation of domicile from place of work and the feminiza-tion of textile labor had had profound unintended consequences for rural society and politics. The sheer numbers of working women making their way from hamlet to village and circulating in the streets of mill towns and villages inevitably altered and extended the feminine domain within the public realm. Men adapted to changed circumstances as best they could; after all, women's wages were subsidizing inefficient farms now worked full-time by men. Textile towns, villages, and hamlets featured newly demasculinized public spaces now that women were no longer confined to the customary places within village life—the market, the washplace, the neighborhood, the church—and now dominated the public ways as never before, at least at intervals. In demonstrations, at first tentatively, later more systematically, women defined the issues of public debate and public life in terms of their own experience. More opportunistically, women exploited their numbers and their extended public role to politicize the textile villages. Cafés, dances, festivals, weddings, even the innocent game of *boules* afforded an occasion to make a point and pass the hat. These occasions could be turned to suit the purposes of the women of the mills; they became features of a distinctly feminine village sociability.

98. Ibid., 18 April 1906. For a fuller development of these ideas see Raymond A. Jonas, "Equality in Difference? Patterns of Feminine Labor Militancy in 19th-Century France," *Proceedings of the Western Society for French History* 15 (1988): 291–299.

8

Peasants,

Industry,

and Politics

By the eve of World War I, the Isère was sending as many Socialists to the Chamber of Deputies as any department in France. After rather dismal results in the general elections of 1902, the markedly better results of 1906, 1910, and 1914 made the Federation of the Isère one of the most powerful in the SFIO. The prestige conferred by the election of five SFIO deputies to the Chamber hoisted the Isère into the loftiest ranks of SFIO federations, a position ordinarily occupied by federations from such urban and industrial departments as Nord, Seine, and Bouches-du-Rhône.

Moreover, these changes would last. In the interwar period the Isère remained a Socialist department; the Communists never succeeded in electing a candidate before World War II. Candidates who adhered to the principles of the Third International never received the support of more than 6 percent of registered voters in the department, and then only in 1924, when enthusiasm for the Bolshevik Revolution was at its peak. In 1928, when SFIO candidates were backed by 26 percent of the electors, only 5 percent of all eligible voters cast ballots for Communists. In fact, Communist candidates never survived the first round of voting. Even Jean-Pierre Raffin-Dugens, former deputy and the most prominent of the figures from the old Fédération de l'Isère to join and remain with the

Communist party, failed as a candidate.[1] The Socialists never looked back from their victories of 1910 and 1914. They consistently sent four and sometimes five deputies at each renewal of the legislatures of the Third Republic through 1940.

How to account for such strong allegiance? And what precisely did these Socialist victories signify? In a sense we already know the answer. Identification with the Socialists was a product of a relationship, established at the most basic levels of rural society, between Socialist institutions and the working people of the department. The efforts of the Union des Syndicats and the Federation of the Isère converged in the 1906 campaign to mobilize the working women of the Isère. Almost certainly their efforts succeeded beyond their wildest dreams as the women Max Cance described as "a flock of sheep" who needed to be shaken out of their "torpor" shook the towns and villages of the Isère for the better part of the year.

The 1906 strike involved thousands of workers who walked out of a dozen mills scattered across the Bas-Dauphiné. Their demonstrations mobilized the population and public opinion on their behalf, with the result that the politics of the textile workers redefined the political identity of the communities of the rural Isère, as electoral results soon revealed. Socialist support and coordination of the strike was repaid in 1910 when voters in the Bas-Dauphiné elected three SFIO candidates.[2] By then it was clear that the industry that had sought industrial peace beyond the limits of Lyon had succeeded instead only in conveying the vigor of the *canuts* to the *canutes* of the hinterland.

But then how meaningful was the collectivism of the Socialists as an obstacle to the support of voters? To answer this question we need first to know something about what the party's zealous advocates told their public; we have to know the nature as well as the

1. For details of the breakup of the old SFIO in the Isère see Pierre Barral, *Le Département de l'Isère sous la Troisième République* (Paris, 1962), pp. 435–438. For electoral details see pp. 557–561.

2. The candidacies of "renegade" followers of Zévaès in 1906 confused voters and split the Socialist vote. The *zévaèsiste*-faction had disappeared by 1910, so 1910 is a better measure of the appeal of the SFIO in the Isère. On the *zévaèsiste* controversy see chap. 1.

origins of socialism in the Isère. What the Socialists put in their public program matters less than what they said when they went before the voters in an attempt to win their votes. It is one thing to call one's party the party of collectivization; it is quite another to say so in front of a crowd of property-owning peasants.

The Socialists in the Isère made no effort to conceal their commitment to collectivization; the term appeared in numerous pronouncements and editorials, and party candidates described themselves as *collectivistes*.[3] In an article titled "Socialists Can Only Be Collectivists" a Dr. Greffier, official and sometime candidate for the Federation of the Isère, attacked the view expressed in the rival Radical daily *Petit Dauphinois* that a republican government could "include Socialists but . . . [not] collectivists." "True Socialists," Greffier insisted, "are all collectivists."[4]

Nor is there any evidence that the message changed appreciably with the audience. In 1906 a Socialist candidate named Brizon took his campaign to the tiny commune of Fontaine, on the outskirts of Grenoble. There, "before a packed audience . . . presided over by M. Pugnet, municipal councilor and cobbler," he told his audience: "I am a collectivist and if you aren't, don't vote for me. Vote for the bourgeois."[5] The fact that he made his statement and presumably others like it during the 1906 campaign is significant because it indicates that Brizon was an SFIO candidate, and thus suggests ideological continuity between the old POF and the newly unified SFIO on the issue of collectivization.

On the face of it, it does seem to require a powerful imagination to believe that peasants voted Socialist primarily because they wanted to hasten the day when their land would be collectivized. But as J. Harvey Smith has shown for the skilled vineyard workers and Tony Judt for property-owning peasants in the Var, everything

---

3. Barral and implicitly François Goguel, in the works listed in the Bibliography, express skepticism that French peasants actually supported collectivization. The same view is expressed by Georges Pélissonnier in his *Etude sur le socialisme agraire en France* (Dijon, 1902). Carl Landauer describes the confusion in the POF on the question of collectivization in "The Guesdistes and the Small Farmer," *IRSH* 6 (1961): 212–225, and in "The Origin of Socialist Reformism in France," *IRSH* 12 (1967): 81–107, he attributes reformism in the Socialist party of the twentieth century to concessions made to peasants by Socialists in the nineteenth century.

4. *Droit du Peuple*, 10 July 1898.

5. Ibid., 18 February 1906.

depends on context.[6] Skilled vineyard workers and even small peasant proprietors need not feel threatened by collectivization when it conforms to their collective work routine or their relation to the land. Socialists in the Isère, while insisting upon their identity as collectivists, defined their commitment to collectivism in such a way that it posed no threat to the small farmer.

The Socialists of the Isère could have it both ways—they could be both collectivists and friends of small property-owning peasants— and they could do so in good conscience. Their position hinged on a definition of the place of land in the system of agricultural production and on the distinction they maintained between "individual" property (good) and "capitalist" property (bad). The position of the Isère Socialists evidently owes something to the position worked out at a series of meetings in Paris in August and September 1894, in anticipation of the Nantes party congress. According to police accounts, the proposal was constructed with the active participation of Jules Guesde and Paul Lafargue; Lafargue presented the report at the congress. The POF emphasized the similarities between the positions of the small peasant and the artisan. The nettlesome item, of course, is the peasant's land—obviously a form of property, however small and inefficiently exploited.

In 1894 the POF had resolved this difficulty by assimilating the land of the peasant to the tools of the artisan. In this sense, the peasant, like the artisan, is an "owner-operator." Unlike the large agricultural property owner or the industrialist, the property-owning peasant "exploits no one" and "need not expect to see his land taken from him."[7] Even as a property owner and an occasional employer of agricultural day laborers, the small peasant exploited no one and therefore was not subject to collectivization. In fact, the small peasant was invited to join "the workers of town and field" in the struggle for socialism.[8] Here was a significant rhetori-

6. J. Harvey Smith, "Work Routine and Social Structure in a French Village," *Journal of Interdisciplinary History* 3 (1975): 357–382; Tony Judt, *Socialism in Provence* (Cambridge, 1979).

7. On the preparatory meetings see Archives de la Préfecture de Police, Ba 1484, reports dated 15 August and 6 September 1894. Quotations are from "Rapport présenté au Congrès de Nantes (1894), par le citoyen Lafargue, au nom du Conseil national du POF," cited in Pélissonnier, *Etude sur le socialisme agraire*, p. 146.

8. Lafargue and Guesde were roundly criticized by Engels and the German

cal shift, from a critique of private property to a critique of exploitation.

Socialists in the Isère insisted upon the validity of just such a distinction. In April 1902, in a meeting of the Conseil Général de l'Isère, the Socialist representatives Morel and Mistral—the same Mistral who later, as mayor of Grenoble, would symbolize socialism in the Isère for his generation—read their common position on small property into the minutes of the meeting. The statement contained nothing that could be construed as threatening to the small peasant proprietor. It began with the entirely orthodox statement that "the producers will not be free until they are in possession of the means of production." Whereas in industry the means of production are so centralized "that they can be restored to the producers only under a collective form . . . it is not the same now in France in the agricultural domain, [where] the means of production, the soil, in many cases are still owned individually." Even if peasant property is doomed to disappear, the Socialists need do nothing to hasten that day.

The small peasant proprietor deserved the defense and support of the Socialists, the statement went on. Why? Because the small peasant had not yet been expropriated by capitalism. Mistral and the Socialists of the Isère insisted upon collectivism not only as a desirable form of social organization but as compensation for the collapse of small property. They thus asserted that while the large farms, the railroads, the mines, and the factories had to be returned to the producers under collective form, no less important was socialism's duty "to support and maintain the farmer/owner on his patch of land [and defend him] against taxation, against usury, and against the new seigneurs of the land." In other words, not only must Socialists do nothing that might jeopardize the small peasantry's tenuous hold on the land, they had an obligation to defend the small peasant.[9] The statement reveals a shift of position from non-

---

Socialists for "opportunism." The German Socialists had been through similar quarrels with their own leadership in Bavaria. See Madeleine Rebérioux, "Le Socialisme français de 1871 à 1914," in *Histoire générale du socialisme*, ed. Jacques Droz, 3 vols. (Paris, 1974), 2:165–166.

9. See *Droit du Peuple*, 11 April 1902. Paul Mistral was himself of peasant background. He went on to become deputy of the Isère before being elected mayor of Grenoble.

intervention in the certain decline of the small peasant proprietor—the conventional view—to active intervention in defense of the smallholder. Exploitation, not property itself, was the issue, and since peasants exploited no one, they remained securely on the right side of a moral chasm.

On the wrong side were ranged *les gros.* A Socialist campaigning in St-Joseph-de-Rivière began a speech by addressing the interests of his audience as workers ("Who would dare to suggest that workers in the countryside are unresponsive to socialism? That's wrong") and concluded by addressing their interests as peasants, suggesting that socialism would mean a more equitable distribution of land than the current arrangement, under which "29,000 big landowners own more land than 7.3 million small proprietors."[10] Such statements revealed an acute sense of audience. The position of Socialists in the Isère on the property question, far from alienating peasant voters, placed the Socialists in the popular role of defender of the small peasant.

Socialists took pains to fashion a minimalist program with the same advantages, one that showed unambiguously that the Socialists had the immediate interests of small property owners at heart. The elements of this program included the abolition of all indirect taxes and the transformation of all direct taxes into a single, progressive tax on annual incomes over 3,000 francs, a figure that safely sheltered most small farmers. They demanded an end to all taxes on farmland cultivated by the owner and on inheritances of such land. Finally, they proposed that the state help the communes to buy agricultural machines to be "placed free of charge at the disposal of the farmers."[11] These proposals, if implemented, would eliminate most of the major burdens on small farmers and provide them with some of the advantages currently enjoyed only by large-

10. "La Propagande rurale à St-Joseph-de-Rivière," ibid., 3 April 1905.
11. *Droit du Peuple,* 29 April 1906. For comparison with the agricultural program of the POF, see esp. the *comptes rendus* of the 1892 congress at Marseille (Musée Sociale, Paris, C 7). The agricultural program of the SFIO before 1914 was principally the work of Auguste Compère-Morel (his more important publications are listed in the Bibliography). Compère-Morel was of peasant background and helped to elaborate the Socialist approach to rural questions, particularly at the SFIO congresses of 1906 (Limoges) and 1908 (Toulouse). See also Georges Lefranc, *Le Mouvement socialiste sous la Troisième République,* 2 vols. (Paris, 1977), 1:168–170.

scale farmers. In short, this was a program neatly tailored to the interests of peasants.

Moreover, the Socialists were steadfast supporters of the aims of these peasants in their capacity as workers in the textile industry, by their explicit identification with the textile unions, and by providing a forum in *Droit du Peuple* for communication among the far-flung workers of the rural silk industry. In the departmental Conseil Général the Socialists placed particular emphasis on improvement of work conditions in the textile mills, by proposing, for example, that work inspectors be elected "by the men and women workers." When the Millerand-Colliard law reduced the workday to ten hours in facilities that employed women and minors, workers welcomed the shorter workdays. But since the law made no provision for an increase in piece rates, it had the effect of reducing workers' income. As a consequence, workers were put in the position of having to demand special dispensations from the law "in order to guarantee a regular day's wage." Socialists in the Conseil Général objected to the way this reform was implemented locally. The debate took on considerable symbolic value because the Conseil Général included a textile factory owner.[12] The fact that these initiatives preceded or coincided with Radical confrontations with workers from Draveil to Decazeville only made political choices that much easier. Socialist militants and candidates in the Isère elaborated a vision consistent with the defense of peasant property—and well adapted to the Isère's socially heterogeneous households and communities of peasants and workers.[13]

Among the principal effects of rural industry were not more secure peasants but peasants who in time began to resemble urban workers in their reliance on income from wages—and in their politics. The spread of the rural silk industry, first in fits and starts, later in earnest, initiated the formation of a regional working class, a

12. *Droit du Peuple*, 9 October and 20 November 1898, 11 April 1902. On the function of such legislation in gender differentiation in the work force see Mary Lynn Stewart, *Women, Work, and the French State* (Kingston, Ont., 1989).

13. Madeleine Rebérioux, *La République radicale? 1898–1914* (Paris, 1975), pp. 111–116; Jacques Julliard, *Clemenceau briseur de grèves* (Paris, 1965); and Donald Reid, *The Miners of Decazeville* (Cambridge, Mass., 1985). For a discussion of how the POF's earlier inflexibility on this question had driven the likes of Hubert Lagardelle toward syndicalism, see Jeremy Jennings, *Syndicalism in France* (New York, 1990), pp. 87–88.

process already well under way by 1884 but brought to its political fulfillment through the collaboration of Socialist militants in 1906 and after. The textile workers discovered their common regional interests in combat, particularly in combat supported and organized by the Socialist party and the Union des Syndicats.

As women took up wage work in the silk industry, conventional gender relations and boundaries in rural society inevitably changed. These changes had obvious implications for the division of labor in the privacy of the peasant household. But they also influenced the gendering of the public realm in village society, because women so visibly dominated the public scene in textile villages. Women workers colonized and feminized significant moments and institutions in the public life of textile villages—dances and cafés, weddings and *boules*—as they sought to mobilize rural public opinion in support of their cause or to stake out territory on their own. As the reporter from the *République de l'Isère* noted after he witnessed the women beating the strikebreaker's brother, anyone who observed these events could see that these were not ordinary struggles between capital and labor. Gender relations overlay relations of power within the public and private realms. The women of the mills not only redefined village life, by their actions they redefined the political.

In mobilizing women, the Socialists of the Isère avoided some of the mistakes committed by their counterparts in French Flanders, whose marginalization of women, according to Patricia Hilden, led women eventually to reject them.[14] The Socialists of the Isère did not fashion a consistent theoretical position for women, and in fact their efforts to organize and support the silkworkers flatly contradicted statements made by Jules Guesde (who, it should be pointed out, was not a presence in the Isère) and echoed by Charles Auda (who frequently was) to the effect that in a workers' paradise, women would look after the home. Even so, in most practical efforts, the Socialists of the Isère valued women's participation. Their support for the 1910 feminist program and campaign of Elisabeth Renaud shows that the Federation of the Isère, far from trivializing women's concerns, supported them publicly and finan-

14. Patricia Hilden, *Working Women and Socialist Politics in France, 1880–1914* (Oxford, 1986).

cially; the prominent positions in the Federation accorded Angèle Roussel and Jane D'Helmay suggest that the federation was a place where women could be confident that their voices would be heard. As for the working women of the villages and towns, what choice did Socialists have but to conclude along with Max Cance that *this* was the working class of the Isère? The preponderance of women in the Isère's mills forced the Socialists to come to grips with issues they almost certainly would otherwise have avoided. In this sense, the Socialists' flexibility and adaptation to women's concerns mirrored their overtures toward peasants. Socialism in the Isère built a constituency—workers, peasants, women—characterized less by class than by a shared sense of alienation from the institutions that wielded social and political power.

At the root of it all rested the paradox that the conditions that prepared the way for the emergence of a rural Socialist electorate were created by the convergence of two independent initiatives: the effort made by marginal peasants to shore up their inadequate holdings of land and the desire of manufacturers to flee the militant proletarianized artisans of Lyon. The impact of rural industry was diverse—on demography, on household composition, on the sexual division of labor, on the rhythms of rural life, on environment and habitat, on the gendering of village society, on rural public opinion, on political attitudes and the symbols deployed to represent them—and reveals a story of opportunism, resistance, and mutation for the textile industry, for peasant women rapidly becoming workers—for socialism. Industry was not a steamroller; it had to conform to the contours of peasant society. Business had its own cycles and rhythms, but they overlaid rather than replaced the original patterns of rural life.

Socialism adapted too. Political reorientation in the Isère worked to the benefit of the Socialists in the first decade of the twentieth century, as peasant-worker households turned to the party of working people. Because their prior and enduring interest in the land ruled out any perspective that transcended property or region, most of these textile workers never developed a sense that their interests extended much beyond the boundaries of the Isère or the Lyon textile industry. Theirs was a regional identity; they were peasants and workers of this place, this community where they clung tenaciously to the land and a way of life, not members of a category.

And yet it is the dynamic and flexible quality of socialism in the Isère that must be emphasized. For in their zeal to appeal to a peasantry in the grips of proletarianization and to women mobilized politically but not electorally, and driven in part by their enthusiasm for electoral success, they departed from the canonical and succeeded in crafting a program with obvious breadth and local appeal. In this sense, socialism in the Isère expressed a keen sense of a milieu with specific human, material, and moral features. It bore the unmistakable stamp of the terrain it had come to occupy.

Bibliography

PRIMARY SOURCES

Archives Nationales (AN), Paris

BB 18   Procureurs généraux
   1824   Religion, usine
   1902   Enquête sur les internats industriels, 1892.
   2209   Rapports sur les élections de 1902.
   2210   Rapports sur les élections de 1902.
C   Assemblées
   1331   Elections générales, Assemblée législative (28 May 1849–2
         December 1851).
   1511   Election partielle, Assemblée législative, 10 March 1850.
   3021   Enquête sur la condition des classes ouvrières, 1872–1875
         (région du Sud-Est).
   3025   Rapports des sous-commissions, annexes des procès-verbaux.
   3026   Rapports des commissions, procès-verbaux de la Commission.
   3350   Situation des ouvriers en France, par département.
   4836   Elections générales, Grenoble, St-Marcellin, 1889.
   4837   Elections générales, La Tour-du-Pin, Vienne, 1889.
   6091   Elections générales, Grenoble, La Tour-du-Pin, 1902.
   6092   Elections générales, St-Marcellin, Vienne, 1902.
   6355   Elections générales, Grenoble, 1906.
   6356   Elections générales, La Tour-du-Pin, 1906.
   6357   Elections générales, St-Marcellin, Vienne, 1906.
   6623   Elections générales, Grenoble, 1910.
   6624   Elections générales, La Tour-du-Pin, 1910.
   6625   Elections générales, St-Marcellin, 1910.

6966 Elections générales, Grenoble, 1er et 2e arrondissement, 1914.
6968 Elections générales, La Tour-du-Pin, 1914.
6970 Elections générales, St-Marcellin, 1914.
F 1 C III 5 Esprit public
F 7 Police générale
12316 Congrégations religieuses non-autorisées (Gironde à Isère), 1880–1901.
12325 Congrégations religieuses non-autorisées, documents généraux (Ain à Isère).
12360 Sociétés et associations: Autorisations et surveillance, Hérault à Lozère, 1870–1912.
12385 Sociétés campagnonniques, 1870–1912.
12387 Culte catholique: Affaires diverses, affaire de Châteauvilain.
12477 Agissements cléricaux, 1872–1908.
12488 Congrès socialistes, Paris (1876), Lyon (1878), Marseilles (1879).
12491 Congrès de la fédération nationale des syndicats, 1886–1895.
12494 Congrès divers, 1899, 1900.
12499 Activité socialiste dans les départements, Haute Garonne à Loire, 1900–1913.
12514 Attentats anarchistes, Ain à Nièvre, 1892–1900
12523 Congrès régionaux.
12542 Elections législatives, Gard à Nièvre, 1902–1906.
12545 Elections législatives, Gard à Vosges, 1905–1906.
12546 Elections aux Conseils généraux, 1904.
12547 Elections municipales, Ain à Jura, 1904.
12553 Notes sur la situation politique, 1899–1905.
12723 Agitation révolutionnaire par département, 1893–1914.
12734 Situation politique et économique des départements, questions ouvrières, 1900–1910.
12767 Enquêtes économiques et sociales, industries textiles, 1900–1911.
12785 Grèves, Gironde à Isère, 1906.
12788 Grèves, Eure à Nièvre, 1908.
12793 Groupements, syndicats jaunes: Renseignements généraux et série départemental, 1901–1909.
12886 Paris, socialistes, blanquistes, allemanistes, 1894–1901.
13057 Anarchistes, communistes en province, 1911–1915.
13060 Activité anarchiste dans les départements, Herault à Yonne
13567 Bourses du Travail, 1896–1916.
13568 CGT, organisations et activités, 1903–1915.
13570 CGT, unions départementales des syndicats, 1908–1913.
13604 Notes, rapports et presse concernant les Bourses du Travail et l'Union des Syndicats, 1908–1913.
13819 Travailleurs du textile (1905–1929), activité des syndicats du textile (1905–1908).
13820 Travailleurs du textile (1905–1929), activité des syndicats du textile (1909–1913).

F 12   Commerce et industrie
  4509a Situation industrielle, Isère, 1876–1886.
  4658 Grèves et coalitions, Herault à Lozère, 1880–1889.
  4670 Grèves, Ain à Maine et Loire, 1893.
F 20   Statistique
  501   Etat civil des ouvriers appartenant aux dix principaux établissements manufacturiers dans chaque département, 1849–1850.
F 22   Syndicats et grèves
  66   Isère, syndicats ouvriers.
  67   Isère, syndicats ouvriers.
  68   Syndicats patronaux, fédérations.
  166   Travail dans l'industrie, Isère.
  167   Grèves, 1905–1906.
  168   Grèves, 1907.
  170   Grèves de 1908, 1916, 1918.
  234   Grèves, 1852–1904.
  439a Travail des femmes et des enfants, infractions à la législation, 1886–1937.
  466   Travail des femmes et des enfants, commissions départementales, Isère.

Archives Départementales de l'Isère (ADI), Grenoble

8 M   Elections législatives
  37   Elections législatives de 1906.
  41   Désistements, registre de déclarations des candidats, procès-verbaux du recensement des votes.
51 M   Affaires politiques
  25   Campagne d'Italie (1859), Boulangisme dans l'Isère (1888), affaire Max Régis (1899).
  26   Affaire Dreyfus, 1898–1906.
52 M   Correspondances diverses, rapports de police.
  57   1880–1892.
  58   1883–1898.
  59   1891–1901.
  60   1897–1900.
  61   1901–1906.
  62   1907–1914.
  69   Propagande syndicale, affiches, 1896–1912.
  74   Renseignements politiques, correspondance, 1903–1913.
53 M   Police générale, police et gendarmerie, rapports de police.
  15   1860–1875.
  16   1876–1885.
  17   1886–1897.
  18   1898–1899.
  19   1900–1915.

55 M   Police générale: Réunions publiques et privées, conférences
  1   Réunions publiques et privées; mouvement syndical, clubs, banquets, conférences politiques, etc., 1850–1914.
  2   Réunions publiques et privées, etc., 1895–1908.
  3   Réunions publiques et privées, etc., 1909–1924.
123 M   Population: Recensement quinquennal, dénombrement
  3   1861–1876.
  6   1891.
  8   1901.
  10   1911.
  51   Dénombrement de 1896, canton de Voiron.
  53   Dénombrement de 1896, cantons de Pont-en-Royans et Rives.
  54   Dénombrement de 1896, cantons de Roybon et St-Etienne-de-St-Geoirs.
  55   Dénombrement de 1896, cantons de St-Marcellin.
  57   Dénombrement de 1896, cantons de Bourgoin.
  59   Dénombrement de 1896, cantons de Grand Lemps.
  60   Dénombrement de 1896, cantons de Morestel.
  61   Dénombrement de 1896, cantons de Pont-de-Beauvoisin.
  62   Dénombrement de 1896, cantons de St-Geoire-en-Valdaine.
  64   Dénombrement de 1896, cantons de Virieu.
138 M   Statistiques industrielles
  3   Etats relatifs aux industries textiles, filatures de chanvre lin, coton, laine, 1809–1884.
  10   Situation industrielle, 1852–1862.
  11   Situation industrielle, 1863–1868.
  12   Situation industrielle, 1869–1876.
  13   Situation industrielle, 1877–1880.
  14   Situation industrielle, 1881–1884.
  15   Situation industrielle, 1885–1887.
  16   Statistiques sommaires des industries principales, 1852–1895.
162 M   Industrie et travail; documents concernant l'organisation du travail
  1   Enquête sur le travail agricole et industriel, arrondissement de Grenoble, 1848.
  2   Enquête sur le travail agricole et industriel, arrondissements de Vienne, St-Marcellin, et La Tour-du-Pin, 1848.
  3   Correspondance générale, statistiques, 1853–1885.
  4   Correspondance générale, statistiques, 1892–1904.
  5   Correspondance générale, statistiques, après 1895.
  11   Travail des enfants dans l'industrie.
  12   Statistiques industrielles, 1869–1877.
163M   Industrie et travail: Salaires
  1   Salaires industriels.
  2   Vérification du taux normal et courant des salaires et de la durée de la journée de travail.

166 M   Grèves des différents corps de métiers
     1   1858–1877.
     2   1878–1890.
     3   1891–1895.
     4   1896–1899.
     5   1900–1901.
     6   1902.
     7   1903.
     8   1904–1905.
     9   1906–1908.
    10   1909–1917.

Archives de la Préfecture de Police

    32   Troisième Congrès ouvrier régional de l'Est tenu à Lyon en juillet
          1880. Sixième congrès de la région de l'Est tenu à St-Etienne en
          avril 1881.
  1444   Tisseurs en tous genres, 1872–1882.
  1472   Le Socialisme, 1893–1896.
  1473   Le Socialisme, 1897–1914.
  1476   Le Socialisme en province.
  1482   Les Guesdistes, 1882–1895.
  1483   Les Guesdistes, 1882–1895.
  1484   Les Guesdistes, 1882–1895.

Published documents

Assemblée Nationale. *Commission d'enquête sur l'industrie textile: Procès-Verbaux.* 5 vols. Paris: Imprimerie de la Chambre des Députés, 1906.
Direction du Travail. *Statistique des grèves* . . . [title varies], *1893, 1894, 1895, 1897, 1899–1914.* Paris: Imprimerie Nationale, 1894–1915.
Ministère de l'Agriculture. *La Petite Propriété rurale en France.* Paris: Imprimerie Nationale, 1908–1909.
Ministère du Commerce, de l'Industrie. Office du Travail. *Bulletin de l'Inspection du Travail, 1902, 1903, 1904, 1905, 1906, 1907, 1908, 1909, 1910, 1911, 1912, 1913.* Paris: Imprimerie Nationale, 1903–1914.
Statistique Générale. *Résultats statistiques du recensement des industries et professions (dénombrement général de la population du 29 mars 1896).* Paris: Imprimerie Nationale, 1899–1901.
_____. *Résultats statistiques du recensement général de la population effectué le 5 mars 1911.* 2 vols. Paris: Imprimerie Nationale, 1911.

Newspapers

La Croix (Paris), 3 July 1885–30 April 1886.
Le Droit du Peuple (Grenoble), 1 August 1897–17 May 1914, weekly to 1900,

then daily. Consulted each issue through 1902, thereafter all issues in years of general elections and selected issues in nonelection years (issues published after Socialist Federation congresses, during strikes, etc.).

L'Ouvrière Textile, 1904–1909.

Le Ralliement, 29 January–5 March 1893, weekly.

La République de l'Isère, 1906.

Le Reveil du Dauphiné, 1870–1871.

Other Published Primary Sources

Ardouin-Dumazet, Victor. *Voyages en France.* Vol. 9, *Le Bas-Dauphiné.* Paris: Berger-Levrault, 1903.

Baud, Lucie. "Les Tisseuses de soie de la région de Vizille." *Mouvement Socialiste* 2 (June 1908): 418–425. Also reprinted with foreword by Michelle Perrot as "Le Témoignage de Lucie Baud, ouvrière en soie." *Mouvement Social* 105 (December 1978): 139–146.

Bonnin, Bernard, René Favier, Jean-Pierre Meyniac, and Brigitte Todesco. *Paroisses et communes de France: Dictionnaire d'histoire administrative et démographique.* Vol. 38, *Isère.* Paris: CNRS, 1983.

Garden, Maurice, Christine Bronnert, and Brigitte Chappe. *Paroisses et communes de France: Dictionnaire d'histoire administrative et démographique.* Vol. 69, *Rhône.* Paris: CNRS, 1978.

Guerry, Emile. *Les Syndicats libres féminins de l'Isère.* Grenoble: St-Bruno, 1921.

SELECTED SECONDARY SOURCES

Accampo, Elinor Ann. *Industrialization, Family Life, and Class Relations: Saint Chamond.* Berkeley: University of California Press, 1989.

Agulhon, Maurice. *1848; ou L'Apprentissage de la République.* Paris: Seuil, 1973. Published in English as *The Republican Experiment.* Cambridge: Cambridge University Press, 1983.

———. *Marianne au combat: L'Imagerie et la symbolique républicaines de 1789 à 1880.* Paris: Flammarion, 1979.

———. *La République au village.* Paris: Plon, 1970.

Agulhon, Maurice, Gabriel Désert, and Robert Specklin. *Apogée et crise de la civilisation paysanne de 1789 à 1914.* Vol. 3 of *Histoire de la France rurale,* ed. Georges Duby. Paris: Seuil, 1976.

Althusser, Louis. *For Marx.* London: New Left Books, 1977.

Anderson, Perry. *Considerations on Western Marxism.* London: New Left Books, 1977.

Anderson, Robert. *France, 1870–1914.* London: Routledge & Kegan Paul, 1977.

Ardouin-Dumazet, Victor-Eugène. *Les Petites Industries rurales.* Paris: J. Gabalda, 1912.

Armengaud, André. "Industrialisation et démographie dans la France du XIXe siècle." In *L'Industrialisation en Europe au XIX^{3}siècle*, 187–200. Paris: CNRS, 1972.

——. *La Population française au XIXe siècle*. Paris: PUF, 1971.

Augé-Laribé, Michel. *La Politique agricole de la France de 1880 à 1940*. Paris: PUF, 1950.

Auzias, Claire, and Annik Houel. *La Grève des ovalistes*. Paris: Payot, 1982.

Barral, Pierre. *Les Agrariens de Méline à Pisani*. Paris: A. Colin, 1968.

——. "Aspects régionaux de l'agrarisme français avant 1930." *Mouvement Social* 67 (1969): 3–16.

——. *Le Département de l'Isère sous la Troisième République (1870–1940)*. Paris: A. Colin, 1962.

——. "La Sociologie électorale et l'histoire." *Revue Historique* 238 (1967): 117–134.

Barrelle, Henri. "Notes sur le développement industriel récent dans l'agglomération de Saint-Marcellin." *RGA* 18 (1930): 201–207.

Bennet, Jean. *Regard sur le passé: L'Isère, haut lieu de la mutualité*. Etampes: Société Régionale d'Imprimerie et de Publicité, 1962.

Benoit-Builbot, Odile, Margaret Maruani, and Florence Terray. "Domination et révolte des femmes au travail." In *La Sagesse et le désordre: France, 1980*, ed. Henri Mendras. Paris: Gallimard, 1980.

Bercé, Yves-Marie. *Croquants et nu-pieds*. Paris: PUF, 1972.

——. *Fête et révolte: Des Mentalités populaires du XVIe au XVIIIe siècle*. Paris: PUF, 1976.

Bernard, Paule. "Un Exemple d'industrie dispersée en milieu rural. Deux Vallées en Bas-Dauphiné: La Bièvre et le Liers." *RGA* 40 (1952): 133–157.

Bernstein, Eduard. *Evolutionary Socialism*. New York: Schocken, 1975.

Bezucha, Robert. *The Lyon Uprising of 1834: Social and Political Conflict in the Early July Monarchy*. Cambridge: Harvard University Press, 1974.

——. *Modern European Social History*. Lexington, Mass.: D. C. Heath, 1972.

Blanchard, Raoul. "Une Emeute ouvrière dans l'Isère." *Revue d'Histoire de Lyon* 13 (1914).

Blet, Henri, *La Population du département de l'Isère en 1846 et 1936*. Grenoble: Allier, 1951.

Bligny, Bernard, Pierre Barral, Aimé Bocquet, Pierre Bolle, Bernard Bonnin, Vital Chomel, André Laronde, Jacques Solé, Jean-François Troussier, and Pierre Vaillant. *Histoire du Dauphiné*. Toulouse, 1973.

Bloch, Marc. *French Rural History*. Berkeley: University of California Press, 1973.

Bois, Paul. *Paysans de l'Ouest*. Le Mans: M. Vilaire, 1960.

Bon, Frédéric, and Jean-Paul Cheylan. *La France qui vote*. Paris: Hachette, 1988.

Bonnefous, Georges. *Histoire politique de la Troisième République*. Vol. 1, *L'Avant-guerre*. Paris: PUF, 1956.

Bonnevay, Laurent. *Les Ouvrières lyonnaises à domicile*. Paris: Guillaumin, 1896.

Boswell, Laird. "How Do French Peasants Vote?" *Peasant Studies* 16 (1989): 107–122.

Bouillon, Jacques. "Les Démocrates-socialistes aux élections de 1849." *Revue Française du Science Politique* 6 (1956): 95.

Bouvier, Jeanne. *Mes Mémoires, ou 59 années d'activité industrielle, sociale et intellectuelle d'une ouvrière*. Poitiers: L'Action Intellectuelle, 1936.

Bovier-Lapierre, Edouard. *De l'influence du milieu physique sur le développement économique: Le Département de l'Isère*. Paris: Lacose, 1906.

Boxer, Marilyn J., and Jean H. Quataert. *Socialist Women*. New York: Elsevier, 1978.

Braun, Rudolf. "The Impact of Cottage Industry on an Agricultural Population." In *The Rise of Capitalism*, ed. David Landes. New York: Macmillan, 1964.

Brunet, Roger. *La Carte, mode d'emploi*. Paris: Fayard, 1987.

Brustein, William. "A Regional Mode of Production Analysis of Political Behavior." *Politics and Society* 10 (1981): 355–398.

———. *The Social Origins of Political Regionalism: France, 1848–1981*. Berkeley: University of California Press, 1988.

Burguière, André. "Demography." In *Constructing the Past*, ed. Jacques Le Goff and Pierre Nora, pp. 99–122. New York: Cambridge University Press, 1985.

Burns, Michael. "Politics Face to Face: Rural Reactions to Boulangism and the Dreyfus Affair in France, 1886–1900." Ph.D. dissertation, Yale University, 1981.

———. *Rural Society and French Politics*. Princeton: Princeton University Press, 1984.

Bury, J. P. T. *Gambetta and the Making of the Third Republic*. London: Longmans, 1973.

Cameron, Rondo. *Essays in French Economic History*. Homewood, Ill.: Irwin, 1970.

Capdevielle, Jacques, Elisabeth Dupoirier, Gérard Greenberg, Etienne Schweisguth, and Colette Ysmal. *France de gauche, vote à droite?* Paris: Presses de la Fondation Nationale des Sciences Politiques, 1988.

Centre Régional de Documentation Pédagogique. *De l'histoire régionale à l'histoire générale: Dossier documentaire, Isère, 1787–1972*. Grenoble: Centre regional de documentation pédagogique, 1974.

Chaline, Jean-Pierre. "Les Contrats de mariage à Rouen au XIXe siècle: Etudes d'après l'enregistrement des actes civils publics." *Revue d'Histoire Economique et Sociale* 48 (1970): 238–275.

Chambers, J. D. "Enclosure and Labor Supply in the Industrial Revolution." *Economic History Review* 5 (1952–1953): 319–343.

Champier, Louis. "L'Equilibre économique du Bas-Dauphiné septentrional de la fin du XVIIe siècle au milieu du XIXe." *Evocations*, October 1949.

Charlety, Sebastien. *Histoire de Saint-Simonisme*. Paris, 1896.

Charpentier, Armand. *Le Parti radical et radical-socialiste à travers ses congrès*. Paris: Giard & Brière, 1913.

Chatelain, Abel. "L'Emigration temporaire des peigneurs de chanvre du Jura méridional avant les transformations des XIXᵉ et XXᵉ siècles." *Etudes Rhodaniennes* 21 (1946): 166–178.

———. "La Formation de la population lyonnaise: Apports savoyards au XVIIIᵉ siècle." *Revue de Géographie de Lyon* 26 (1951): 345–350.

———. *Les Migrations temporaires en France, 1800–1970.*

———. "Les Usines-internats et migrations féminines dans la région lyonnaise." *Revue d'Histoire Economique et Sociale* 48, no. 3 (1970): 373–394.

Chayanov, A. V. *The Theory of Peasant Society.* Homewood, Ill.: Irwin, 1966.

Chorier, Bernard. "Réaction aristocratique et poussée sociale dans une cellule rurale de Bas-Dauphiné: St-Hilaire-de-la-Côte, 1659–1835." In Bernard Chorier, Gilbert Garrier, Pierre Guichard, and Gérard Sabatier, *Structures économiques et problèmes sociaux du monde rural dans la France du Sud-est.* Paris: Belles Lettres, 1966.

Clapham, J. H. *Economic Development of France and Germany, 1815–1914.* Cambridge: Cambridge University Press, 1936.

Clarkson, L. A. *Proto-industrialization: The First Phase of Industrialization?* London: Macmillan, 1985.

Clerget, Paul. "Les Industries de la soie dans la vallée du Rhône." *Etudes Rhodaniennes* 5 (1929): 1–26.

Cobb, Richard. *The People's Armies.* Trans. Marianne Elliott. New Haven: Yale University Press, 1988.

Cole, Alistair, and Patrick Campbell. *French Electoral Systems and Elections since 1789.* Brookfield, Vt.: Gower, 1989.

Coleman, D. C. "Proto-Industrialization: A Concept Too Many." *Economic History Review* 36 (1983): 435–448.

Compère-Morel, Adéodat. *Le Programme socialiste de réformes agraires.* Paris: M. Rivière, 1919.

———. *Les Propos d'un rural.* Beauvais: Audaille, 189?.

———. *La Question agraire et le socialisme en France.* Paris: M. Rivière, 1912.

Conk, Margo Anderson. *The United States Census and Labor Force Change: A History of Occupation Statistics, 1870–1940.* Ann Arbor: University of Michigan Press, 1980.

Converse, Philip, and Roy Pierce. *Political Representation in France.* Cambridge: Harvard University Press, 1986.

Copley, Antony. *Sexual Moralities in France, 1780–1980: New Ideas on the Family, Divorce, and Homosexuality.* London: Routledge, 1989.

Corbin, Alain. *Archaisme et modernité en Limousin au dix-neuvième siècle.* 2 vols. Paris: M. Rivière, 1975.

Cote, Léon. *L'Industrie gantière et l'ouvrier gantier à Grenoble.* Paris: Société Nouvelle, 1903.

Coughenour, C. Milton, and Louis Swanson. "Work Statuses and Occupation of Men and Women in Farm Families and the Structure of Farms." *Rural Sociology* 48 (1983): 23–43.

Courgeau, Daniel. *Study on the Dynamics, Evolution, and Consequences of*

Migrations. Vol. 2 of *Three Centuries of Spatial Mobility in France.* Paris: UNESCO, 1983.

Crafts, N. C. R. "English Workers' Real Wages during the Industrial Revolution: Some Remaining Problems." *Journal of Economic History* 45 (1985): 139–144.

Cross, Gary S. *Immigrant Workers in Industrial France: The Making of a New Laboring Class.* Philadelphia: Temple University Press, 1983.

Crouzet, François. "Agriculture et révolution industrielle: Quelques réflexions." *Cahiers d'Histoire* 12 (1967): 67–85.

———. *Description topographique, historique et statistique des cantons du département de l'Isère.* Grenoble: Prudhomme, 1869.

Dallas, Gregor. *The Imperfect Peasant Economy: The Loire Country, 1800–1914.* Cambridge: Cambridge University Press, 1982.

Derfler, Leslie. "Reformism and Jules Guesde: 1891–1904." *IRSH* 12 (1967): 66–80.

Dowd Hall, Jacquelyn. "Disorderly Women: Gender and Labor Militancy in the Appalachian South." *Journal of American History* 73 (1986): 354–382.

Dowd Hall, Jacquelyn, Robert Korstad, and James Leloudis. "Cotton Mill People: Work, Community, and Protest in the Textile South, 1880–1940." *American Historical Review* 91 (1986): 245–286.

Dreyfus, Paul. *Histoire du Dauphiné.* Paris: PUF, 1972.

Droz, Jacques, ed., *Histoire générale du socialisme.* Vol. 2, *De 1875 à 1918.* Paris: PUF, 1974.

Dupâquier, Jacques, ed. *Histoire de la population française.* Vols. 2–4. Paris: PUF, 1988.

Dupeux, Georges. *Aspects de l'histoire sociale et politique du Loir-et-Cher.* Paris: Mouton, 1962.

———. *French Society, 1789–1970.* Paris: A. Colin, 1972.

Durkheim, Emile. *Socialism and Saint-Simon.* Yellow Springs, Ohio: Antioch, 1958.

Duveau, Georges. *1848: The Making of a Revolution.* New York: Pantheon, 1965.

Esmonin, Edmond, and Henri Blet. *La Révolution de 1848 dans le département de l'Isère.* Grenoble: Allier, 1949.

Fauvet, Jacques, and Henri Mendras. *Les Paysans et la politique.* Paris, 1958.

Fiechter, Jean-Jacques. *Le Socialisme français de l'affaire Dreyfus à la Grande Guerre.* Geneva, 1965.

Fohlen, Claude. *L'Industrie textile au temps du Second Empire.* Paris: PUF, 1956.

Friedlander, Dov. "Demographic Pattern and Socio-economic Character of Coal-Mining Populations." *Economic Development and Cultural Change* 22 (1973): 39–51.

Gachon, Louis. "Le Partage d'activités entre l'agriculture et l'industrie dans les familles paysannes de la montagne des Vosges." *Revue Géographique de Lyon* 27 (1952): 45–46.

Galbert, Comte de, and Charles Génin. *L'Agriculture dans l'Isère au XIXe siècle.* Grenoble: Dupont, 1900.

Galeski, Bertrand. *Basic Concepts of Rural Sociology.* Manchester: Manchester University Press, 1972.

Garavel, Jean. *Les Paysans de Morette.* Paris: A. Colin, 1948.

Garrier, Gilbert. *Paysans du Beaujolais et du Lyonnais.* Grenoble: Presses Universitaires de Grenoble, 1973.

———. "L'Union du Sud-Est des syndicats agricoles avant 1914." *Mouvement Social* 69 (1969): 17–38.

Gay, Peter. *The Dilemma of Democratic Socialism.* New York: Collier, 1962.

Gerschenkron, Alexander. *Economic Backwardness in Historical Perspective.* Cambridge: Harvard University Press, 1962.

Giddens, Anthony. *The Class Structure of Advanced Societies.* New York: Harper & Row, 1973.

Ginet, Jean. "La Main d'oeuvre agricole saisonnière dans le Bas-Dauphiné." *RGA* 21 (1933): 337–339.

Godart, Justin. *L'Ouvrier en soie.* Lyon: Nicolas, 1899.

———. *Travailleurs et métiers lyonnais.* Lyon, 1909.

Goguel, François. *Chroniques éléctorales.* 3 vols. Paris: Presses de la Fondation Nationale des Sciences Politiques, 1983.

———. *Géographie des élections françaises.* Paris: A. Colin, 1951.

———. *La Politique des partis sous la Troisième République.* Paris: Seuil, 1946.

Goldberg, Harvey. *The Life of Jean-Jaurès.* Madison: University of Wisconsin Press, 1962.

Gonnard, René. "L'Industrie lyonnaise de la soie et la concurrence mondiale." *Revue Economique Internationale,* 2, 15–20 August 1905, 259–299.

Grantham, G. W. "Scale and Organization of French Farming, 1840–1880." In *European Peasants and Their Markets: Essays in Agrarian Economic History,* ed. William N. Parker and Eric L. Jones, pp. 293–326. Princeton: Princeton University Press, 1975.

Gratton, Philippe. *Les Luttes de classes dans les campagnes.* Paris: Anthropos, 1971.

———. *Les Paysans français contre l'agrarisme.* Paris: Maspéro, 1972.

Guilbert, Madeleine. *Les Femmes et l'organisation syndicale avant 1914.* Paris: CNRS, 1966.

Gullickson, Gay L. *Spinners and Weavers of Aufray: Rural Industry and the Sexual Division of Labor in a French Village, 1750–1850.* New York: Cambridge University Press, 1986.

Habermas, Jürgen. *Jürgen Habermas on Society and Politics.* Ed. Steve Seidman. Boston: Beacon, 1989.

Hajnal, John. "Two Kinds of Pre-industrial Household Formation Systems." *Population and Development Review* 8 (1982): 449–494.

Hareven, Tamara K. *Family Time and Industrial Time: The Relationship between Family and Work in a New England Industrial Community.* Cambridge: Cambridge University Press, 1978.

Hause, Steven C., and Anne R. Kenney. *Women's Suffrage and Social Politics in the French Third Republic*. Princeton: Princeton University Press, 1984.

Hilden, Patricia. "Class and Gender: Conflicting Components of Women's Behavior in the Textile Mills of Lille, Roubaix, and Tourcoing, 1880–1914." *Historical Journal* 27 (1984): 361–386.

————. *Working Women and Socialist Politics in France, 1880–1914*. Oxford: Oxford University Press, 1986.

Hohenberg, Paul. "Migrations et fluctuations démographiques dans la France rurale, 1936–1901." *Annales* 29 (1974): 461–497.

Houston, Rab, and K. D. M. Snell. "Proto-industrialization? Cottage Industry, Social Change, and Industrial Revolution." *Historical Journal* 27 (1984): 473–492.

Hunt, Lynn. *Politics, Culture, and Class in the French Revolution*. Berkeley: University of California Press, 1984.

Hutton, Patrick H. *The Cult of the Revolutionary Tradition: The Blanquists in French Politics*. Berkeley: University of California Press, 1981.

Irvine, William D. *The Boulanger Affair Reconsidered: Royalism, Boulangism, and the Origins of the Radical Right in France*. New York: Oxford University Press, 1989.

Isambert, F.-A., and J.-P., Terrenoire. *Atlas de la pratique religieuse des catholiques en France*. Paris: CNRS, 1980.

Jennings, Jeremy. *Syndicalism in France: A Study of Ideas*. New York: St. Martin's Press, 1990.

Johnson, Christopher H. *Utopian Communism in France: Cabet and the Icarians, 1839–1851*. Ithaca: Cornell University Press, 1974.

Johnston, Ronald J., Fred M. Shelley, and Peter J. Taylor. *Developments in Electoral Geography*. London: Routledge, 1990.

Jolly, Jean, ed. *Dictionnaire des parlementaires français*. Paris: PUF, 1970.

Jonas, Raymond A. "Peasants, Population, and Industry in France." *Journal of Interdisciplinary History* 22 (Autumn 1991): 177–200.

————. "Visualizing Population in History" *Historical Methods* 24 (Summer 1991): 101–109.

Jouanny, Joseph. *Le Tissage de la soie en Bas-Dauphiné*. Grenoble: Didier & Richard, 1931.

Judt, Tony. *Marxism and the Modern French Left*. Oxford: Oxford University Press, 1986.

————. *Socialism in Provence*. Cambridge: Cambridge University Press, 1979.

Julliard, Jacques. "La CGT devant la guerre (1900–1914)." *Mouvement Social* 49 (1964): 47–62.

————. *Clemenceau briseur de grèves*. Paris, 1965.

Kaplan, Steven L., and Cynthia J. Koepp. *Work in France: Representations, Meaning, Organization, and Practice*. Ithaca: Cornell University Press, 1986.

Katznelson, Ira, and Aristide R. Zolberg, eds. *Working-Class Formation: Nineteenth-Century Patterns in Western Europe and the United States*. Princeton: Princeton University Press, 1986.

Kayser, Jacques. *La Presse de province sous la Troisième République*. Paris: A. Colin, 1958.

Kemp, Tom. *Economic Forces in French History.* London: Dobson, 1971.

Kolakowski, Leszek. *Main Currents of Marxism.* Oxford: Oxford University Press, 1978.

Laffond, Charles. "L'Industrie de la chaussure à Izeaux." *RGA* 34 (1946): 69–85.

Landauer, Carl. "The Guesdistes and the Small Farmer." *IRSH* 6 (1961): 212–225.

———. "The Origin of Socialist Reformism in France." *IRSH* 12 (1967): 81–107.

Landes, David, ed. *The Rise of Capitalism.* New York: Macmillan, 1964.

———. *The Unbound Prometheus.* Cambridge: Cambridge University Press, 1969.

Landes, Joan B. *Women and the Public Sphere in the Age of the French Revolution.* Ithaca: Cornell University Press, 1988.

Le Bras, Hervé. *Les Trois Frances.* Paris: Seuil, 1986.

Lefranc, Georges. *Le Mouvement socialiste sous la Troisième République.* 2 vols. Paris: Payot, 1977.

Le Jeune, Yvonne. "Structure professionnelle d'une petite ville industrielle du Bas-Dauphiné: Voiron." *RGA* 42 (1954): 713–733.

Lehning, James R. *The Peasants of Marlhes: Economic Development and Family Organization in Nineteenth-Century France.* Chapel Hill University of North Carolina Press, 1980.

Léon, Pierre. "Les Grèves de 1867–1870 dans le départment de l'Isère." *Revue d'Histoire Moderne et Contemporaine* 1 (1954): 272–300.

———. "La Naissance de la grande industrie en Dauphiné." *RGA* 40 (1952): 601–613.

———. *La Naissance de la grande industrie en Dauphiné (fin du XVIIᵉ siècle–1869).* 2 vols. Paris: PUF, 1954.

———. "A travers les revues: Etudes récentes d'histoire économique régionale." *Cahiers d'Histoire* 6 (1961): 481–485.

———., ed. *Colloque internationale des sciences humaines sur l'industrialisation en Europe au XIXᵉ siècle.* Lyon, 1970.

Lequin, Yves. "Classe-ouvrière et idéologie dans la région lyonnaise, 1870–1914." *Mouvement Social* 69 (1969): 3–20.

———. *Les Ouvriers de la région lyonnaise, 1848–1914.* 2 vols. Lyon: Presses Universitaires de Lyon, 1977.

———. "Sources et méthodes de l'histoire des grèves dans la seconde moitié du XIXᵉ siècle: L'Exemple de l'Isère (1848–1914)." *Cahiers d'Histoire* 12 (1967): 215–230.

Leroy, Maxime. *Histoire des idées sociales en France.* Paris: Gallimard, 1950.

Leroy-Beaulieu, Paul. "Les Ouvrières de la Fabrique." *Revue des Deux Mondes* 97 (1872).

Lévèque, Pierre. "Libre pensée et socialisme." *Mouvement Social* 57 (1966): 101–141.

Levine, David. *Family Formation in an Age of Nascent Capitalism*. New York: Academic Press, 1977.

_____., ed. *Essays on the Family and Historical Change*. College Station: Texas A&M University Press, 1983.

Lichtheim, George. *Marxism: An Historical and Critical Study*. London: Routledge, 1974.

_____. *Marxism in Modern France*. New York: Columbia University Press, 1966.

_____. *The Origins of Socialism*. New York: Praeger, 1969.

_____. *A Short History of Socialism*. London: Fontana, 1970.

Lida, Clara. "Agrarian Anarchism in Andalusia." *IRSH* 14 (1969): 315–337.

Lindert, P. H. and J. G. Williamson. "English Workers' Living Standards During the Industrial Revolution." *Economic History Review* 36 (1983): 1–25.

Linz, Juan J. "Division of Labor and Voting Behavior in Europe." *Comparative Politics* 8 (1976): 365–429.

Lloyd, Robert C., and Kenneth P. Wilkinson. "Community Factors in Rural Manufacturing Development." *Rural Sociology* 50 (1985): 27–37.

Lorcin, Jean. "L'Utilisation des listes nominatives en démographie historique." *Cahiers d'Histoire* 12 (1967): 183–192.

Loubère, Leo. *Radicalism in Mediterranean France, 1848–1914*. Albany: State University of New York Press, 1973.

Lukacs, George. *History and Class Consciousness*. Cambridge: MIT Press, 1968.

Luxemburg, Rosa. *Selected Political Writings*. New York: Monthly Review Press, 1971.

McBride, Theresa. "The Long Road Home: Women's Work and Industrialization." In *Becoming Visible*, ed. Renate Bridenthal and Claudia Koonz, pp. 280–295. Boston: Houghton-Mifflin, 1977.

_____. "Social Mobility for the Lower Classes." *Journal of Social History* 8 (1974): 63–78.

Maitron, Jean, ed. *Dictionnaire biographique du mouvement ouvrier français*. 43 vols. to date. Paris: Editions Ouvrières, 1964–.

Manuel, Frank E. *The New World of Henri de Saint-Simon*. Cambridge: Harvard University Press, 1956.

_____. *The Prophets of Paris*. New York, 1962.

Marchegay, Albert. *La Propriété paysanne en France*. Paris: Jouve, 1902.

Margadant, Ted. *French Peasants in Revolt: The Insurrection of 1851*. Princeton: Princeton University Press, 1980.

Marie, Christian. *L'Evolution du comportement politique dans une ville en expansion: Grenoble, 1871–1965*. Paris: PUF, 1966.

Mayeur, Jean-Marie. *Les Débuts de la Troisième République*. Paris: Seuil, 1973.

Medick, Hans. "The Proto-industrial Family Economy." *Social History* 3 (1976): 291–314.

Mendel, Franklin. "Proto-industrialization: the First Phase of the Industrialization Process." *Journal of Economic History* 32 (1972): 241–261.

Mendras, Henri. *Sociétés paysannes*. Paris: A. Colin, 1976.

Merlin, Pierre. *L'Exode rural*. Paris: PUF, 1971.

Merriman, John M. *The Agony of the Republic*. New Haven: Yale University Press, 1978.

———. *The Red City: Limoges and the French Nineteenth Century*. New York: Oxford University Press, 1985.

Milhaud, Albert. *Histoire du radicalisme*. Paris: Société d'Edition Française et Internationale, 1951.

Minge, Wanda. "Household Economy during the Peasant-to-Worker Transition in the Swiss Alps." *Ethnology* 17 (1978): 183–196.

Mitchell, Harvey. *Victors and Vanquished: The German Influence on Army and Church in France after 1870*. Chapel Hill: University of North Carolina Press, 1984.

Moch, Leslie Page. *Paths to the City: Regional Migration in Nineteenth-Century France*. Beverly Hills, Calif.: Sage, 1983.

Morand, Marius. "L'Outillage de la Fabrique lyonnaise du tissage de la soie." *RGA* 3 (1916): 318.

Moreau, Jean. "L'Industrie de la soie dans le département de l'Isère." *RGA* 15 (1927): 615–625.

Moss, Bernard. *The Origins of the French Labor Movement: The Socialism of Skilled Workers*. Berkeley: University of California Press, 1976.

Newell, William H. "The Agricultural Revolution in Nineteenth-Century France." *Journal of Economic History* 33 (December 1973): 697–731.

Nicolas, G. A. *L'Organisation sociale de l'industrie du tissage de la soie*. Paris: Société générale, 1923.

Nordmann, Jean-Thomas. *Histoire des radicaux, 1820–1973*. Paris: Table Ronde, 1974.

Nye, John Vincent. "Firm Size and Economic Backwardness: A New Look at the French Industrialization Debate." *Journal of Economic History* 47 (1987): 649–669.

O'Brien, Mary. *The Politics of Reproduction*. London: Routledge, 1981.

Ozouf, Mona. *Festivals and the French Revolution*. Cambridge: Harvard University Press, 1988.

Pariset, Ernst. *Histoire de la Fabrique lyonnaise: Etude sur le régime social et économique de la soie à Lyon depuis le 16³ siècle*. Lyon, 1901.

Pélissonnier, Georges. *Etude sur le socialisme agraire en France*. Dijon: Venot, 1902.

Pennetier, Claude. "Le Socialisme dans les départements ruraux français: L'Exemple de Cher (1850–1921)." 2 vols. Thesis, Université de Paris I, n.d.

Perrot, Michelle, *Les Ouvriers en grève: France, 1871–1890*. 2 vols. Paris: Mouton, 1974.

———, ed. *Une Histoire des femmes. est-elle possible?* Marseille: Rivages, 1984.

Perrot, Michelle, and Annie Kriegel. *Le Socialisme français et le pouvoir*. Paris: Etudes et Documentation Internationale, 1966.

Pessieux, Auguste. *Etude monographique des créations sociales*. Valence: Legrand, 1907.

Pfister, Ulrich. "Work Roles and Family Structure in Proto-industrial Zurich." *Journal of Interdisciplinary History* 20 (1989): 83–105.

Pic, Paul, and Alphonse Amieux. *Le Travail à domicile en France et spéciale-ment dans la région lyonnaise.* Paris, 1906.

Pic, Paul, and Justin Godart. *Le Mouvement économique et social dans la région lyonnaise.* 2 vols. Lyon: A. Storck, 1902.

Pinchemel, Philippe. *Structures sociales et dépopulation rurale dans les campagnes picardes de 1836 à 1936.* Paris: A. Colin, 1957.

Pinkney, David. *Decisive Years in France, 1840–1847.* Princeton: Princeton University Press, 1985.

Pitié, Jean. *Exode rural et migrations intérieures en France: L'Exemple de la Vienne et de Poitou-Charentes.* Poitiers: Norois, 1971.

Plessis, Alain. *De la fête impériale au mur des fédérés: 1852–1871.* Paris: Seuil, 1973.

Pouthas, Charles-Marie. *La Population française pendant la première moitié du XIXe siècle.* Paris: Institut National d'Etudes Démographiques, 1956.

Price, Roger. "The Onset of Labor Shortage in Nineteenth-Century French Agriculture." *Economic History Review* 28 (1975): 260–279.

———, ed. *Revolution and Reaction: 1848 and the French Second Republic.* London: Croom Helm, 1975.

Rebérioux, Madeleine. "Un groupe de paysans socialistes de Saône-et-Loire à l'heure de l'unité (1905–1906)." *Mouvement Social* 56 (1966): 89–103.

———. *La République radicale? 1898–1914.* Paris: Seuil, 1975.

Reddy, William. "Family and Factory: French Linen Weavers in the Belle Epoque." *Journal of Social History* 8 (1975): 102–112.

———. *The Rise of Market Culture: The Textile Trade and French Society.* Cambridge: Cambridge University Press, 1984.

Reid, Donald. *The Miners of Decazeville: A Genealogy of Deindustrialization.* Cambridge: Harvard University Press, 1985.

Reiter, Rayna R., ed. *Toward an Anthropology of Women.* New York: Monthly Review Press, 1975.

Reybaud, Louis. *Etude sur le régime des manufactures.* Paris, 1859.

Reynier, Elie. *La Soie en Vivarais: Etudes d'histoire et de géographie économiques.* Paris: Largentière, 1921.

Rondot, Natalis. *L'Industrie de la soie en France, 1894.* Lyon: Mougin-Rousand, 1894.

Roth, Guenther. *The Social Democrats in Imperial Germany.* Totowa, N.J.: Bedminster, 1963.

Roualt, François. *Géographie agricole du département de l'Isère.* Grenoble: Drevet, 1907.

Rousset, Henri. *La Presse à Grenoble.* Grenoble: Gratier, 1900.

Rude, Fernand. *L'Insurrection lyonnaise de novembre 1831.* Paris: Domat-Montchrestien, 1944.

———. *Le Mouvement ouvrier à Lyon de 1827 à 1832.* Lyon: Federop, 1977.

Sahlins, Marshall. *Historical Metaphors and Mythical Realities.* Ann Arbor: University of Michigan Press, 1981.

Schmidt, Charles. "Encore un document rélatif à l'histoire du machinisme en France." *Révolution Française* 45 (1903): 66–70.

Schorske, Carl. *German Social Democracy, 1905–1917*. Cambridge: Harvard University Press, 1955.

Scott, Joan. *Gender and the Politics of History*. New York: Columbia University Press, 1988.

———. *The Glassworkers of Carmaux*. Cambridge: Harvard University Press, 1974.

Segalen, Martine. "The Family Cycle and Household Structure: Five Generations in a French Village." In *Family and Sexuality in French History*, ed. Robert Wheaton and Tamara Hareven, pp. 253–271. Philadelphia: University of Pennsylvania Press, 1980.

Sewell, William. *Work and Revolution in France: The Language of Labor from the Old Regime to 1848*. Cambridge: Cambridge University Press, 1980.

Shade, William G. "New Political History: Some Statistical Questions Raised." *Social Science History* 5 (1981): 171–196.

Shanin, Teodor, ed. *Peasants and Peasant Societies*. Aylesbury: Penguin, 1976.

Sheridan, George J., Jr. "Household and Craft in an Industrializing Economy." In *Consciousness and Class Experience in Nineteenth-Century Europe*, pp. 107–128. New York: Holmes & Meier, 1979.

———. "Perfection and Intelligence: Technique, Invention, and Social Ideology among the Silk Weavers of Lyon, 1830–1880." Paper presented at the 16th Annual Conference of the Western Society for French History, UCLA, November 1988.

Shorter, Edward, and Charles Tilly. *Strikes in France, 1830–1968*. Cambridge: Cambridge University Press, 1974.

Siegfried, André. *Tableau politique de la France de l'Ouest sous la Troisième République*. Paris: A. Colin, 1913.

Silvestre, Claude. *L'Union du Sud-Est des syndicats agricoles*. 2 vols. Lyon: Legendre, 1900.

Skocpol, Theda. *States and Social Revolutions*. New York: Cambridge University Press, 1979.

Smith, J. Harvey. "Work Routine and Social Structure in a French Village." *Journal of Interdisciplinary History* 3 (1975): 357–382.

Soboul, Albert. "The French Rural Community in 18th and 19th Century France." *Past & Present* 10 (1956): 78–95.

———. *Paysans, sans-culottes et jacobins*. Paris: PUF, 1966.

Sonn, Richard. *Anarchism and Cultural Politics in Fin-de-Siècle France*. Lincoln: University of Nebraska Press, 1989.

Sorlin, Pierre. *La Société française*. 2 vols. Paris: Arthaud, 1969.

Sowerwine, Charles. *Sisters or Citizens? Women and Socialism in France since 1876*. Cambridge: Cambridge University Press, 1982.

———. "Workers and Women in France before 1914: The Debate over the Couriau Affair." *Journal of Modern History* 55 (1983): 411–441.

Stewart, Mary Lynn. *Women, Work, and the French State: Labor Protection and Social Hierarchy, 1879–1919.* Kingston, Ont.: McGill-Queen's University Press, 1989.

Stiehm, Judith H., ed. *Women's Views of the Political World of Men.* Dobbs Ferry, N.Y.: Transnational, 1984.

Stone, Judith F. *The Search for Social Peace: Reform Legislation in France, 1890–1914.* Albany: State University of New York Press, 1985.

Tackett, Timothy. *Religion, Revolution, and Regional Culture in Eighteenth-Century France: The Ecclesiastical Oath of 1791.* Princeton: Princeton University Press, 1987.

Taylor, Peter J., and Ronald J. Johnston. *Geography of Elections.* New York: Holmes & Meier, 1979.

Thiervoz, Robert. "L'Industrie en Valdaine et ses répercussions démographiques, sociales, et électorales." *RGA* 42 (1954): 90–92.

Thompson, E. P. *The Making of the English Working Class.* New York: Vintage, 1966.

——. *The Poverty of Theory and Other Essays.* New York: Monthly Review Press, 1978.

——. "Time, Work-Discipline, and Industrial Capitalism." *Past & Present* 38 (1967): 56–97.

Tilly, Charles. "Did the Cake of Custom Break?" In *Consciousness and Class Experience in Nineteenth-Century Europe,* ed. John Merriman. New York: Holmes & Meier, 1979.

——. *The Vendée.* Cambridge: Harvard University Press, 1976.

Tilly, Louise. "Individual Lives and Family Strategies in the French Proletariat." In *Family and Sexuality in French History,* ed. Robert Wheaton and Tamara Hareven, pp. 201–223. Philadelphia: University of Pennsylvania Press, 1980.

Tilly, Louise, and Joan Scott. "Women's Work and the Family in Nineteenth-Century Europe." *Comparative Studies in Society and History* 17 (1975): 36–64.

——. *Women, Work, and Family.* New York: Holt, Rinehart & Winston, 1978.

Tilly, Louise A., Joan Scott, and Miriam Cohen. "Women's Work and European Fertility Patterns." *Journal of Interdisciplinary History* 6 (1976): 447–476.

Tufte, Edward R. *The Visual Display of Quantitative Information.* Cheshire, Conn.: Graphics Press, 1983.

Trempé, Rolande. *Les Mineurs de Carmaux.* 2 vols. Paris: PUF, 1971.

——. "Le Réformisme des mineurs français à la fin du XIXe Siècle." *Mouvement Social* 65 (1968): 93–107.

Valette, Aline. *Femmes et travail au XIXe siècle: Enquêtes de la Fronde et la bataille syndicaliste.* Ed. Marie-Hélène Zylberberg-Hocquard and Evelyne Diebolt. Paris: Syros, 1984.

Van Davidson, Rondel. *Did We Think Victory Great? The Life and Ideas of Victor Considérant.* Lanham, Md.: University Press of America, 1988.

Vigier, Philippe. *Essai sur la répartition de la propriété foncière dans la région alpine.* Paris: SEVPEN, 1963.

_____. "Lyon et l'évolution politique de la province française au XIXᵉ siècle." *Cahiers de l'Histoire* 12 (1967): 193–207.

_____. *La Seconde République dans la région alpine: Etude politique et sociale.* 2 vols. Paris: PUF, 1963.

Walton, Whitney. "Political Economists and Specialized Industrialization during the French Second Republic." *French History* 3 (1989): 293–311.

_____. "Working Women, Gender, and the Putting-Out Industry in Mid-Nineteenth-Century France." *Journal of Women's History* 2 (1990): 42–65.

Warin, Robert. *Les Syndicats jaunes: Histoire du mouvement jaune.* Paris: Jouve, 1908.

Weber, Eugen. *Peasants into Frenchmen.* Stanford: Stanford University Press, 1976.

Willard, Claude. "Les Attaques contre Notre-Dame de l'Usine." *Mouvement Social* 57 (1966): 203–209.

_____. *Le Mouvement socialiste en France, 1893–1906: Les Guesdistes.* Paris: Editions Sociales, 1965.

Wolf, Eric. *Peasant Wars of the Twentieth Century.* London: Faber, 1969.

Wright, Gordon. *France in Modern Times.* Chicago: Rand McNally, 1974.

Zelnik, Reginald E. *Labor and Society in Tsarist Russia: The Factory Workers of St. Petersburg, 1855–1870.* Stanford: Stanford University Press, 1971.

Zévaès, Alexandre. *Histoire des partis socialistes in France.* Vol. 12, *Le Parti socialiste de 1904–1923.* Paris: Rivière, 1923.

Zylberberg-Hocquard, Marie-Hélène. *Féminisme et syndicalisme en France.* Paris: Anthropos, 1978.

_____. *Femmes et féminisme dans le mouvement ouvrier français.* Paris: Editions Ouvrières, 1981.

Index

Library of Congress Cataloging-in-Publication Data

Jonas, Raymond Anthony.
  Peasants, industry, and politics in rural France : the Isère in the early Third
Republic / Raymond A. Jonas.
      p.   cm.
  Includes bibliographical references and index.
  ISBN 0-8014-2814-9
  1. Rural industries—France—Isère—History—19th century. 2. Peasantry—
France—Isère—History—19th century. I. Title.
HC277.I8J66   1994
305.5'633'094409034—dc20   93-30896